REPORTS OF MY DEATH

Reports of My Death

BY

KARL SHAPIRO

Algonquin Books of Chapel Hill

1990

published by
Algonquin Books of Chapel Hill
Post Office Box 2225
Chapel Hill, North Carolina 27515-2225
a division of
Workman Publishing Company, Inc.
708 Broadway
New York, New York 10003

Portions of this book, some in different form, have appeared first in the following publications: *New York Quarterly* (No. 27, Summer 1985, "Present State of American Poetry," pp. 78–91); *The American Scholar* (Vol. 55, No. 1, Winter 1985/86, "The Golden Albatross," pp. 77–96); *Triquarterly 62* (Winter, 1985, "From *Scratchings*, a Study of the Making of a Poet," pp. 161–76); *Triquarterly 60* (Spring/Summer 1984, "From *Scratchings*, a Study of the Making of a Poet," pp. 61–82); *Delos* (Vol. II, No. 1, Spring 1989, "Life in a Schloss," pp. 79–98); *The CEA Critic* (Vol. 48, No. 3, Spring 1986, "At Auden's Grave," pp. 10–20); *Contemporary Authors Autobiography Series* (Vol. VI, 1988, Gale Research Company, Penobscot Building, Detroit, Michigan 48226, pp. passim).

Library of Congress Cataloging-in-Publication Data
(Revised for vol. 2)
Shapiro, Karl Jay, 1913–
Poet : an autobiography in three parts
Contents: v. 1. The younger son—v. 2. Reports of my death.
1. Shapiro, Karl Jay, 1913–   —Biography.
2. Poets, American—20th century—Biography.
PS3537.H27Z474   1988   811'.52   88-6204
ISBN 0-945575-28-9 (v. 2)

10 9 8 7 6 5 4 3 2 1

First Edition

If you live in the capital of voodoo,
Better learn to watch your soup.

ILLUSTRATIONS

REPORTS OF MY DEATH

BOOK I

Career Poet

1.

It was 1945. He was a civilian again, and for good this time. He gathered his wife and after a brief stay in Baltimore, until they could regain the little apartment in New York, they returned to their place in Washington, also too small. Where could they go? There had been no building anywhere for years except for the military and soon hundreds of thousands of soldiers were beginning to come back. The *New Yorker*'s art critic was getting a divorce and his wife, a sculptor, was going to give up their house in the country, far up in Connecticut, in an area where writers and editors lived and painters like Arshile Gorki and Peter Blume, and where Hart Crane used to visit and near where he had written "Quaker Hill" and got drunk on highly fermented apple cider, and all the *New Republic* writers lived and everybody spoke French because they were the people of the famous literary Exile of the Twenties which they would all write about forever after.

The poet was enthralled, his wife was ecstatic with relief though she was already pregnant, had been pregnant since the second month of his return and there would be no doctor or hospital around for miles and not even a grocery store for miles and they had no car, but a famous poet had said he was going to England the moment he could and he would rent his Model A Ford to the poet if he would come and get it.

They made the move. An aspiring novelist drove them there in a large strong car in which he hauled bricks. He had become a bricklayer and did itinerant jobs to make enough money for a few months and then go to his house that he was building himself and build and write until he ran low on money and went off on his itinerant bricklaying. All the writers admired his way of handling his life.

The house had been designed for a sculptor with big plans, it was all two-story living room or studio for massive work but there were no statues, only miniatures standing on a sideboard, not models or "sketches" but just miniatures, a diminution of power and ambition, he decided, but in one corner hung a real Calder, a rust rooster in pure abstraction hanging from the high rafters and barely turning with the motion of the breeze. Calder too lived not far away, though close-by in this rocky unfarmable area did not exist. The nearest neighbor was an invisible half-mile away and most twice that and more. He saw a deer across the ravine, then another, and went out on the big screened porch and spotted a giant tortoise waddling away.

He had come to this retreat, for that was what he quickly discovered it to be, newly famous and was treated with deferential respect, respect for the big prize he had won, which was the one poetry prize in America that even ordinary people knew about and was mentioned in almost every newspaper in the land, because it was a newspaper prize that celebrated newspaper writers primarily but also the best novelist of the year, or so it was assumed, and also the best poet, and deference because he was new and young, though he didn't think of himself as young but among the writers of the bohemian Exile he was only a fledgling and was only nineteen when Hart, as they called Crane, jumped off the *Orizaba* in the Caribbean while the wife of one of the Exiles was waiting for him in her stateroom. They talked about Hart so much that the poet, who loved Crane, began to hate him and began to feel uncomfortable around the Exiles with their French and their hearing aids and their fancy cooking, and he knew he would not be happy here in the midst of the Lost Generation. He didn't want to be their mascot or protégé and had always felt that the attempt of the Exile's wife to "save" Hart Crane from homosexuality was lunacy and might have driven him overboard, that and the way the educated Exiles had treated this bumpkin from Ohio, genius or not, with their devastating criticism. But this new poet had snatched the brass ring and the Prize was their Prize and like it or not he was something of their captive.

He could never decide whether he was really happy to have the Prize. Like every writer he wanted, demanded recognition from his fellows the writers and was delighted to have a passport to the ordinary world which the Prize provided, but he had always held the Prize in low esteem. It was a middlebrow honor at best and it had always been given to *intelligible* writers, those with a large reading public, and he knew that a large reading public was the most suspect readership of all, especially in America where the reading level was never above sixth grade even among college graduates.

He was at his wife's apartment and still in uniform when the news came. One of the judges of the Prize, whose name was synonymous with anthology, spilled the beans to the poet's wife on the telephone and swore her to secrecy. They were overjoyed and the poet was beside himself. He had proved himself to his family and friends and all the other non-writers who had never taken him seriously and had wondered what kind of future he could have, if any. But the magical name of the Prize was common, universal knowledge, and he knew that forever after whenever his name was mentioned in the newspapers or a magazine it would be coupled with the Prize and that the Prize-givers would never let anyone forget that they were the founders and donors of the Prize, which was after all only a newspaper prize, and the poet knew that the poets would use it against him. After all, Eliot and Pound and Cummings and Williams and Hart Crane had never won the Prize or even come close. They won prizes like the Dial, which Americans had never even heard of. It was not until after the War that the poets set up a counter-prize and it would be many years before the poet won that one. Meanwhile he basked in the common acceptance of his achievement and felt very grateful for his wife's part in what was now becoming a career.

All the poems in the winning book had been written while he was overseas except one, a satire on himself written in the style of Andrew Marvell, and there were as many love poems to the Melbourne girl as to the Baltimore girl and the book was well-titled *V-Letter*, for victory-letter, as the photostats of mail from overseas were called, and the book would be reprinted in England on bad butcher paper at the dead-end of the War and copies of the American edition would be put into ships' libraries of the U.S. Navy which he would not know about until years later when ships were decommissioned and people would send him copies from the U.S.S. *This* and the U.S.S. *That*, and that, to him, though it wouldn't be to the other poets, was the major achievement, so maybe he deserved to win the Prize that he felt so ambivalent about.

After a while he began to call it the Golden Albatross because he knew fairly well that he would always be able to get lectures, even jobs, even good jobs, doing what he wanted in and around poetry, and he wouldn't have to sit behind a librarian's desk answering silly questions about how to address a duchess or which zoos keep unicorns, and he knew that people who had never read a book, much less a book of poetry, much less Rimbaud or Hart Crane, would know that he had won the Prize. It didn't matter whether for cartooning or "covering" a battle or writing poems, he had won the Prize and that made him special with all rights and privileges appertaining thereto and he was hands off to ordinary occupations and preoccupations and could go his own way and do practically whatever he liked, even to not paying his bills. He would have to fight to keep the Golden Albatross from owning him. But meanwhile the Exiles had him and his precious Prize, had him both ways, as a new young local celebrity and as a Prize-winner they could upstage, and the poet didn't like the spot he was in with these French-speaking ex-expatriates who wrote for all the liberal magazines and were now country squires really and were out to make him and his wife one of their commune.

He went to Cape Cod where the famous old poet Conrad Aiken lived and picked up the Model A and went to Boston with him to a museum, but the poet was anxious to get back to where he was still sorting himself out and passed up the opportunity to go to a literary party and meet New England writers and poets, and got in the antique car and drove back to the sculptress's house without stopping except for gas and not even for food.

There were guests, the poet's mother, his sister and her husband, back from the War in Middle Europe, the wife's friends, mostly girl friends, and one handsome blond giant, some aristocratic New Yorker who had been a high-ranking officer in the Army and jocularly ordered the poet around, calling him playfully Sergeant, while he did outside chores which the poet didn't know how to do, such as putting up huge porch screens to keep the wasps out. The big studio room was full of wasps which terrified his wife, but the poet swatted them with his hand and was never stung, they were so sluggish, he said, after the lightning-quick red centipedes that got you before you saw them in New Guinea and sent you howling with pain and racing around the tent while the tent-mates roared with laughter.

They visited back and forth with the Exiles and listened to their histories of the great world that had gone into their writings, for they were all living in the past and had only contempt for the present, and the poet wondered if that would happen to him in time and he prayed it wouldn't. Well-known, not known, and famous writers showed up at their parties, some whose names he knew only from anthologies or even encyclopedias and he was awed, always polite, and not quite at ease in this new world of established professionals.

There was a Southern Poet of a practical turn of mind who was

[7]

visiting one of the nearby Twenties people for the weekend and who asked the young poet about next year. Where was he going next year? Would he be interested in becoming the poetry consultant at the Library of Congress? It could be arranged. Of course it would mean a move to Washington, D.C., not exactly the cultural capital of the world or even the U.S.A. Without thinking or, in a sense, caring, the young poet said yes. It was done, he found out later, not without literary bloodshed, for a woman poet who had already been asked to fill this post had to be postponed. What disappointment and fury this shift entailed the young poet never really found out. It was his first introduction to cultural politicking and he didn't know the rules of the game and never would, though he would see enough to learn that power has a shining nakedness like electricity and can turn lives off and on with a touch of the finger.

Why had the Southern Poet done the young poet this extraordinary favor? Was it the same kind of favor Professor Hazel had done him in getting him the scholarship to Johns Hopkins? Cannily the young poet knew it was. Given the talent, even when others had equal or better talent, one could be chosen, but there were other factors and chief among them Manners—Deportment, in fact. The old Southern charm, the soft laugh, the sharp impersonal reproof, the quality of voice. Not so much the looks but the look, the way eyes met or did not meet, and above all the ability to be silent at just the right place. Vaguely the young poet was aware of such things, not because he had studied or even cared about them, but because that was what he himself liked in others, why he preferred Southerners or Europeans to almost all Americans of the writing ilk. His officers in the Army had been Southern and they had tacit understandings with him having to do with place. The young poet had been born barely below the Mason-Dixon line but barely was sufficient.

So then, it was his Southernness that was opening doors as well as his now accepted poetry—and the Southern Poet was honoring this new talented Southerner whom he had praised highly in reviews and the fact that the newcomer was a Jew was all to the good. Hadn't Judah P. Benjamin, the Secretary of State of the Confederacy, been a Jew? Jews made good Southerners. All his life the young poet would profess his Southernness and, making known this characteristic to a stranger, even a truck driver from Texas or Alabama, would exchange a brief glance of complicity, almost a secret shake. And the displaced woman poet was a New Englander besides, or was he making too much of this? He thought not.

Thus he was knighted as a Member of the Establishment, and it was as if he had won the Prize a second time and had had an oak-leaf cluster added to the Congressional Medal of Honor. He had not really wanted a job, if it was a job, and hadn't done anything about it and was still not adjusted to the idea of having to have a job, when he had been gainfully employed, as they say, for four years in the Army and had done what he was told, more or less, and gone where he was sent. For he had no choice and no real objection of the kind that people go to federal penitentiaries for, and was paid practically nothing like all soldiers for risking their lives, which was not what they were drafted for, nothing heroic but only to sit behind typewriters or stand behind counters in sheds and do what they were told and make their beds.

So the whole idea of a job hadn't quite sunk in, especially as he had won the Prize and part of him felt that jobs were beneath him, like a prize ram at the county fair with a blue ribbon hanging from its neck and not knowing why it was there, and all he had to do was to stand in his stall and munch grass and be stared at. The Exiles were surprised that he was not more excited. Hart Crane would have jumped out of his skin and the poet thought, poor Hart Crane, he wished he had known him, they would have understood each other in a flash and nobody would talk about Hemingway shadowboxing in front of the window of the Ritz bar before he went in.

He didn't really enjoy the year in the beautiful deer-strolling, rock-studded countryside of Connecticut, and felt sad most of the time, cut off from everything, even the Army and the War. He and his wife were in the nearest town, New Milford, when Germany surrendered, and the people were dancing and drinking in the streets and he didn't feel anything, not even glad it was over, because he had become part of the war-state-of-mind and didn't think it was over and didn't think it would ever be over because nobody knows how not to make war. It was almost like a celebration of the local high school football victory, it was so provincial and stupid, and he wished there was a better way to celebrate victory, especially as they all had sick and wounded and dead in the town from the War and everybody hated Krauts and Japs, the-little-yellow-bastards, and this was the thing to do. He went home depressed.

The pregnancy got bigger and everyone walked on eggshells about to hatch, and in the winter they drove to New York where they had rented a furnished two-room apartment and sat and waited while she visited the doctor every other day. She was going to the Doctors' Hospital in front of the Queensborough Bridge which the poet liked because it resembled a steel candelabra. It was a superior hospital for superior people and he could not remember how she had gotten into it at all, a hospital where menus were delivered to the room by what looked like orderlies but which might have been stewards, and a *wine list*. The poet had never seen a wine list in his life and looked at the curious French titles without prices and didn't know what to make of it.

The baby was born famous, presided over by the Golden Albatross, for her arrival was broadcast by a world-known columnist from the dark backward and abysm of journalism all over the nation and to "all you ships at sea" that in Babylon a child was born to the Prizewinner. The poet was elated and uneasy simultaneously for himself and the child and mother, and the nurses came to look at this alert dark-eyed child that was already lifting its head up, like a turtle, the poet said, and peering around, though he was told she couldn't really see anything except light and shadow.

The bricklayer-writer came with his car after a week to drive them all back to the studio-house and the poet insisted on driving, even on the twisty icy road along the Housatonic River in the dark, while the bricklayer sat white-knuckled beside him and the wife and the baby sat in the back, and he drove too fast and the writer said whatever you do don't touch the brake. But they reached home and ever after the poet remembered this drive with pure horror and wondered if he had been trying to kill everybody.

The house became a nursery with the big screened-in crib on rubber wheels, screened on all sides and on top because of the wasps which were always inside the high studio somehow and the poet stayed up nights rocking the crib back and forth on wheels because the moment he stopped pushing the crib the baby woke up and yelled as only the newborn know how to do. The baby now became the center of the writer-artist community, for there hadn't been a baby of crib-size in the area for years, and all the wives and mistresses of the writers and artists came to pay homage and bring country-style gifts, preserves and knitted things and home remedies for chapped bottoms and constipation and handmade toys to hang up in view of the screened-in domicile of the newcomer. The poet learned to cook bottles and make formulas and wash diapers and took pleasure in it, not even stopping to complain but actually preferring to take care of the child himself for some reason as if he were both mother and father in one, and his domesticity became a topic of conversation and witticisms and even the great poet William Carlos Williams wrote him a letter addressed to Papa Shapiro, this salutation displeasing the poet for some reason, but then Williams was a famous baby doctor in his part of New Jersey and had seen a lot of papas in his time and would see a lot more, but the poet took it as some kind of demotion.

The winter spun along with days and nights mixed with bottles and diapers and visitors and even dinner parties and the poet writing in the nursery-studio in between and driving the Model A to the grocery, when one day he received the formal letter from the

Library of Congress informing him of his appointment as Consultant in Poetry and stating his salary, which seemed immense, and asking him if he objected to signing a loyalty oath and setting a date for an introduction to the Librarian himself.

The Library of Congress was a place he felt an almost proprietary interest in because it was Thomas Jefferson's library, it had been his idea and his books to begin with. The poet already knew a lot about the Library from having studied it in his library course and was very impressed that the Librarian was the only person appointed for life in the whole government except the members of the Supreme Court, that the President himself chose him and the Senate had to approve the appointment. The poet-librarian Archibald MacLeish had nevertheless resigned to become the head of UNESCO—Educational-Scientific-Cultural, the poet spelled out to himself—a bigger kind of responsibility, and had been replaced by a Texan who was not a poet and whom he would meet. The Library by now was the savior of Culture with a capital C and famous poets in exile from fascism were given consultantships, Alexis Leger (St. John Perse) from France, Juan Ramón Jiménez from Spain, for instance, and the poet would walk with these figures himself down the gilt and marble corridors as in a dream, and the Library had copied on film hundreds of thousands of Chinese works from antiquity which were in danger of destruction by the Japanese, and the Russians who were already gouging into China for keeps.

One of the Exiles would return the Model A to the Cape and they made their goodbyes to the "commune" and boarded the train to Washington, or rather Virginia, where the poet had rented a furnished apartment in Arlington, as close to Washington as they were able to get. It was an apartment in a "complex" totally devoid of character, where government minor officials and civil servants lived and all of a certain age, all with babies and toddlers pushed in strollers up and down the sidewalks by young mothers who all had college degrees from State Colleges and who read the *Nation* and the *New Republic* where the poet published some of his poems, a bit of news which got about in the Complex somehow, so that the poet was sometimes greeted on the sidewalks with indications of recognition.

The date for his meeting with the Librarian of Congress came and the poet dressed with careful nonchalance—he would never know how to dress for an "occasion" and fretted about it endlessly until after decades of experimentation he discovered that the secret was to dress inconspicuously in clothes of passable quality that should not draw attention for being too new or expensive or too shoddy. To have run-down heels was fine, but to have a flapping sole was not, the point being that no one should have to come to the rescue of someone else's clothes, that no one should have to ever notice someone else's clothes except impressionistically like a blob in a pointillistic landscape. He imagined that the new Librarian was a gentleman of about fifty-five in crumpled tailor-made clothes and a pongee shirt with a black stringy tie, black for the recently dead President who had had him on the list of possibles. He would have "shrewd blue eyes" and a couple of facial tics indicating quick ratiocination and courtesy, et cetera.

The poet was not ushered into the Librarian's office but was told by a lone secretary that the door was open and to walk right in. A stocky man in a blue suit got up in a kind of crouching position and held out his hand. The secretary had shut the door. "Shapiro," the Librarian said as a complete sentence, and he looked at the poet.

"Shapiro," the Librarian of Congress said, "we don't want any Communists or cocksuckers in this Library."

When the sadistic dentist was battering the poet's impacted tooth with his electric battering-ram and picking out pieces of the porcelain and maybe fragments of jawbone the poet thought he had fainted but didn't really know, but he would never forgive the outrage as long as he lived. But that was a mere annoyance like a fly insisting on settling on your nose while you are trying to carry on a conversation with a prince, compared with this bolt of electricity that went all the way through him and smashed him heart and soul. It broke something in him that would never heal, as if one of his children had attacked him with a butcher knife. Here was a man in charge of the greatest Library in the world, as the poet thought of it, who had been appointed to be the keeper of the books until he died, appointed by the President of the United States for life and approved by the Congress of the United States, and whose opening salute to his new Consultant in Poetry in American Letters was on the level of addressing a soldier clearing out a latrine.

I should get up and leave, he thought, but he sat there speechless and heard the voice turn conciliatory and soft, and the Texan, as the poet now saw him, opened a drawer in his desk and hauled out a quart of bourbon and two glasses, and they drank while the poet remembered idiotically that alcoholic beverages are forbidden by law on Capitol Hill where the Library of Congress sits facing the Capitol itself and next door to the marbly Supreme Court which wasn't about to rush in and snatch away the Librarian's bottle. The Librarian asked if the poet had found a place to live and he said yes and said where and the dialogue petered out and they shook hands and the poet went his way. He said nothing to his wife about the conversation except that it was friendly; but the shame of it would never leave him.

In a sense it steeled him and he would do the job well, he would make it a job worth its name and he would show the redneck Texan that a kike knew what a library was better than he ever would, and in fact after a year on the job the Librarian himself asked him to stay on for a second year, which had never been done before, and the poet declined. A few years later he would meet the Librarian at a gathering in Paris, for this Librarian had also resigned to be head of UNESCO, and they chatted like old friends. And that was the last time the poet saw him or heard of him.

He went to his job or sinecure in the ridiculously beautiful mas-

sive building which had been built in the fin de siecle period
of American architecture, when the nation was flooded with big
Yankee dollars and robber barons and gold and silver and lead
and copper and coal mines, and oil was beginning to be thought
of as black gold, and all the half-educated architects went crazy
with textbooks and tried to fit Babylonian with Doric and Ionic
and Corinthian and Colonial and Christopher Wren and Gothic and
Spanish Renaissance and anything else they could throw in the pot,
and up went the Library of Congress with a million tons of marble
and slate and tile and steel, for steel and iron girders were becoming
fashionable.

The poet's office was on the top floor in a great room that had
been a lounge of some kind, and it faced the massive Capitol across
the park which made the poet's heart swell when he went out on
the little balcony which was part of the architecture of the old afflu-
ent age, wrought-iron balconies à la Paris and New Orleans, mostly
New Orleans. But to the poet's dismay the big room was furnished,
as he was told by the functionary who was assigned to show him
around, with authentic sixteenth-century Italian Renaissance furniture (as he would say) and glassware and museum quality rugs
(as he would say) except for a modern desk of an ordinary kind that
faced the Capitol dome across the way. All the Renaissance furniture was loaned by the wife of the Attorney General of the United
States to the Library for the Poet's Office. The poet never touched
anything in the room except his desk, and he felt uneasy around
those billowy golden tables and sideboards and chairs that glowed
at him and his common American utilitarian desk with its six steel
drawers and a typewriter sitting anachronistically on top. He was
planted inside a museum room which should have had a red silk
braided rope to keep the public out, but this was his *office*. And
to go with the grandeur he was informed that he was to hire a secretary as soon as possible. It was the poet's first secretary and he
was startled, but was told that applicants would be coming for the

next few days and he was to decide what qualifications they were to have.

The poet sat in his modern swivel chair and looked at his private museum and began to wonder about qualifications for secretaries, and immediately began to wonder what it was *he* was supposed to do that would require *him*, much less a secretary. A Consultant should do something, he thought, such as consulting or being consulted, about poetry, about American poetry. It was very puzzling and there was no secretary to consult or anybody else and he began to panic. Maybe the job wasn't a job at all, there were no "hours," he was responsible to no one that he knew of, there was no superior as in the Army and maybe it was just a Fellowship for writing poems, not necessarily inside his private museum. He had a sudden idea and picked up his phone and called the head of the Music Department, who was the only person in the Library who had written him a note and said if you need any advice come and see me, signed Harold Sponder.

He went to Sponder who had a vast office in the basement of the Library, not a view of the Capitol dome, but which was strewn with music manuscripts in a blizzard and phonograph and tape equipment and loudspeakers. Sponder came and gave him a hug and said he was looking at the new Bach manuscripts that nobody knew even existed and that all good librarians were banditti and that they had the best "fences" and were getting it all, especially as they were getting it from Hitler's banditti who had gotten it from Napoleon and Napoleon Barbiche, etc. He sat the poet down and told him what to do, pointing to the radios and tape recording machines.

"You do this," said Sponder. "A, get a secretary who works her fingers to the bone. Not young. No beauty. B, you write the best poets, beginning with the momzer T. S. Eliot, to come to the Library of Congress to record their own poems for recordings under the label of the United States of America. Get Eliot to record *The Waste Land*, insist on it, and if he squawks for royalties we'll give him royalties. Nobody else gets royalties. We have a grant from Rockefeller for this, a small fee for recording and no royalties except in emergencies. C, you interview Americana figures for the archives. I've already lined up Thomas Wolfe's sister who is a pain in the ass, and a Confederate General who was really a corporal but who is what the L.C. needs to keep Congress off its back in case they investigate that subversive T. S. Eliot. You get the idea? You are part of the Music Department."

The poet enjoyed this hucksterism and saw what he was talking about, and understood that he now had a job. This was what libraries were all about and Sponder hadn't called him a Communist or a cocksucker and he felt a partnership with this music curator in the basement of the great Library.

In two days he had hired a secretary, but too hastily. He had talked to about twenty women, they were all women, and picked the one, a Canadian who had been in the Royal Canadian Air Force, on the ground of course, but who was a naturalized American, who knew literature and poetry and who had been in charge of an air force flight school. He wrote a note to the Librarian and said he had hired a secretary and was visited almost immediately by a somber man who said that he had no power to hire anybody, and would be from now on following these instructions, and laid a thick pamphlet on the poet's desk.

The poet leafed through the Instructions and in a flash saw that he was back in the Army, as it were, that the Army was the government and the government was the Army and that that was where the language or the un-language came from. In order to hire a secretary, he fathomed, one had to make a series of suggestions to a superior, though he had no superior that he had been told about, and then write a request which would be considered, etc., at various levels until at some point his, or someone else's, suggestion or recommendation would be taken seriously and given to Someone with a capital S who might approve one or another of the recommendations, or might not.

But in fact it didn't happen that way, maybe because in his ignorance he had had the temerity to write directly to the Librarian who had busted him down to buck private, for the next day he was informed by telephone that Miss Armstrong was to be his secretary and was told that she would report for work in two days. He had picked right, she remained the secretary for the Poetry Consultant for twenty years, for one difficult poet after another for twenty years, for which, the poet thought, she deserved the Congressional Medal.

He did the interviews with the Confederate "General" who in spite of his great age and resplendent uniform was a crushing bore and a liar, and with the sister of Thomas Wolfe who was worse, but it was just before the age of the Literary Interview which would be even more boring and mendacious than those with a Confederate General soi-disant, but he started the recordings of poets reading their poems in the hot little Rockefeller recording studio in a purlieu of the vast Library. Eliot agreed to record *The Waste Land* but he would do it in the laboratories of the RCA in New York, even though he was on his way to Washington to visit his teacher Ezra Pound at St. Elizabeth's mental hospital where Pound held court, and Eliot asked for a contract with royalties as Sponder had said, and which after all he had a right to.

If there is such a thing as a literary life—and the poet knew there was such a thing and had read about it, so that he shared the common view that writers have a life that no one else can participate in and that is superior to every other kind of life—he would now get as close to it as he ever would in his own life before he discovered that he didn't really belong there and was being kicked out of its orbit as fast as he came close to the magic circle. Not that this made him any different from many other writers and poets who were sucked toward the flame, moths that they were, but that he didn't know about the peripherals. They were all considered sports, eccentrics, oddballs, runaways, even traitors committing the treason of clerks against the priesthood of writers and artists, against Culture itself. Meanwhile he was just a new bright luna moth fluttering toward the soft sweet fire to the oohs and ahs of the feathered assembly with long bills and sharp eyes who only seemed to pay little or no attention.

But yes, they paid attention, it was part of their job to dance attendance on the newcomer, to indoctrinate him, admit him to the closed doors and the secret names and special gestures of the great or near-great or self-styled great and the once-great. After all, they had appointed him, anointed him in conclave, and he wasn't so stupid as to be unaware of his debt, his acknowledgment, his honor. He was polite, even well-mannered in his self-invented way and was even credited with a kind of charm, a mixture of shyness and boldness, of downcast eyes and glares, of sheepishness and bared fangs and could roll over and play dead and also bite and not let go, but he didn't know this and didn't practice anything, and could not ever predict his own behavior with anybody and usually left a literary gathering thinking he had disgraced himself for good.

He met the Living Anthology, poets he had never dreamed of being with in what seemed to be drawing rooms, and would listen well, respond tolerably well, he thought, be serious for a moment, witty for a moment, the way those non-conversations went. He was surprised to see that nobody ever spoke about poetry or about literature, which was absolutely taboo except at dinner tables where non-literary people such as wives were seated between Lions and one was expected to be addressed by these lower orders about sacred subjects, if only to elicit a crack they could then repeat to their bridge partners or neighbors. "Conversational" was tangential to everything, no "shop," certainly no considered opinions except maybe politics, which was contrary to the lingua franca of middle-class books of etiquette, the only common ground of the classes, of the human race. Soon it would be bandied about as a slogan for all people on the make that Everything was Political, including fucking and Mozart and the spiral nebulae. The poet was interested to hear the general talk concentrated more or less on Politics, engaged in even by the actual present Attorney General of the United States and a Supreme Court Judge, with poets and their wives present and various functionaries who wielded great power here and there but who were completely unknown to everybody so that nobody could even remember their names after the introductions. He began to comprehend that conversation was bite-sized in this atmosphere, that one took a bite and a sip and then said excuse me and moved off to another bite and sip, and that although nothing was ever said that meant anything, what was said mattered and might stick to one's mind like a Band-aid or a bit of poison ivy and keep one itching for weeks.

What he liked best was the brushing of elbows, the slight looks and exchanges of the poets who were great, who were held in awe by the world, even by the stuffy diplomats he had begun to meet at these meets, who prided themselves on having one of these Lions at their house like a political triumph and who looked down on everybody who came as a matter of course and even to consider them as toadies, as Second or Third Secretaries or even clerks who had somehow crashed the party. The poet conceived a loathing for these monsters who had been appointed by the President and approved by the august Senate because they were so rich with money they had inherited or swiped fair and square from the American people, like the Irish Joe Kennedy who had been given the whiskey franchise in exchange for the Massachusetts Catholic vote and who was made Ambassador to the Court of St. James.

He stood with the other poets and writers and wives and unknowns and glanced from time to time into another room, where sitting beside the fire T. S. Eliot was in close converse with St. John Perse, actually talking about Eliot's translation of Perse's *Anabase*, which the French poet had reservations about, Perse told the poet the next day at the Library. What he really cherished to remember was a moment when he was talking to the French poet and a woman appeared in the doorway of the room behind the poet's back and

the Frenchman's face lit up like a sunrise and he excused himself
and went to her.

The Consultant's office with its fine view of the Capitol and its
Renaissance furniture was soon a hallway of poets, come on errands
so various that he was glad he had hired a secretary to shoo some
of them away. Most of them pleaded, or demanded, the Privilege
of the Taxpayer, saying that because they paid taxes, paid for the
Library of Congress, the Library was obliged to house the letters
and poems of their uncles and aunts and of themselves, and even
to publish them. Classrooms of children came to peer in with their
teachers because of the view of the Capitol across the way. Photographers traipsed in and out for various reasons until the poet and
his efficient secretary devised various methods of exclusion such as
keeping the doors closed and even locked, posting a small notice
of a phone extension for appointments. He could never write in the
Renaissance room, not a word, but learned to dictate to the secretary who knew how to make fourteen copies of everything and
gradually reduced the tension of the high office to a minimum so
that he could come and go and take poets to lunch or beer across
the street where a line of rundown shops and counter restaurants
provided the only entertainment on the august Hill.

He settled into a routine and spent hours in the dreamy stacks,
for he had permission to wander everywhere as a Consultant, and
could finger volumes that should have been under glass and even
open boxes of manuscript that the Library was forbidden to publish
for seventy-five years. He would run into the famous Consultants
on these tours and stop and sit down and talk, and the famous sad-
looking Jiménez gave him a copy of one of his books of poems with
his inscription. The poet was constantly sensitive to the fact that
he was living in a treasure-house, and he trod softly between the
bureaucrats who kept the gilded establishment up and the treasures
themselves. He didn't really like the job and still smarted under the
branding insult of the Texan. If only even a scintilla of it had been

true he could have taken it in stride, but it was all part of a kind of dossier he thought dated back to the ROTC Second Lieutenant Jewish lawyer who hated anybody who didn't think like him and had sat on the Baltimore draft board and put a checkmark against his name and got him into the first peacetime Army. Now the head of the noble Library of Congress got the whole "story" from the FBI and the poet was permanently under their cloud, no matter what, he who had been briefly in the hush-hush OSS and was asked to be in the newborn CIA and all his life he wondered if he shouldn't have said yes, I'll be one of your gumshoes, and could see himself lying dead in a ditch in Yugoslavia en route to a Writers Conference in Zagreb.

He didn't have to work hard, but he did. He didn't have to work at all, as he knew it was a non-job, a title-job without duties, but he invented the job, made it a place for poets to come and put their works down on wax, along with statements from other people who were sent to him, such as the relatives of famous writers, like Thomas Wolfe's sister, the self-promoted Confederate generals. It didn't matter really, it was all history, and libraries are all history and he was a librarian and understood and loved it, loved even the Renaissance furniture which he was afraid to touch and the houses he went to in Georgetown where the silent great lived who ran the whole government and the War and by now the World, and every-one knew that and accepted it as a matter of fact, because who else was going to run it?

He committed his first adultery in the far little apartment in Arlington where the baby was sleeping and the wife visiting her father dying in a Baltimore hospital, during a blizzard winter such as exists only in Maryland-Virginia where the wet water-laden snow is half ice and cracks down great trees and telephone poles and electrocutes children coming from school and makes cars skid into crowds or into the Potomac and bodies cannot be recovered for months. The white-haired artist had come from Australia and the three had had dinner together and the wife had gone to her father's bedside and the poet slept with the artist and was just dressed when the wife came home exhausted and the three went to sleep together in the same double bed because the snow was too heavy for anyone to drive home to where the artist lived. Although there was no "affair" that ensued, no anything but an enduring sweet regard for one another, even among all three, one of those episodes like a fragrant passing breeze that leaves nothing in its wake but a delightful whiff.

2.

The Consultantship was only for a year, which didn't bother the poet who couldn't see a year ahead and saw no reason to, but one day he was invited to give a lecture at his old school, Johns Hopkins, for a few faculty of the English Department "on a subject of his own choice." He had an unlikely choice, prosody, a secret love the very name of which had been forgotten except among the old philologists who still had the upper hand in their corner of the small famous university. The poet had always had a penchant for this crotchety disestablished subject whose tomes had gathered dust for a century in vast libraries which coveted such things. He had done an entire bibliography of it on the q.t. for his personal predilection. He knew that most prosodists were batty Brits, eccentrics from the eighteenth century mostly who sat in country houses trying to figure out the versification of metrical feet in Elizabethan soliloquies and because they couldn't succeed invented a Theory and then decorated the Theory with a Notational System. The poet found this not only charming but satisfying, he could have talked for days with these nuts, he was such a nut himself and he loved the people who devised these screens to keep themselves from milking cows or beating servants for stealing the silver.

He wrote his lecture, contrasting the stress and foot system of Saintsbury with the "temporal" system of the American poet and musician Sidney Lanier, also a Baltimorean of sorts and a Southern Gentleman of high repute from the Civil War days.

"The obscurities of recent versification," he said, "are explained as an attempt to introduce prose structures into regularly metrical lines," and he explained the reunification of the two systems as a fusion of two older systems, a fusion of the North and the South, as it were.

The Johns Hopkins English Department offered him a job. He took it.

He didn't and did want to go back to his old school where he was a sophomore still, but to do that he had to reestablish his physical presence in Baltimore again where all his family lived, and would go there, cum wife and child, and there was no question about it and it was all settled. The Library of Congress appointment had already fixed him in a constellation which a part of him accepted and even approved. He would be a Professor and see what that was like.

Generally speaking, a poet in the Academy is neither flesh, fish nor fowl, even if he is a scholar—rare to impossible in one person— and is a kind of literary curiosity or biological specimen, someone who has stepped out of the context of literature for a moment to visit with those who write the books about the writers. He may or may not be happy or comfortable there, he may or may not work there, either at teaching or writing, and his stay is always unpredictable even when he has been handed Tenure for life. Poets of course are even more unpredictable than other writers, overwhelmed as they are by the moment they inhabit and finding it difficult to connect yesterday with tomorrow. It is not that poets have bad habits in comparison with the better-behaved segments of society, but that they tend not to have habits at all, and this is expected by the better-behaved segments of society who would be suspicious of a poet who sharpened his pencils before he sat down or who did push-ups at six every morning. Characteristically the poet didn't know what to expect from his new job which carried the title of Associate Professor, with tenure, but he was taken aback when he asked his

Chairman what he was going to teach and the Chairman answered, you don't have to teach at all if you don't want to. This alarmed the poet and he took the answer to mean that he could invent his own courses. He wasn't, he knew, what is called a Poet or Writer in Residence, and strangely he would never be offered that title until after he retired.

He immediately set about constructing a course in modern poetry the way he had set about writing his verse essay in the Army, by plotting it with outlines, by chronology and Tendency, and using history instead of philosophy as most of the real professors did, using biography as most of the professors didn't, and emphasizing prosody above all, which had become anachronistic and which he hoped to revive somehow. But it was all a mistake, he found, and almost at once found himself lost in a thicket of minor writers whose works and names had long been forgotten but which he believed he had to hack his way through before he got to the treasure. What's worse, he wrote the lectures out, in sentences, as he had never learned to lecture from notes and didn't trust himself to stick to the subject, and so wrote laborious essays which he then stood up and read, aware that this is the deadliest form of teaching, even if the lecturer is reading masterpieces off the page. He wrote what amounted to a book of essays about people like Austin Dobson and William Watson and Richard Le Gallienne, cursing himself for getting into this quagmire, while pipe-smoking graduate students dutifully took notes, and he went home and wrote more such lectures as if deliberately avoiding the treasure which was lying all around in heaps and which he told himself he was saving until he got to the Twenties, when everything happened at once and suddenly the whole sky was lit up with the new American poetry.

He could find no good excuse for this pedantry, unless it was a way of finding his road back to where he had left off before he was drafted, the road back that led him to Prosody, his secret love. And if these all but worthless poets were nothing else they were at least prosodists and they would lead to a real prosodist like Robert Bridges, who was just another kind of milksop, but who would lead to Gerard Manley Hopkins who was a stallion under his Jesuit skirts. The poet had before long written so many of these lectures beating around the bush that it was too late to pull out, and he plowed on, boring himself to despair.

But there was another course, a seminar for writing poetry and fiction, which compensated for the lecture course, and he and his writing colleagues sat around for hours at night with the handful of aspiring poets and fictioners, and real work was accomplished, the poet felt. Everything was rewritten twenty times and subjected to the frontline fire of equals and competitors, though the poet would take over and plead with them not to turn writing into a horse race, that there was nothing competitive between them because nobody could possibly write anyone else's lines, and that if they were thinking of honoraria and emoluments they were barking up the wrong tree and they could worry about that when they were proofreading their first book. But he knew he was wrong and was talking like an Old Master because he had already won all those blue ribbons, and he ought to keep his mouth shut in front of these burning young men and women whose jealousies were perfectly natural and in fact necessary for them. You don't acquire wisdom without success, you can't afford it, and they were too young and unpublished to be wise and know-it-all like him, and their eyes burned through him. In a way he envied them their novitiate and their smouldering, and he remembered the happiness of the anguish and the centipede stings of rejection that had sent him howling, as a great poet had put it, to his Muse.

It was all new and had a name which the poet would try to make opprobrious and would never succeed,—Creative Writing. For the university was dabbling in blueprints for writing factories and they were the blueprint. There had been one such experiment, way out on the plains of Iowa, and it was already a monumental success and a model for other English Departments, which had fallen into acedia and ennui and backbiting boredom and had in fact run out of gas, as the poet put it, and had become narcissistic and bitter and brittle and were ready to fly apart at the first brickbat from an administrator. Greek and Latin had long since been abolished or at least demoted, even at Oxbridge, and Literature with a capital L was on the proscribed list. Creative Writing appealed to the psychologists as a playground for them. The sociologists, all the Social Sciences loved the idea, making monkeys out of writers, though they didn't put it quite that way, and the Administrators seized the opportunity to justify their seriousness as the business end of the establishment and to get bigger salaries and blacker silk suits. But so far they were left alone and hadn't yet been organized.

Someone had heard of a poet who was in Phipps Clinic, the psychiatric ward of the famous Hopkins hospital, and someone had seen his poems, prose poems, the mention of which made the poet's mind fly open. He and a colleague went to visit the hospitalized poet whose name was two first names, George John, and with his poems was an introduction written by Gertrude Stein herself a couple of years before at the end of the War when John was in Paris with the American Field Service and had left the poems with Miss Toklas. Gertrude Stein searched all over for this American poet and couldn't find him, but wrote an introduction to the prose poems which she sent to the missing poet, who had them and the small introduction on his lap when the visitors came and arranged for him to sit in on the seminars if he was willing. He came to the seminars and said nothing but listened and had appointments with the teacher-poet in his office.

George would come into the office and shut the door first, as if the poet was his psychiatrist and they would talk for an hour, a psychiatric hour, the poet thought. He could never remember what they talked about, because what poets talk about is usually difficult if not impossible to remember, for such conversations are open at both ends and everything leaks away. Such conversations are exercises in avoiding the way other people talk, so that what is said is beside the point. It is just a living notebook, a flexing of styles, a wiggling of vocabularies and locutions. People who are not writers are usually horrified at what poets "talk about," thinking that all they talk about is sex and money, like truck drivers in a bar. When in fact the poets are not talking about anything at all but only listening to the way the other person is working his way out of a phrasal situation, which is always a trap, shadowboxing for a real encounter with the typewriter.

The poet was happy to find that there was no social life at the university because there was no campus enclosure, no *communitas* as in most such establishments, and because this was Baltimore, where social meetings are highly important and are kept in the family, so to speak. In spite of its great liberal philosophy Hopkins was a cabal of snobbery of the worst kind, of local bluebloods who lived in blue-blooded sections of the city, and the very university sat in the middle of a neighborhood where Jews, for instance, were not allowed to buy or rent houses. So the poet, when he pointed this out to the visiting poet Spender and his wife as they were being taxied to the campus to read his poems, was curious to hear the reaction of the British pair. How disgusting, they said, and the poet felt confused and wondered if he had been, for want of a better word, impolite.

He went to one dinner with his wife at the apartment of a leading Wordsworth scholar who lived in the sanctity of the pure neighborhood, and they had to wear evening clothes to eat in the building's public dining room. The poet rented a tuxedo and wondered what Wordsworth would have thought of the proceedings and the tall handsome bachelor professor of Wordsworth with silver buckles on his shoes or pumps, which the poet couldn't take his eyes off of.

There began the infighting about Creative Writing, the scholars who wanted to ditch the program, the ones who were friendly, and the writers themselves who had everything to lose, and battle lines were drawn. The poet's Chairman was a canny and clever politician, a whisperer as a good politician has to be, a keeper and purveyor of secrets, and the poet was aghast at the maneuvering, the phone calls, the lunches, the late-night calls, the hints he was supposed to be privy to, and he felt hurt at what he believed was the general low behavior of everybody involved. He hated politicking and didn't understand it and wanted to get away.

He had been given an office, which he loved, in the tower, the Lantern, as architects call it, of the not very old Georgian edifice, an unfinished room where there were not supposed to be offices or people, an attic room with a window that overlooked the campus. He was alone there, nobody knew where he was and he wrote poems, one about his anxiousness over being in a place where he didn't feel at home, where he felt an intruder. His feelings about the internecine war began to alienate him from his position, the poet-in-the-tower bit, and he felt he was on display in secret, that he was a rare book in the library and was being looked at through a glass showcase, even that he was the pawn that would win or lose the chess game between the old guard and the new guard. He wanted to get away.

Men who had been his professors a few years before were now his colleagues and the poet felt fraudulent, unprepared. He had no history of professorism, he had no schooling really, a smattering of history and Latin and the English poets he had read himself, a smattering of French, no German, no Italian. He went to the seminar of a famous Dante professor and bought the Grandegent edition and felt totally defeated with the cosmology and theology and the beautiful language he knew he would never learn. English was still the greatest mystery of his life.

He had started to paint, unaccountably, when he first began to teach at the university in Baltimore, it was just something he could not resist doing, there were no ideas of "creativity" that drove him in this direction, no special interest in painting as such, no crutch for his poetry, no connection of any kind, only the desire to use paint and color. He bought an easel and set it up in his little study in the little apartment where there were now two babies, maybe he painted because painting was quieter than the typewriter and wouldn't disturb the children. Yeats had described Michelangelo lying on his back up on the scaffold unfolding the universe, "His mind moves upon silence," said Yeats. Silence was blessed. He even remembered the Army as silent because he had learned the trick of not hearing his tent-mates, the sounds of domesticity were louder. He didn't paint things, he couldn't draw and had no intention of learning, that was for artists. He envied people who could do portraits and felt it was some kind of magic but he never could. He remembered in high school sitting next to a friend who decorated his copybooks with faces of the teachers and students, neat cartoons that captured a likeness without trying, sometimes he would pass a drawing to the poet who would gape at a naked girl sitting in front of him though the girl didn't know she was being undressed, the drawing passed from hand to hand to snigger over. The poet wished he could draw naked bodies but hadn't the wherewithal.

He bought oil paints and studied the strange names, burnt umber, cadmium, cobalt, large tubes of white and black and a green bottle of turpentine. He began to love the smell of turpentine and even linseed oil that brings a shine to paints. His idea was to paint something that didn't exist, he said, a new shape, the shape would engage blobs of color nearby, they would begin a kind of dialogue. Like all amateurs he used too many colors and saw that things began to cancel each other out, one had to use restraint, one had to edit out the mischievous colors and stick to two or three in various tones. He didn't use canvas at first but painted on pieces of plywood or whole wood or heavy cardboard and only kept a painting around for a few days and would then paint over it up to seven times and he never showed anyone these efforts, it never occurred to him, any more than he would show the draft of a poem although he knew other poets did.

Two rich old ladies named Cone had given money to the public museum to build a separate wing to house their gift of a huge Matisse collection, and he would spend hours studying these brightly faded nudes and French Riviera windows and flowers and wallpapers and Mediterranean views. One was the famous Blue Nude, fascinating in its distortions of the body. He wondered how the artist had achieved a kind of two-dimensionality as if he had unlearned all that he knew about perspective or as if he were trying to reinvent the postcard. The poet believed they were masterpieces. The two-dimensionality influenced not his painting but his poems and a fellow poet was later to describe him as a neo-primitive, a classification he liked whether it was meant as a compliment or not. He would never stop painting these—pictures, they were hardly that —and would never hang one anywhere except in his study or in the garage when he had a house. Standing before his easel he would lose himself exactly as if he were writing a poem. Hours would pass like minutes and there was the same strange physical sense of concentration as if every nerve fiber in the body had become one nerve. He began to understand what was being called action painting; there is a kind of duel between the blank board or canvas and the painter; what is put down on the canvas fights back in a sort of birth pang—not that any masterpieces were about to be born. It must have been like that in chaos or in limbo when everything was flying off in different directions in a hopeless attempt to pull something together; it was this chaos in modern painting that hung in all the museums and that the art dealers were getting rich on. The art critics were having a field day, the Rosenbergs and Greenbergs and Herbert Reads. It was like an intellectual blank check. The public wanted to be enlightened or given an ax handle to beat the artists with, and they got both. Terminology is the fruit of criticism, and big terminology reared its thousand heads—abstract expressionism, minimalism, analytic cubism. The radical ism is all you need for ammunition. Ism is supposed to be the golden key that lets you into the garden. The obvious things were almost never mentioned, such as where did all the people go, where did objects go, in what warehouse in the museum of the sky are they banished? He loved these empty paintings, the Pollacks and Rothkos and Stills, more than he did the literary-political-mythopoeic Picassos. He loved the Matisses in which the human face and figure was not human; it too was in a state of becoming. Sometimes the wallpaper absorbed the nudes and the flower vases, it was hard to tell what was actually being represented. It was a mirror world, man had gone into painting and come out on the other side, the same with sculpture.

But what about poetry; had Eliot and Pound taken poetry that far, or Joyce or Gertrude Stein or Apollinaire? They couldn't, hard as they tried. Mallarmé had gone the whole distance in *A Throw of the Dice* and come out with blank paper. The one thing you couldn't banish in poetry was words. Poets were stuck with the written word and that was that. You could bend them and stretch them, you could torture them to death and cut them in little pieces, but miraculously they joined segments again and started wriggling and moving and mating. The poet's exercise in painting was telling him words wouldn't behave like paint or pure sound or marble and steel; they were definition bound. This was why almost every word in the dictionary had three or seven or fifty-five different and opposed meanings. You could kill a set of definitions but the word remained alive, unkillable like some primitive organism which the human race will never get rid of. A poem, even a bad poem, was harder to kill than a cockroach. The poet, even the bad poet, breathed the fire of life into the words and they started on their careers generating new words and images and ideas, aimlessly it seemed, and the entire job of the poet was to keep some kind of control over the fire he had started. What is called style indicates these controls, brakes, firebreaks, back-fires. You started a fire and then had to fight fire with fire. The entire corny as well as philosophical jargon of criticism used the figure of fire, awful expressions such as words tipped with flame, esthetician-rhetoric of the hard gemlike flame, fire of creativity, burning words. He had written his poem about the Hebrew alphabet as a kind of heavenly fire that conflagrated history, eternally consuming the Jews.

He was amazed that criticism never got anywhere. To this day philosophy professors could be heard making fun of Aristotle's explanations of poetry, while others passionately defended him. The very fact that man needed poetry to be defended proved its inflammability and volatility. It was like liquid nitroglycerin sloshing around in a tank truck. Plato knew what he was talking about when he warned Utopia to give poetry a wide berth. Criticism was supposed to put the fire out; poets should avoid it like the plague. In some centuries of great poetry there was no criticism at all, but in anxious and disintegrating times criticism was everywhere with its fire hoses trying to quench the flame, and even the poets hopped on the critical fire engine. To be an important poet in the twentieth century you had to be a critic too, an incredible state of affairs, but in a society where sanitation is an ideal you don't want poetry to get out of hand. Maybe the poets knew that they were endangered and were writing criticism in self-defense, the way various groups of pessimists were learning to use guns in case of a holocaust which practically everybody expected would come unless the leaders of nations could quiet the uproar.

The poet had caught the critical disease early. The very first time he had faced a public audience was to give a talk on modern poetry, not to read poems, which was just as well, considering the state of his poetry at the time. He had wanted to bring the gospel of modern poetry to whoever would listen and there was an invitation at the posh Jewish temple where the young people had a literary group. There he talked or rather read his observations about Eliot and Pound and Williams and Joseph Auslander. How Auslander got in there he wasn't sure but anthologies in those days weren't too picky and most of his poetic knowledge came from these collections and from Untermeyer's doughy notes. This kind of criticism, or whatever it was, was proselytizing and not firefighting, but he had tasted criticism on his tongue and he liked the sharp flavor. He was not yet aware that the critics, the real ones, were at this point arming themselves to the teeth and were on the verge of capturing the kingdom of poetry itself in a kind of fascist coup d'etat. It would go on like that until the end of the century.

All the same his own pull toward the art—he thought of criticism as an art—was ingrained and indelible like a tattoo, and in spite of all the turmoil it got him into he would never give it up. He plunged deeper and deeper into it and became a polemicist like Mencken, outraging everybody including himself, so that sometimes when he was asked about his criticism he would say things like It's what I call mad dog criticism. He would find that he had plenty to be mad about inside and outside poetry, and he didn't see why he should be excluded from the arena of Litcrit, especially as he was to become an editor of poetry magazines and literary, that is to say, noncommercial magazines and made an unenviable reputation as good editor. Randall Jarrell wrote to him saying he liked sending his essays and poems to him because as Jarrell said, You're not like an editor at all.

Jarrell knew what a magazine editor was, a ball-cutter, an assassin. Poets quaked in their beds when they published a new slim volume in fear Jarrell would review it in The *Nation* where he was poetry editor. He had got caught himself by Jarrell when he published a new book; Jarrell busted him back to buck private. The poet was deeply hurt but curiously not resentful. He didn't credit such a good poet or critic as Jarrell with a common motive like jealousy, and maybe he is right, he thought, and would never again read the book that Jarrell demolished.

Gradually it dawned on him or on his subconscious thinking that it was necessary for poets to engage in the critical battle because the world of poetry was in flames, and you either had to become a firefighter or go up in smoke yourself, and if you could handle a hot weapon like criticism you might as well use it. In fact he wanted to use it, the way boys like to handle guns. There is something about handling a gun that brings the love out of you to the surface. The old cliché is that the gun is a sexual weapon and so it is, certainly one of the reasons why war is so popular in human history and why women wilt at the sight of men in uniform. Criticism is a deadly weapon, no matter how many mealy-mouthed Arnolds or sublime Longinuses or snapping-turtle Eliots you have on tap, it's guerrilla warfare, every critic behind his tree and shooting his friend in the back. If poetry is a mug's game (T. S. Eliot) what is criticism?

Eliot was the poet's first love among the living poets. He began to comprehend Eliot's loathing of poetry. *I loathe poetry* Eliot would say from time to time. This was pure criticism, meaning on the manifest level that he loathed what passes for poetry in the usual world, but on the latent underground level that he really loathed poetry in the highest empyrean, that it was only a fake of the transcendental reality. Poor Uncle Tom was only a reborn Christian after all. Tom's a-cold, wrote Stephen Spender in a poem that he showed the poet. Spender said he was writing about Eliot. Eliot in his sad life wrote so little and the world made so much of it, giving the example of the minimum, but his criticism was voluminous and powerful and drove through Europe and America like Rommel in the desert. It was breathtaking, scripture from Sinai, it thundered and wrote obiter dicta in stone tablets. Was the poet going to be Mosaic and smash the tablets in front of the people and proclaim a new dispensation—away with the Tradition, away with Classicism and so forth? He would; why not?

In time he found he was to make a formulation of his own, not to confront a pro like the Eliots and Pounds, but to save himself for what he thought was the poetry. He had plenty of help and aid and comfort from his compatriots. It was no accident that his first love had been Whitman and his late love Williams, both of whom the archbishop, as he was already known in literary circles, loathed, as he loathed poetry. This game of swatting the tsetse, as T. S. Eliot's friend Aiken called it, occupied the poet off and on all his life, until he reached the climacteric in one lecture which ricocheted around the country for years, he called it "T. S. Eliot, the Death of Literary Judgment." It was a zinger, but this act of valor did not in the poet's mind diminish his real admiration for Eliot, his love in fact.

It was the very paralysis of Eliot, like the sibyl upside down in the bottle and shrunk to a bat, that made the crippled Eliot an object of love. He had sacrificed himself to the poetry fire and been shriveled by the flame. He was an icon, a walking cadaver in his tailored English clothes. Unlike the calm prolific polished senatorial loftily occult and magical William Butler Yeats, the spider Eliot crept into sainthood and Nobelhood tortured and befouled with vision, an actual martyr in a world where martyrs did not exist, only victims of hit men and murder factories. On the one hand there was the poetry, the legitimization of the broken line, the broken stave, the broken image, the heap of broken images as Eliot called them. On the other hand was the quester's dream of putting them back together again, or rather of hoarding them as holy relics, for inspiration and succor. He knew it was a hopeless task, the holy water was polluted and the wafer stank, but he was already a ghoul, he had been a ghoul from the start.

He had long had a theory that ghosts had not yet crossed the Mississippi. T. S. Eliot was born in St. Louis and it haunted him all his life, being born in St. Louis; ghosts had been brought from New England and had emigrated as far as the Mississippi and then stopped. Eliot went back to Boston. Did he know that he was the first American ghost or ghoul to cross Ole Man River? He must have, he crossed all the rivers, look at all the rivers in his poetry, the Plate, the Ganges, the Virginia rivers, every, almost every continent, rivers, the river Thames sweats oil and tar, London Bridge is falling down. Eliot knew; he had the genius to turn his back on the West and go home to the old ghosts and shades, had himself burned to ashes and buried in a small ancestral churchyard in England, leaving the West to the big pink gay Walt Whitman, to Hart Crane and bitter Jeffers and his American enemy Doc Williams.

All this seeped through to the poet while he was still young, still in love with the W's, still hypnotized by the Eliots and all those who absented themselves from the felicities of St. Louis and Paterson, New Jersey. He was aware of all the visits Eliot made to the New World, casting his shadow over the grim academies, sowing the seeds of doubt in the hearts of the young, defining Culture step by step, the Ideal Society step by step, a microcosm of the about-to-fall British Empire, everyone would be British in this neo–New World, everyone a Christian with a pocket handkerchief.

Home had already turned into a hell in the little apartment with two babies: the new son screaming all night and the woman next door banging on the wall because the baby was keeping her from her sleep and she had to go to her job; and the cockroaches in the living room where the poet had built bookcases out of bricks and the insects laid their eggs between the bricks and he had to tear the whole thing out; and the older child rolling her walker down a flight of concrete stairs; and a secondhand car that caught on fire in the middle of Eutaw Place and he grabbed the child and fled and left the car and never heard of it again. And the FBI.

They came to him, the FBI, two big young men in perfect suits and gleaming sneers, to talk about a woman he had known fifteen years before, a schoolteacher he had gone to Tahiti with, and he was curious and let them come in. They went into the bedroom where he had set up an easel and was trying to learn to paint and they said sneering things about Modern Painting, about him of course, and asked him to try to remember where the woman who went to Tahiti had put her furniture that summer when she went away with him. He couldn't remember anything like that and they grilled him about it because they said she was up for promotion to Major in the WACs and they had to check. He couldn't remember, he didn't know. He was getting fed up with Baltimore and its past, his past which he didn't want to remember anyhow.

The Hiss Case broke, Alger Hiss the darling of Johns Hopkins, who was worshiped by all the professors and the chancellor and the deans and the bluebloods who wouldn't let Jews in their neighborhoods. The poet followed the case and knew that Hiss was guilty as hell, as they all did but weren't about to throw their darling to the wolves. He even wrote to the accuser, an unsavory Henry Luce character, and told him what he knew about two of the Communists mentioned in the testimony called variously and interchangeably Carpenter and Zimmerman, who were both death-pale and pockmarked and wore long black overcoats and black Homburg hats all the time even in the summer at the Communist bookstore on Eutaw Place. The Accuser asked the poet to visit him but the poet would have no part of that. He was just shaking the hand of the Accuser for smoking these bastards out.

He felt he had become a kind of focal point of infection. The Bollingen "Case" followed him, especially him because he was a victim of it, the Jew who wouldn't let it rest, who would fight it all his life as the last straw on his camel's back that broke his equanimity for good.

How something important happens is the business of historians and newspapers, the effect it has is the business of philosophers and writers and especially poets. Poetry makes nothing happen, a great poet had announced, and this aphorism caused only a mild surprise among people who think that poetry ought to make something happen, especially in a land where results are taken more seriously than causes. But if poetry makes nothing happen, poets can make all hell break loose, and in fact seem to have a penchant for it.

The Library of Congress is too tasty a dish to ignore and the poets who had been there began to taste of it. Why not, they thought, some of them thought, found a kind of Academy to direct the taste of this barbarous country and provide it with standards of excellence? ("Standards of excellence" was to become a political slogan shortly, borrowed from the poets, perhaps, who were discussing prizes more or less innocently.) Why not do something to counteract the Golden Albatross Prize, such as create a new Prize, a real one, not one donated by a journalist, so the poet thought they thought. Money of course is no problem for poets, in the first place because they seldom have any and in the second place because they don't believe in it, this being the main reason why monied people shell out money for poets and artists. The monied people can't believe that there are people who don't believe in money, and keep holding it out to them the way scientists hold out cheese to rats. Of course the philanthropists rarely give money directly to poets and artists, nobody wants that kind of burden of responsibility, but they give away millions indirectly, inventing Foundations with their names on the letterhead and their gold preserved for their families in the name of the Foundations. Scholarships, fellowships, above all, Prizes, the poets knew all this like the backs of their hands. Some of them had the ear of persons so rich that they hid themselves in remote chateaux in remote countries and came home only for family funerals. The right poets had the keys to these kingdoms where they were more than welcome, where they were medicine for the hurt minds of the anxious very-rich who all felt like minor archdukes about to be shot at in a restaurant or in their anonymous cars. Very-rich had become perilous, it had always been perilous but now was more so, as everybody had a gun and an ideology. The right poets, the right painters, even the millionaire Communist artists were all balm to these worried monied heirs and heiresses who would now extend their largess to include them, not like a Mozart who was treated like a domestic and was seated below the salt, but like family members or exiles from one of the old brocaded empires. Money was no problem.

The poets who had had the Consultantship formed themselves into a committee, then a fellowship, and denominated themselves Fellows in American Letters of the Library of Congress, a windbag title like the Society of the Cincinnati which General Washington was attached to before Thomas Jefferson put a stop to it as a potential hereditary officer corps, as this was to be in the same sense, a hereditary elite writers' corps which would call the cultural shots.

The money came to the Fellows like a tame pigeon. The heir to the biggest aluminum fortune in the world, who lived in Switzerland where he had been analyzed by Carl Jung on Lake Bollingen, donated the money, as the poet believed, via T. S. Eliot, now the most famous poet in the civilized world. And Eliot, no longer an American, was made an honorary member of the new Fellowship of American Writers to donate the Prize to the Library of Congress, though non-American writers were not supposed to be members of the Fellows.

A meeting of the Fellows was called and the poet felt happy to visit the Library which he loved and to see the poets all in one room with its mellow golden Renaissance furniture, and to see the great Eliot in the flesh, whose most famous poem he had arranged to be recorded on wax for posterity. The Prize was to be given for the best book of poetry of the year before, and there were two candidates, William Carlos Williams's *Paterson* and *The Pisan Cantos* of Ezra Pound. The poet had read both and knew that the Williams poem was probably his best, anyhow his most ambitious work, and knew that the Pound *Cantos* were also his best, although the whole thing had been sloppy and ill-conceived from decades back. It was like one of those panaceas or Rube Goldberg machines that Americans patent because it is a land of cranks and crackpots who think that their invention is going to save the world. Now Pound was sitting not far away in St. Elizabeth's Hospital for the criminally insane, under indictment for high treason to the United States for years of broadcasts for Mussolini and the Axis against the U.S.A. with filthy Hitlerian diatribes against the Jews. New York was Jew York and

Roosevelt was Rosenveldt and kikery was the cause of everything wrong with the world, and the Jews were even worse than niggery because they were and so forth and so on. This was what *The Pisan Cantos* were primarily about, except for Pound's self-pity for having been caught and put in a cage until he was sent back for his treason trial, which would never take place because of the Bollingen Prize which of course he got, and because of the indifference of the people in the White House who weren't all that crazy about The People of the Book.

They, the rest of the Fellows, the poet remembered, had all gone to lunch together, or so he thought, because they all came in together, the best and most famed of poets and novelists of the time, while he was sitting on the window sill looking at the Capitol across the way and musing about American architecture.

Aiken, who had rented him his car, Auden, Louise Bogan, Eliot, Tate, Katherine Anne Porter, Robert Penn Warren, and the youngish Robert Lowell sneering and shifty-eyed and sycophantic and a half-dozen others took chairs and thought casually that the Prize should go to Pound and what did the poet, the Jew on the window sill think, and he said yes and that was the end of the meeting. Allen Tate wandered over to him and said that *that was a very Christian thing for him to do*, and Auden said about Pound that everybody is anti-Semitic some time, Auden who had a Jewish lover notoriously unfaithful and heartbreaking to the great poet, and Louise Bogan spoke to the Jew on the window sill and said she had been married to a Jew for twenty years though she hadn't known he was. People got up, the poet got up and passed some words with T. S. Eliot about a study of Eliot he had just read by a nun, and they joked a little about nuns writing literary criticism, and the poet left.

At home he started to brood and feel sick and he drank whiskey, which his wife objected to on general principles. He played with the two babies a while and gradually began to feel horrified, began to feel that he had been tricked and made a fool of, began to feel

[42]

a Judas which was what they wanted him to be, wasn't it, with the new Catholic convert Robert Lowell licking T. S. Eliot's boots and the new Anglican convert Auden licking his wounds over his Jewish lover, and giving the Prize to Ezra Pound under indictment for high treason, he who had done more for Hitler than any English-speaking person in the world and who was holding seminars at this moment probably in St. Elizabeth's Hospital for the criminally insane, or whatever they called it, and who was going to be let out because he was a poet. It was all right for poets to hate Jews, because they were poets and said that poetry makes nothing happen. There would be a meeting of sorts next day before the press release went out. The Library put a lot of emphasis on Press Releases, in case Congress thought they were acting independently of them. The poet knew what he had to do, what he should have done hours ago, stalked out of the room and never come back, never spoken to these poets again. He would do it tomorrow, knowing with the innate sadness of the Jew that from then on the door of their Establishment would be closed, or half-closed to him, in the same way that he would never be invited to their Clubs where things were decided once and for all and that from then on he would be considered just another refuser.

He went and changed his vote in favor of Williams, with a note that he could not endorse an anti-Semite for the Prize.

The newspapers were delighted with the outcome. Who could ever write an article about the stodgy Library of Congress, that hideous pile of freak architecture that collected Gutenberg Bibles and wasted the taxpayers' substance? Now here was something, a bunch of longhairs giving away what they called Government money to a fascist traitor who was about to be hanged, they hoped, and all led by T. S. Eliot, not even an American citizen but himself a traitor to the United States, and so forth and so on. Never mind that Eliot had won the Nobel Prize, there was dirty work afoot.

The Baltimore papers, like all the newspapers, made a story out

[43]

of the Prize. The poet began to be besieged, in some quarters he was a hero, a Jewish hero to the Jewish papers, in others he was a philistine, a bourgeois, a pinhead who didn't appreciate modern art.

He was visited by a strange movie-type self-styled Communist who telephoned first from Boston saying he wanted to interview the dissenter, in order to publish an article in the *Saturday Review of Literature*. The poet tended to be suspicious of persons who declared Communist allegiance but allowed him to come. To have a witness, he asked his Chairman if the interview could take place in the Chairman's office instead of his own tower. He asked the Chairman to be there and just listen, pretend to be working. The poet was being OSS.

The Communists' costume was too good to be true. He wore a brown felt hat pulled down over one eye and a slovenly suit and he chomped on a fat smelly cigar which he seldom took out of his mouth, and he talked cleverly and offhand about the Moscow Trials of the Thirties and the Hitler-Stalin Pact and what did the poet think of Henry Wallace and the Hiss case? He said he was commissioned by the *Saturday Review* to expose the fascist plot on Capitol Hill, those were his words, but of course the article would be based on this or future interviews. The poet answered that he didn't know of any fascist plots on Capitol Hill, that he opposed the Prize as rotten judgment on the part of the jury and as some kind of misplaced and mistimed act of friendship for Pound or for poetry, but that he wouldn't be a party to an attack on the Library or the government because of this mistake.

The movie Communist left with the cigar in his mouth and the poet and his Chairman looked at each other and laughed briefly, The *Saturday Review* then engaged the Harvard poet-professor Robert Hillyer who detested modern poetry to do their bidding, he knew nothing about the shabby business but wrote fluently and at length.

Though he partly understood and sympathized with Hillyer, he was furious with all the participants in this charade—Hillyer, the Communist with the fat cigar; the famous poets who were honoring the infamous meshugena momzer Pound; the Librarian of Congress who seemed pleased that Pound had won their prize; the newspapers with their carefully calculated misunderstandings of something so dreadful; the Jews who congratulated the dissenter on his "stand," for he didn't have a "stand." He was furious with the heir to all the aluminum dollars in the world sitting beside Lake Bollingen with the great counter-Freudian Jung, and probably slightly embarrassed that he had stirred up such an unpleasantness.

Now he himself was invited to Harvard to deliver the annual Phi Beta Kappa poem and to read it at the meeting of the founding chapter, the Alpha Chapter at Harvard, and he set about writing a longish academic Yeatsean poem about teaching "creative writing" really. It was a good dull poem, just right for the occasion, and he walked in a small procession by the side of the President of the school who didn't seem to know he was there, the poet in a black hot heavy suit like an undertaker (he would never know what to put on), in the sweltering Cambridge weather, and he read his poem to polite applause and sat through a raging Phi Beta Kappa oration by a Harvard firebrand. He stayed with his friend Matthiessen at his elegant apartment in elegant Louisburg Square and slept on the sofa and the next day returned to his home, his job, his unsettled mind.

He already felt both wanted and out-of-place, somehow fraudulent and peaceless like an animal tortured by boys. If there was a chance to leave he would leave, to go where?

3.

He got the chance. A letter came from Chicago asking him if he would be interested in editing *Poetry* magazine. The present editor, a good poet, was not working out as an editor and would be leaving before long, and would he come to Chicago, at their expense, and talk things over? He could stay with one of the Board Members on the North Side or one of the Board Members on the South Side; the Blue and the Gray again, the poet thought, elated at the idea of leaving the East Coast behind. Something told him that the choice of where to stay, North or South, was very important, maybe even crucial. Where there was poetry there would be fights. There were always people—rich people, bored people, people on the make one way or another—who wanted to stick in their thumb and pull out the plum called poetry, art, culture.

He chose the North Side, maybe because the South Side was where he had lived as a child among the quarantine signs and death hanging over the children from scarlet fever and diphtheria, where his little friend had been lost in the park. He was put up in a beautiful room high in a skyscraper apartment house with doormen and curbmen to open car doors, and women in silk dresses in the wood-paneled elevators. The view looked west out over the smoky Chicago jungle stretching forever away in poverty and near poverty, but this was the Gold Coast where the old rich and the new rich lived and ran things in the Loop, and sat on boards of the Art Institute and the University and the Opera and the Symphony and the Newberry Library, the same few people who ran all the things having to do with art and music and higher education and yes poetry. *Poetry*, the magazine, was one of the plums and he was asked to be the plum-keeper.

But he was worried. What had happened to the present editor? Had he resigned, had he been fired, and if so, why? Well, he discovered, the other editor had been manipulated, ideologically, as it were, by one or more of the New Critics, especially the Southerner poet-critic who had given the Consultantship job at the Library of Congress to the poet editor-elect, and who was T. S. Eliot's right-hand man and the chief *philosophe* of the New Criticism. Or perhaps the new Aristotelians at the University of Chicago had had a hand in the choice of the absent young editor who, the editor-elect was told, was acting in a very unstable fashion, riding subways all night long to think and write poems, and who, after he had gotten his Ph.D. at the University of Chicago couldn't face a class, he was that unstable, and had to give up his first assistantship and just quit. So the intellectuals and the *philosophes*—the poet was to learn that in Chicago everybody who amounted to anything at all spoke French and belonged to the Alliance Francaise and sprinkled their conversation with French buzzwords—the intellectuals and *philosophes* decided that the poet with the Ph.D. who couldn't face a class should be the editor of *Poetry* magazine and give it some philosophical stiffening and starch and publish poems that had some appeal to people who had heard of Quintilian. It was only a trial balloon, like the invention of the Bollingen Prize for Pound, the poet thought, beginning to be convinced; and the editor frankly was acting too much like a *philosophe* and not a litmus paper for poetry, any kind of poetry that had quality, within limits of course, the way the little lady Founder of the magazine had picked poems and hadn't let the tail of criticism wag the flying horse. The poet was supposed to smell a rat in all this, but he didn't care and only wanted to know whether the absent editor had *resigned* or not. He had, he was told.

The little lady Founder was a poet and a Chicago blueblood, as such things go, and had started the magazine thirteen months before the poet was born. Because she was a poet herself and had even given the big Ode at the Chicago International Fair in the late Nineties she was known as a successful poet and could be admitted to the offices of the very rich in the Loop and get money to found her magazine, which was such an immediate and extraordinary success in the literary world that it practically put Chicago on the cultural map all by itself. Of course the lady Founder had editorial genius and rounded up the new free verse poets who were springing up all over the Middle West and putting New England and New York poets in the shade. All the Sandburgs and Lindsays and Masterses were right there for the picking, and the young American Ezra Pound in London asked the editor or rather told her that he would be the foreign editor and send Chicago the best of England and France, and an international tone was set from the beginning. Even "The Love Song of J. Alfred Prufrock" got printed, somewhat over the protest of the lady Founder, whose taste was still mostly on the side of her Ode to the Chicago World's Fair and the strophes of some of her friends who lived in the better parts of the city. And so the magazine started off as a sensation and never stopped being one. The foremost poetry magazine in the English-speaking world, it was called, and became not only the voice of poetry but as Mr. Eliot was to name it when the new editor asked for an endorsement, an institution. And what better place for such an institution than Chicago? the poet thought.

The Founder died in 1936 while crossing the Andes on foot, the kind of thing that Founders do, but the magazine was by now an institution and did not die with her. Everyone decided that a new editor could be found, and they picked a famous University of Chicago professor.

When he quit after a year, a poet was chosen next, a shy well-educated reclusive fellow who had translated *Les Fleurs du Mal* with the glamorous Edna St. Vincent Millay. The present editor-elect regarded this Baudelaire translator as the best editor the magazine had ever had, not solely because he was the one who had accepted the Baltimorean's first poems for the great magazine but because he had published MacNeice and Auden and Dylan Thomas before any of their names were hallmarks of the new poetry. He had won the Golden Albatross himself when he was young and people said it killed his poetry, for he never published after that except for *The Flowers of Evil* and in fact began to bury himself in French poetry, which Chicago approved of. At least this fellow wasn't a *philosophe* or a New Critic and he lived in a lugubrious hotel across from Lincoln Park and devoted himself to editing like a monk, but he was drafted too when the War came and never returned to the magazine after that but lived in Sea Island, Georgia, with his mother and became a fine and distant memory, and it was in this military interregnum that the magazine worried along as best it could with this substitute and that, until they made it uncomfortable for the poet who was being manipulated, it was said, by the New Critics and the Aristotelian critics, and the Board decided to ask the Baltimore poet to step in.

That is a precise way of putting it, stepping in, for the renowned, penurious, tightly guarded symbol of Chicago culture had from its inception been far more than a Little Magazine for poetry. It was an embattled talisman as precious as a Midwestern holy grail, with its old shabby offices on the Near North Side where a small ghetto of millionaires clustered together in their mansions and apartment houses.

There was no meeting of anything like a Board or a Committee. People who sit on real boards for banks and hospitals, universities, operas, anything where there is a lot of money at stake, don't have meetings for a carefully pauperized arm of culture, no matter how far-reaching its influence may be. Instead someone makes a telephone call about something else and then says somewhere along the line, "By the way, what do you think of getting rid of that editor at *Poetry*; isn't he sort of an *embarras de richesses*?" and when there was what amounted to a family consensus the editor would be taken to lunch by one of the members of the crepuscular Board, not one woman among them, and told that the magazine was going into a new phase or new budget or something of the kind.

There was no budget, it had always been a hand-to-mouth operation and would so remain through the century, the best way in fact to run or not run such a tough little sensitive plant. The businessmen knew how to do these chores and enjoyed them. Everything was by word of mouth. The poet had noticed in the Library of Congress that when he had to visit one of the field officers of the operation they never had even a single piece of paper on their desks, as if paper was vulgar and was needed only by those lower bureaucrats who had to make sixteen copies of everything. But the luncheon for the unwanted editor would have the same effect as a Board meeting or a firing squad, and there would be no fuss except on the intellectual edges.

He met all the South Side members, mostly people tied to universities, not bankers or lawyers on their way to the State Supreme Court, and they approved him too, he thought, because it was obvious he had no ax to grind and was understandably ignorant of the internecine politics of the city, even though he had made the mistake, from their point of view, of joining the North. One of them was a professor of semantics at Illinois Tech, a Japanese born in Canada who lived with his wife in a vast apartment with no furniture in it, or so it appeared, and the professor, whose wife was on the staff of the magazine and was big and sweet and Dutch-American, did all the talking and went barefooted on the tatami mats that covered the vast floors. He would become president of San Francisco State University where he stopped a campus demonstration by the simple device of pulling the plug on the loudspeaker. He wasn't a semanticist for nothing and knew that to cut communications you cut the cord; this simple act made him famous all over the United States and he was elected to the national Senate from California and might have gone higher if he hadn't fallen asleep so often in the Senate.

The new editor met other professors, those who had known the Founder and had ideas about the preservation of the Intention. He met friends of the fired editor who grilled him closely about the Board and what they were up to.

And he met the secretary, the only other paid person on the staff, because poetry is always treated as a charity case and he and the secretary got paid enough, barely enough, to have the honor of having the job. She was the last of the Founder's staff, and had over the fifteen years since the Founder died become the Founder herself, she thought, and the poet felt alerted in a sense to the fact that she was the editor, not he, and he would have to have her advice and consent about everything.

She took him to the previous editor's office and simply pointed to the desk. It was a very small room that looked out on a parking lot, and the desk was an enormous rolltop desk made of heavy oak, and the rolltop was up and there were stacks of manuscripts a yard high all across the desk and a large table that took up most of the rest of the room, also piled high with unanswered manuscripts, hundreds, thousands of poems, and the poet's heart sank. There were photographs on the wall of people like Rupert Brooke and D. H. Lawrence and Edgar Lee Masters and one of the Founder, and the poet made a joke about her desk with all its pigeonholes and he wondered what one put into the pigeonholes, indicating that he would get rid of the desk as some kind of symbolic gesture of getting rid of, replying to, all the manuscripts that poured in day after day from all over the world. He would be the first person to get rid of the desk, he thought, he hated rolltop desks, he didn't know why, he wasn't going to lock everything up, he had no secrets, he prided himself.

He had a couple of months to go at Johns Hopkins in Baltimore, and the secretary said she would mail the manuscripts to him in boxes so he could get started reading, and she talked about the old days and they parted, and the poet knew he could not work with her because she was living in the past and had seen too many editors come and go and none of them could ever measure up to the Founder.

Like his father when he had come to Chicago to find an apartment for his young family, he found an apartment, with the help of his new rich friends who knew everybody who owned the right kind of places to live. It was a new apartment "complex," not within walking distance to his office but it was good enough, even though it was across the street from a sausage factory. But then the whole city was redolent with the smell of meat, which was what Chicago was all about, and when the wind blew from the South where the Southern Faction lived, the stench of the abattoirs hung over the North Side too.

For the poet the parting from Baltimore was anything but difficult, even at the University where there was a small shock wave among the faculty. To abscond to an editorship was a matter to be weighed, but to head up *Poetry* magazine was something of a palliative; it was not only the sole journal of its kind that enjoyed an international reputation, but it was penniless and fought for its life month by month, and the poet was going there in a knight-errant role to defend its very existence. A renowned philologist who had been knighted by the government of Iceland because of his translations of the sagas expressed such sentiments to the poet and wished him well; they were all sorry he was going, he said.

The poet was not sorry. The closed hermetic campus had begun to suffocate him, Baltimore had begun to smother him with caresses and he was hyperventilating. He had no plans, he would never have plans except to be left alone to stick to the only thing he knew, the poem, in one way or another. He could never be a papa even if he fathered a thousand babies, could never be a husband or even a citizen, though he admired citizens—*allons, citoyens!*—

and would never mount a barricade or go to a prison for the intellectually righteous, though he very well might stand in the middle of a battle between the Haves and the Havenots and get shot like one of Tolstoy's fools or saints, and never know what hit him. He had already developed an outsider's stance, not what people would call alienation, though he would use the word, because he liked people on both sides. He wanted to see and observe like an observation balloon, and he knew that nothing is a better target than an observation balloon.

The family, the mother and the many cousins and uncles and aunts, were disappointed that he was fleeing the coop, but knew that he had made an irreversible and important decision, one that would add to rather than subtract from his name and theirs, though the poet had nothing of the sort in mind but was acting purely out of pique and exhaustion and chagrin and not ambition. He had no ambition except one, the obvious one, to write good poems, but now he felt he had been contaminated in some way by events, that the very people who should have left him alone to do his one and only job—the poets, the librarians, the professors—had muddied his flow, as nobody in the Army had ever done, and sometimes he had a nostalgia for the Army life where he was completely alone to scribble in his bunk and send his poems out on the wind and wave and have glad tidings float back to him months, years later in a bottle washed ashore on a desert island. It began to look like paradise back there in the War and he hoped he wasn't turning into one of those veterans who turn into old soldiers and can't think of anything but the time when every pore tingled with fear and expectation and tomorrows had been eradicated, for all practical purposes. He was disgusted with the way his life was turning out, and could not rejoice in this version of success and happiness, and knew he had neither.

In Chicago his life had a chance to start over, perhaps. For once in his life he was given responsibility, a small total responsibility which he felt he measured up to, because he had no doubts of any kind about the importance and the value of what he was doing. Again, he had no plans, no long-range visions of any future, but only wanted to right the little ship of poetry which was leaking in every plank and had to be bailed out frantically. A reporter from *Time* magazine, which the poet had always a special aversion to as the pseudo-creator of language, came to interview him and asked blandly what his policy was going to be. Reporters naturally think in terms of policy. He was taken by surprise and said that he didn't have any policy and wasn't quite sure what the question was supposed to mean. It is a poetry magazine, he said, and poetry doesn't have a policy, it is an art practiced by artists of language, and if they have a policy it would be to purify the language, he said daringly to the reporter, to purify the dialect of the tribe, and explained that that's how a French poet looked at it. The reporter had nothing to write down and left.

The poet told this as a kind of joke to some of the Board Members, who thought he had made a mistake and had missed an opportunity for some great publicity, which of course he had. Behind his back the Board had actually hired, without pay, a professional publicity director who was going to keep the magazine in the Public Eye. It was a long time before the poet caught on and a long time before he managed to get her out of the office.

Meanwhile there was a major decision he had to make, and he sweated over it. He knew it would be the worst thing he had ever done to a person and that he would never forget it, but never regret it. He knew also in a shadowy way that he was putting a small torpedo into the ship he was now the captain of, and that everything might go to pieces. He knew also that his life as editor depended on it, and that if he didn't do it now while he was still new and shining it would never be done at all. His decision was to drop the secretary, who had in her mind become the Founder herself. He had to fire her.

He fired her, he remembered, on the Fourth of July. He asked her to come to the office and he told her, who had been in that office when he was in diapers, that he had to let her go. He could never remember how he had said it, only that she said nothing and got up and left the building. He sat in his chair for hours and then went home. He had fairly good premonitions about what would happen as a result, the attempts to fire him, the resignations of South Side members, the outrage, tears, a kind of horror at this desecration.

Nor would he ever regret the firing, though he was cowardly enough to let people believe that it was because of his wife, who had been his own editor in the war years and who now because of her success with the poet's writing and his books had been made Managing Editor and had her name on the masthead of the little magazine. But it became immediately apparent that she was no businesswoman and was having trouble with the printer and the advertisers, the tiny few that there were, and she herself already had fired a man, a poet at that, who was trying to get subscriptions and advertising in New York.

Firing was in the air and it was natural for everybody to think that she was behind the firing of the original secretary, and it was not long before the poet's wife would herself be fired, out of the general discontent of the few Board Members who took a hand in watching the pitiful accounts of the magazine which did, come hell or high water, actually pay its contributing poets fifty cents a line for poetry. It was practically the only poetry magazine in the world that did, because that was part of the Founder's purpose, to try to depauperize poets if only with token payment, and somebody had to look over the shoulder of the Managing Editor, and it was in the long run the businessmen who had inherited the original responsibility of keeping the magazine alive who hinted that the poet's wife was in the wrong slot. So she quit peaceably, being four months pregnant, and there was no outcry from anybody, including the poet, who was in the mood for a clean sweep.

It wasn't that the secretary had "done anything," the poet said to himself; it was that she had done too much in gradually assuming critical responsibility for the contents of the magazine over the years and in the comings and goings of editors and especially when there was no editor at all. In this way she had become a pawn for those Board Members, or rather some of their wives, who had certain tastes about poets and poetry and would try to influence the acceptances, sometimes for their friends or themselves. The precedent for this was the Founder herself, who on the one hand printed the then-scandalous poems of Sandburg and Lindsay and Masters and Eliot and Pound but also the poems of what he called the Lake Forest Ladies, the friends of the Founder, the people in the social register of Chicago who belonged to the age of Edward VII prosodically speaking and believed that the Founder's Ode for the Columbian Exposition was a masterpiece. This eclecticism naturally resulted in esthetic crises, as when the annual prizes were chosen and one of the Ladies of Lake Forest won the first prize while Eliot's "The Love Song of J. Alfred Prufrock" received an honorable mention. After all, a magazine that printed Sandburg's "Chicago" to the praises and curses of the newspapers could afford to vacillate on a poem like "Prufrock," which nobody claimed to understand but which radiated some kind of genius, and traditionalism was an ace in the hole during these esthetic crises.

The secretary was only following the lead of her teacher, except that she had no portfolio and was not intended to be editor in the first place. There was even a personal following she had picked up, her friends, not bluebloods but just hangers-on such as always collect around a cultural sideboard. The poet believed he had not imagined any of this and that he had acted just in time. He had fired two women, he didn't fight to keep his wife on the masthead, and he felt he would now have a free hand to do what he had been brought there for. And again he would have to hire a secretary and he looked forward to the assignment, while one of the Board Members who owned a huge textbook publishing company chose a bright young Irishman to be the Managing Editor, if everybody approved. Nobody objected.

The Japanese Board Member and his wife both resigned in outrage at the firing of the secretary; several others who were her friends resigned. He heard remarks about the *style* of his action, Chicago-style one of them said, like a butcher or an Al Capone. The poet was not even stung, and could never tell anyone what he felt, a deep shame as if he had killed somebody in self-defense. Almost immediately she was made editor of a journal of dental technology, a fine-paying job, he heard, but he knew what a comedown it must be, from poetry to teeth. Her friends all disappeared from the office, volunteers who sorted and filed and typed letters and even read manuscripts.

In a fit of ritualistic cleansing he turned housekeeper and librarian; he scanned the groaning shelves of books, already rare, and the *Poetry* magazines that went all the way back to the precious Volume One Number One of October 1912 that had burst upon the literary world like a star shell. They were all dusty and dry and crumpled, and the librarian suddenly decided to have boxes made and get the thousands of copies filed safely away in snug little cartons—black cartons, he decided—and he calculated the number of black boxes he would need and ordered them from a paper company at an expense which the magazine couldn't afford. It would take months to sort and pack the magazines, but he was pleased when it was done and the boxes labeled and lined up on the shelves, though a visiting poet once came in and stood still and said he thought he was in a shoe store. He tried to give away the Founder's rolltop desk, but nobody wanted such a monstrosity until the Chicago Historical Society said they would store it in their basement.

There were three rooms the magazine rented, and where it had been for decades on a side street off Michigan Avenue where the rich shops were. The magazine faced a lamp factory named Rem-

[57]

brandt which discharged red sawdust into the air every ten minutes right at the poetry offices, so that the big front office had a fine coating of redwood dust and it was best not to open the windows. Behind that were two small to tiny rooms for the editors, and the poet took the furthest one, which the previous editors had used. He looked out on the parking lot but kept his own door to the corridor half-open to see the passersby who came and went to what was called the Chicago Models Club. The models, if that's what they were, made him feel lickerish with their high heels and peroxide hair and loud dresses as they came and went to be posed and photographed for nightclubs that hired them, and he wrote a poem about them. The photographer would sometimes bring the poet huge half-dead bouquets from the nightclubs, and the poet would distribute them around the office with sly remarks to and giggles from the volunteers at work. He longed for these women and their sleazy lives, and felt womanless in his cubicle, in his life, as if he were moving in a circle of untouchables among the too-rich or the too-educated, girls who came from the best or the most expensive schools to work a while on the magazine on their work-study programs. He was too innocent to know that his going to bed with them was part of their program. One of these girls from Bennington reproached him years later when they were talking about *Poetry* and her job that spring and said, "Why didn't you seduce me?" He had no answer.

He worked his way through the mountain of manuscripts over the months and began to see daylight. A new volunteer took the great burden off his shoulders by reading the mail as it came and discarding or returning the impossibles, which were about seventy percent of the mail, and passing anything with any merit whatever to him. She was a fine poet and he felt he had discovered her, and accepted a group of her poems for publication and asked her if she would be interested in reading for the magazine. He had struck gold. She slaved at the manuscripts six hours a day for years even after he left, when it was her turn to get fired by a new editor.

She was a red-haired Boston Brahmin beauty heiress poet, and you would think the lonely poet would have fallen smashingly in love with her, but she did not attract him at all, ever through the years though they became lifelong friends and he knew she loved him all her life and would have been happy to be his wife if he had asked. She was used to marrying and he would see her through two marriages and many lovers, one of whom was a black man who broke her arm and put her in the hospital. She came to the magazine overjoyed at the opportunity to live with poems all day long at the famous magazine, but she was very suspicious at first that she had been asked for the wrong reasons. The woman who had been slipped into the offices to make publicity and indirectly to attract money for the poor publication found out that the new volunteer was from a true blueblooded Boston family of bankers, and without mentioning it to anyone put it out to the newspapers, and the Boston poet and blueblood felt she had been deceived and betrayed and said she couldn't work there after all. It took all the poet's powers of persuasion to keep her, and he immediately set about getting the publicity hound off the premises. Another "firing" took place; he was slaying women like flies.

He and the Brahmin became friends and confidants and went to lunch daily at an oversized overdecorated Italian restaurant with whatever poets were around, and they were all around *Poetry* magazine all the time. They drank martinis without counting and the poet learned to talk to her intimately, for the Boston poet became friends with the editor's wife also. He felt immensely grateful to her and put her on the masthead of the magazine as Assistant Editor and a year later Associate Editor, going up the ladder as in the academic world, and she was deeply pleased.

The baby had come and there now were three children, and he needed more work for pay. There was plenty of that available for him, he found out, and he took two extra jobs, one editing the *Journal of Acquisitions* at the beautiful baroque Newberry Library and the other teaching creative writing at the Jesuit Loyola University. He loved all three jobs, walking from one to the other as they were all close by, a half-mile or so in a triangle. The Newberry Library, which owned property, even rented him and his family a dark peaceful railroad apartment with enough rooms, a building they reserved for their employees of the upper echelons, a Victorian edifice with a courtyard and flowers and lawns right on State Street, which Chicagoans boasted was the busiest street in the world.

He worried about his capability in the library job. He couldn't read Italian, much less medieval Latin which he should have been required to know, but when he was editing an article on Frescobaldi or the venerable Bede because of some new acquisition, he could always go to one of the scholars who was working there as a visitor. For it was a scholars' library and the general public was excluded for the most part, except the genealogists who were trying to find a coat-of-arms and who were friendly nuts and didn't bother anybody. He would feel proud and slightly sheepish when the *Journal* appeared and had his name listed as editor, with all that medieval Latin and Provençal and mention of all acquisitions, including James T. Farrell's stomach x-rays which the novelist insisted be deposited in the Newberry because his innards were so important to posterity. The Librarian was a friendly snuffling history professor from Yale, and it was he who hired the poet and gave him carte blanche to come and go as he liked, and all the help he needed for Old French and German and musicology, and took him down to the deep vault with its safes and showed him Columbus's diary and the poet's eyes bulged.

The Jesuit university was a small skyscraper on Michigan Avenue among the posh shops and the long cars and the sparkling shoppers, and the poet went there and was ushered into a small colloquium of priests to talk. One of them asked him, the bona fide Hebrew, whether he believed in Original Sin and Freedom of the Will, and the poet answered with a smile that he would have to ask a rabbi, and that seemed to satisfy the theologians. The poet had had his flirtation with Mother Church and was still considered a catch, he thought. After all, Monseigneur Sheen himself had been put onto him by Clare Boothe Luce, and Mrs. Luce had written him saying she would have the Monseigneur instruct him when he was ready. He could not remember in what context Mrs. Luce had written him.

Unconsciously he began to change the bloodstream of the magazine, diluting the Waspness with infusions of Roman Catholic and Jew. Two young instructors from Loyola were asked to be readers and were put on the staff and would remain many years faithfully editing, and he acquired two Jewish members of the Board and nobody said boo, for fear of appearing what they had always been, a clan of the elite of the city fathers. One of the Jews was a young prominent lawyer who impressed the Board and who in fact had been recommended by one of them; the other was the firebrand financier who had rediscovered Mies van der Rohe living in obscurity in Chicago, where the skyscraper had been born, and engaged him to build glass and steel apartment high rises on the Lake front. He asked a modern French scholar to advise him about European poets and asked a young California critic, a Pound disciple, to be his criticism adviser. It was partly to assuage his feelings of uneasiness about the repercussions of the Bollingen Prize, as he feared that he might be lumped with the philistines because of his vote against Pound, and he was tacking in the direction of the Poundians in order to get as far away from the anti-modernists as possible.

The smoke of battle settled after the resignations and the introduction of the new members, and no mention was ever made of the Late Unpleasantness, as the Board would refer to it in their somewhat quaint English. The poet was learning that in their circle one did not speak of the past either as precedent or as recrimination; the past was for family members or equals. If there was something serious involved, some past event that impinged on the present,

[61]

then one would speak to the family lawyer or lawyers, and every family had lawyers in the family itself as a matter of self-defense. Otherwise one would refer to the past only as honorable recollection or blessed memory, as one spoke of the Founder.

Sometimes the poet thought that his firing of the secretary and the South Side resignations hadn't even occurred, the obliteration was so complete. So this is how it's done, he thought, for he had never encountered ruling class behavior at close range before, and was astonished at the equanimity of the players and what looked like their refusal to have their happiness interfered with. He was right, but there was more to it than that as he would find out. Up to now he had been gaining the impression that the Fathers, as he was coming to think of them, merely tolerated the magazine to please their wives and the Social Register, and as far as he was concerned it was all velvet. But under the velvet lay the predictable claw. He wasn't actually about to be clawed, but he was about to feel the iron hand give his own hand a squeeze as a reminder of who he was.

He had become friends with a youngish German scholar and editor who lived in the pretty Victorian apartment houses of the Newberry Library. He was on the staff of the University of Chicago Press and confided what he said was a scandal of high political importance. He asked for the poet's help. He had written a letter which he wanted *Poetry* magazine to publish, in it he explained the relationship of the scandal with Hitlerism which he had escaped from and which he would continue to fight. After the War he had been sent to occupied Germany with a team to help salvage libraries and art works, which the occupiers were destroying left and right in their search for whiskey bottles and cameras, throwing whole tons of Renaissance books on the trash pile out of the window into the general rubble. The Americans and the Russians were no different from the French and the English. Soldiers are all alike, he said, and his blue eyes blazed like an ice floe.

The University Press, he went on, had accepted for publication the first book on the American concentration camps for the

American-Japanese; in fact it was written by their editor and was called *Americans Betrayed*. It was a good book, he said, and it was in production. Or was until a stop was put on it by the University itself. The brilliant young president, the handsome ex–law dean whom every young Chicago debutante and matron was in love with had stopped the book. Of course it was not his idea to suppress the book, or any book, he would have said, but the Governor of California had asked him to. Governor Warren, who was to become the greatest liberal Chief Justice of the United States Supreme Court, which was to become known to its enemies as the Warren Court, asked President Hutchins not to print that book but to put it aside, because it was Governor Warren himself who instituted the concentration camps and he didn't want to sully his political career. The poet's German friend had written a quiet, judicious letter setting forth the facts and he wanted the poet to print it in the correspondence section at the back of the magazine. The poet read the letter and said he would.

But the letter never reached publication. Someone got wind of the galleys, read the galleys, and the poet had a visit from one of the Board, whose members never showed their faces in the magazine offices except maybe at Christmas or because there was a little cocktail party for T. S. Eliot. A few Board Members called me, the visitor said, and thought that *Poetry* magazine and politics don't mix, that it would really be better if the letter was published in a newspaper or any place. But not here, he said, circling his hand in the air, where it would do no good, you must admit. The poet asked how he had come to see the galleys. Oh, he answered, one of the proofreaders is Dinny, my niece, and she happened to get my wife to hold the copy while Dinny checked the galleys, and Julie, my wife, you know, told me about the letters. Well, of course, I sounded out a few Members who are on the Board of the University, also here and the Library, etc., and we thought we would give you our view.

The poet told his new young staff about the incident, waxing indignant about the U.S. concentration camps and the cynical politicians, and got off the track and started talking about Japanese atrocities in the war and the machine-gunning and bayoneting of amputees in the hospitals and the rape of Nanking, but got back on again, and the staff to his surprise except for the red-headed Boston Brahmin told him that that letter would get nowhere in *Poetry* but would be buried in the stacks and nobody would ever even see it. The German for all his good intentions didn't understand that poetry in America isn't what it is in Europe, and that everybody should try to do something about the University of Chicago Press, but not here at *Poetry*.

The poet sculled, then backtracked and told what he had decided to the German friend, who glowered and then fell silent. He told the poet that the author of the book and chief editor at the Press had already resigned and gone to a Southern university to head their press, and that a poet had taken his place and that the Governor of California and the handsome President of the University of Chicago had smoothed everything over. The poet had smoothed everything over, too; he wasn't ready to tilt against the Establishment so soon after his defeat over the Bollingen Prize. He copped out.

There was peace at his own little establishment or institution as he went from job to job to job through the days, and loved the new baby, and attended the parties with his wife that were given by the aristocrats on Astor Street and State Parkway or at French restaurants where nobody dared speak English unless they wanted a live fly in their dessert. They visited the Boston Brahmin in her Mies van der Rohe house in the suburbs and talked quietly and were not served anything with alcohol, because her husband was a confirmed alcoholic and there was always the danger that he would take a first drink and then disappear for days, weeks or forever. Life and the magazine had struck smooth sailing for the poet, and he found time to write a series of poems about Adam and Eve, inspired by recollections of talks about Wilhelm Reich with his old friend the Reichean psychiatrist. Reich had pointed out something so obvious in the opening lines of Genesis that no one had ever pulled aside the symbolism, or jerked it aside in quite that way, namely that it was a description of puberty in the two sexes and the horror of the knowledge of union. The Hebrew myth was so bald that the believers would always take it for something else, about devils and angels and paradise and stolen ribs and the Second Coming. He was very happy, with the poem in its seven sections in old-style versification and old simplified diction, and took the liberty of publishing it himself in *Poetry*, when he could have had it published anywhere.

Simultaneously a woman appeared on the *Poetry* scene, a woman who was to change him and the magazine and put everyone on a different course. She was not a Member of the Board, but the poet wanted her to be and wondered why there was any opposition to such a person, wife of the Governor of the State, recently divorced, youngish, Social Register, rich, elegant, patron of the arts, as they say, even a poet who had been published in *Poetry* once upon a time. "She has a kind of gamy charm," one of the Board Members said when he suggested her as a new member, and the poet knew that she was not one of their circle and puzzled over it.

It was a presidential election year, and her ex-husband had been nominated candidate for the Democrats to run against Eisenhower, who had only his war record to run on. Adlai, as everyone called him, had won the hearts and minds of the intellectuals and the professors with his periodic sentences and his modest slyly Lincolnesque demeanor and his great and successful governorship, and his ties to the now old tradition of populism and allegiance to Roosevelt, and the hole in his shoe. He was sure to win the election. The rich city Fathers had somehow swung over to his side; he was Illinois personified; he was upper-class, never mind his politics, he had vision and charm and personality, what the journalists would come to call charisma, and the only blot on his scutcheon was divorce, then still a dangerous quantity in puritanical America.

His ex-wife was considered a threat. She had declared herself a Republican, thus aiming a tomahawk at her ex-husband. Newspaper men hounded her about him, and she didn't know how to handle these clever and frequently vicious ferrets. They seemed to be asking about Adlai's sexual nature, the most dangerous ploy of all in American politics. One hint from her about Adlai's sexual normality or otherwise and the ball game would be over for him. She knew this, any child knew this, and in her confusion with the journalists she added a little fuel to a nonexistent fire.

The poet went with her to her mother's palatial apartment to meet Henry Luce and Mrs. Luce and bigwigs whose names he had only seen in magazines, a Republican gathering, and some of the Board Members were there, of course, and wondered what the poet was doing there—as he himself did, except that he was drawing closer to Mrs. Stevenson as a friend and advocate of Board Membership for her. He visited her in her own apartment on Astor Street, but as was his wont had no thought of anything but whatever matters were at hand concerning the magazine, and especially where it was going to live, because their building was going to be torn down for another parking lot.

None of the Board came to the rescue with places to rent, though the poet thought that put together they had to own half of Chicago. As is the custom in matters of patronage they all conversed about the subject but had no concrete proposals. Each waited for someone else to make a gesture, each knowing that the problem would be solved quietly and to everyone's satisfaction and without fanfare. But it didn't work out that way, and the fanfare would take on a national importance in the long run and cause endless heartache and dismay and hostility. In the long run it was the poet who first solved the problem and in the long run again it was the poet who also dissolved it. The Board was "giving him his head" in their strange terminology, and would let him make his own decisions and his own mistakes, and in a sense they were deferring to the "man of imagination," another term used by owners and bureaucrats and just plain businessmen who had come far enough along the way to glimpse the palace of art and might even be able to mess around in it.

Mrs. Stevenson was admitted to the Board. She was too important, too prominent, one might almost say too famous to be ignored, and of course to ignore her would be a scandal of national note in the present presidential race. Whether people, including the Board, were on the side of Adlai or of Ike it was obvious that she belonged to poetry with or without a capital P. It was tacitly decided that she and the poet would take charge of finding new quarters for the little magazine.

With his loyal and by now loving staff behind him the poet took off almost all day with Ellen, the ex–first lady of Illinois, and scouted the Near North Side of Chicago for suitable offices. Suitability meant not just rooms at a decent rent. It meant a certain style, not quite shabby genteel, perhaps even distinctively ordinary, but absolutely Chicago, maybe just west of Clark Street, the Broadway of the city. It was the edge of the vast west side Chicago, which is nearly all of Chicago except for the two or three lines of blocks of the Gold Coast facing the Lake and which run for twenty miles or so north and south along the gentle parabola of Lake Michigan, and where the apartments soar including the new spectacular ones by Mies van der Rohe, and the old mansions sit behind their perfect flowerbeds and black grill fences with fleurs-de-lis spearheads. They looked at the ads in the morning papers, and got in Ellen's enormous Buick convertible and rang doorbells and looked at rooms on a hundred noisy and quiet side streets. The poet, who never knew how to dress, sometimes wore a black shirt and red tie, and at one house which had a for rent sign a woman opened the door and shouted at him—No Puerto Ricans!—and slammed the door, and after that he gave up the black shirt. But nothing they looked at was right, and the ex–first lady would sometimes stop the car along a curb and hint that the search was fruitless and that she had a far more attractive idea if the Board would go along with it. She was somewhat mysterious about it.

One day they found themselves on the South Side along the Lake, though they weren't looking for offices on the South Side because the magazine had been born on the Near North Side, where it belonged somehow. They were only to drop in on a friend of Ellen's, a rich lady who lived alone in a vast Empire-style apartment full of delicate bow-legged chairs and pale tapestries and towering Chinese vases. It was a nice visit, the poet thought, sipping gin and bitters which the lady made herself and looking out at the sailboats on Lake Michigan while the two ladies talked about the mansion on the Lake where Ellen had been born. She was thinking of turning it into an Art Center, Ellen said, and if it could be done, then *Poetry* magazine could have its offices there. The poet was all ears.

Downstairs in the open car she put her white-gloved hands on the big steering wheel and said, looking through the windshield, I have been thinking of taking a Jewish lover. The poet stared at her and said nothing, did nothing.

He would always wonder what stayed him from her. In later years he would say he loved her (because everybody else hated her?) and that he had never had anything to do with her amorously, though nobody believed him because by that time he had earned an unearned reputation for sleeping with everything in skirts. But he must have known at the time that he was in a hold pattern like a buzzard gliding and scanning a cornfield, and he was not ready to plummet.

They drove back to her apartment and she asked him to open a case of wine. There was a little silver crowbar lying on top of the wooden box and he knew how to open wooden cases, like the hundreds of plasma cases he had opened in New Guinea. But he was apprehensive about the wine bottle he withdrew from its packing, and she dusted it off and applied the corkscrew and poured a half glass for each. She asked if he would like to see her house where she was born and grew up. He knew the house, which he called a Loire Chateau, on Oak Street Beach—gray stone and turrets and corbels and steep slate roofs and porte cocheres and high leaded windows. She was thinking of removing the tenants, mostly show-girl types who worked in the nearby nightclubs on Rush Street. The beautiful rooms had been partitioned and cut up for rentals just to keep up with the taxes, and the place was full of squalling babies and gangster types and the smell of cheap cooking. The only person she knew there was her friend, a German baroness who had a fine room on the front overlooking the Lake; the baroness seemed to like the general squalor as well as the address, and was said to be in love with her confessor.

Mansions are always dark inside, the quality of light being one of their attributes, but this mansion, seemingly in a state of perfection on the exterior, was double-dark and a tenement within, almost like a scene in a Dickens novel, the poet thought and tactlessly said to his patroness, as he was beginning to think of her. Ellen had made an appointment with the janitor, or superintendent as he was called, and he let them in and took them through three floors and up the grand staircase and opened closets and storerooms. They even inspected bathrooms and the cellar itself, deserving a better name in its vastness of furnaces and storage rooms and wine rooms with heavy doors and brick walls with the smell of many vintages still hanging ghostlike. They looked at the paved garden in the back, with its fancy fencing and three great oak trees which had given the side street its name. She had already engaged an architect and an engineer, and her lawyers were handling the removal of the tenants who mostly lived by the month without leases, which was probably illegal, she said, for everybody concerned. She was convinced that the Board would go along with her plan, and in any case she and her mother had decided to turn the manse into an Art Center and she was going to devote her life to it.

As usual with important events, the Board did not meet, and

everything was accomplished by telephone and in a sprinkle of French, and there was never a scrap of paper passed from one hand to another nor any fuss or raised voices. Or if there were such things they were kept from him as if he lived in a soundproof world, though of course he was consulted and agreed that the move to the mansion was ideal, especially as they wouldn't have to pay any rent at all and were going to raise the budget by having a writers' cocktail bar in the basement off the garden. Members, bona fide writers only, would pay annual dues and have a place to retreat to meet other poets and writers and bring their honored guests.

The Writers Bar interested the poet not as a bar; he was not interested in bars or barflies or drinkers or drinking. Even in the Army in the jungle, when finally the authorities began to ship beer to the thirsty troops and one was allowed three cans a week, he would give away his three cans while the other soldiers would pay high cash or shoot craps all day to get an extra can. He was interested that the bar could pay the deficit that the magazine was always in, and that the bar would provide a social scene for writers coming and going. Ellen got the poet to agree that photographs of the poets should be blown up to Gutzon Borglum size for the walls of the club or bar or rendezvous. They went through envelopes of tiny pictures that would suddenly and expensively project themselves titanically on the now wooden walls, so that after one had a few drinks they wouldn't look like poets or people or even photographs at all, but only abstractions in black, white and gray. But when one came back into focus one could discern D. H. Lawrence or T. S. Eliot or Harriet Monroe, and immediately be set off on a wild conversational gallop in whatever direction the wind was blowing.

All this transmogrification was gradual and well done. The tenants were eased out quietly to find new tenements, and no fuss. The remodeling was done quietly and very expensively, the floors taken down to the original wood and refinished and good unobtrusive carpet laid, not wall-to-wall which the poet heard was vulgar and suburbia, but leaving exposed the beautiful woods in most places. The ceilings were restored to their white and graceful lineaments, the fireplaces blown out and cleaned, the tiles replaced where damaged, the window sashes put in working order, toilets replaced with replicas of the originals, the butler's pantries rewired for bells— for there would be an English butler and his wife who had the best servant apartment high up under the eaves, and the English butler would enter the poet's office every afternoon at about four with a large pitcher of martinis in case he had guests or just wanted martinis, until the poet told him to stop. The garden was laid with new flagstones and the iron gates painted subtly in dusty black, and all the walls of the poet-editor's office were lined with bookshelves, and the fine unlooked-at collection of original poetry books put there along with the best set of the bound edition of the magazine from 1912. The poet sat in his big carpeted office, with its own bathroom because this had been the main bedroom of the mansion when Ellen was a baby, and he gazed across Michigan Boulevard onto Oak Street Beach, where the picnickers and working-class folk were sunning themselves on the beach or bobbing their heads in the waters of Lake Michigan, and he felt foolish.

The staff had an enormous office next to his, with a bay window under a turret, and the typewriters would clatter and the readers read. The Boston Brahmin decided on a closet, a gigantic closet to be sure but a closet, as she knew about mansions anyhow and closets big enough to store wardrobe trunks and steamer trunks in. She sat in her closet religiously day after day, reading the worst of the mail and passing the possibles on to the editor, who was staring out of the window into Lake Michigan and feeling foolish and in a sense out of work. Sometimes it occurred to him that he was just another English butler who made work for himself to keep his job, that he was bringing poetry to the patrons at four o'clock in the afternoon for anesthesis. He missed the old splintered messy office on Erie Street with a glass sign in the window that was never

[71]

washed that said in Edwardian gold lettering, *Poetry, a Magazine of Verse.*

The Board Members came one by one and admired the premises. A ballet school was renting the first floor, a classical music radio station rented rooms and had elaborate electricity reconverted for its broadcasts, a sculpture class took place elsewhere, offices of the Alliance Française elsewhere, and so on, but the main business was poetry with its capital P. There was even a small apartment reserved for visiting poets from out of town or from overseas, and the huge beautifully proportioned living room where the ballet school did its exercises could be used for readings of a more or less private nature, while the FM radio station could tape or broadcast the readings on the spot. Everything was done easily somehow, the whole operation of moving and settling in and picking up the work of constructing a magazine month after month, and there seemed to be no hitches, what with all the volunteers, so many volunteers that people had to be turned away. A complacent quiet and even a kind of decorum fell over the house, like a stage set before the action.

Ellen would come by almost daily, sometimes to see her friend the baroness next door to his office, or to see some detail of the house. In the humid summer days she would arrive at the second floor slightly breathless and seat herself in one of the Eames chairs, which somebody had donated to the magazine and which she disliked because such chairs throw the body, especially the female body, into inelegant postures, flattening the derriere and pushing it too far back and making it almost impossible for a woman to cross her legs without exposing a great spread of thigh. These chairs, she said, are typical of modern architecture, made to look at, not sit in. She had wanted to put a couple of thronelike carved chairs with tapestried upholstery in his office, but the poet thought the Eames chairs looked better and the old chairs remained in the cellar storeroom. He sat only in his ordinary office swivel chair behind his ordinary office flat-top desk, but which he had catercornered on the far side of the room to be able to look out the window at the silent continuous traffic, and beyond that at the beach with its bathers, and beyond that the sailboats and in the distance the immense iron ore boats coming and going from Duluth to the steel mills at Gary, Indiana. He should have let her have her thronelike chairs, he would think in the future; it was her house, and that was the least he could do for the patroness. But he stuck to the Eames chairs, which sank the body and were an offense to a large woman.

She was large, not big, a little above medium height with dark brown hair and eyes that are called hazel. Her face was broad and well-modeled, he thought, with a proportionately pretty mouth and perfect teeth and fine rosy skin. She looked healthy, like an upper-class, expensively handled, corn-fed Middle-Westerner. He imagined that she was large-boned and yet voluptuous, which had made one of her hostile Board Members refer to her as "gamy" and had inadvertently offended the poet, who looked up to her without knowing why. He thought of her as a lady. Her legs were on the heavy side and he admired that, too; she walked with a trained grace, somewhat slowly and rhythmically like one who is used to being late for appointments and is expected to be. He was fascinated to watch the way she would fling her hand a tiny bit upward and behind her while she was walking away, the gesture of one who is deliberately dropping a handkerchief or a note. Yet he felt no desire for her ever. Her hands were large and plump, and the only time he ever touched her was to kiss her hand once, on idiotic impulse, as he thought of it later, or mischievousness, because she had snatched it away. It was in her living room, and the poet's wife was there and Dylan Thomas and his wife were there, and they were only chatting, and the poet, sitting next to Ellen, suddenly took her hand and kissed it. It might have started the rumor that they were lovers.

She would offer the poet and his wife her country house in Libertyville north of the city, with its private lake and park and rowboats, and her fully equipped gymnasium opening off her bedroom, and its store of special foods and the keys to the wine cellar, and they went once for a weekend. The poet couldn't wait to get back to the city. He tried to write there but couldn't; he wrote in his office.

He wrote a poem about her, but never confided to anyone until years later that she was the inspiration yet would sometimes say at poetry readings when he read the poem that it was not about a car but about a woman he once knew. He called it "Cadillac," and he used a surrealist style which is an intrinsically comic style and would bring laughs at the right lines.

Sometimes he would run into his neighbor, the baroness, in the hall, and she would greet him heartily, almost gleefully. She would emerge from her little apartment, why he could never figure out, in a spattered dressing gown and unkempt red hair, a woman of fifty-something and an official on the school board. The door of her apartment was the one next to his own door, and one morning instead of letting himself into his office he knocked on her door and she opened it in her spattered dressing gown. She said heartily and gleefully that she had been using the plunger and went through a pantomime of plunging into the toilet with the long-handled rubber suction device. She sat down next to him on a worn sofa, her hem fell aside from her thigh, and he put his hand on it. She didn't seem in the least surprised but continued talking while his hand lay on her, until she said, I think you must be very strong. He was puzzled and began to think about the word and what it could possibly mean, until she said, my priest is coming this morning, he should be here about now. The poet withdrew his hand as if it hadn't been there, and he got up without confusion and they smiled and he went to his office. He never saw her after except in the corridor, when she was going to or coming from work, and she always greeted him with the same lusty good humor.

He had been invited to Europe for the first time, to teach in winter at the Salzburg Seminar in American Studies, and in trepidation he accepted. He was not sure why he was afraid, or what it was he feared. The students would all be English-speaking, many of them English teachers in their countries, some of them well-known writers and poets, a few professors in the class, and he would lecture on what he thought he knew best, American poetry. A young novelist named Saul Bellow would lecture on American fiction and an ex-colleague from Johns Hopkins would lecture on American drama. They would all live in a *Schloss,* a castle or palace, in fact the summer palace that the infamous archbishop had built for his mistress in the eighteenth century and where he treated Mozart like a cur. He would go by ship, his old *Queen Mary* in fact, and take the train for Austria from Paris. It sounded like a gift of the gods, but he was afraid, afraid of his ignorance, of the superiority of the European students, of himself, but go he must. He sounded out one of the Board Members, the lawyer who was to become a state Supreme Court Judge. As long as the magazine came out there was no problem, the lawyer said, and he would tend to the leave at the magazine and at the Newberry, and if he wanted, at the Jesuit university. Everything was made so easy for the poet.

His wife was happy at the invitation, even though she would be left alone with the children, but two other women were not in favor of the trip, Ellen and the Boston Brahmin. Ellen acted as if hurt, but said she would arrange for a party in New York to draw in new guarantors of the magazine. The Boston Brahmin simply wished he wouldn't go, but he had already accepted and didn't understand their objections, which he began to resent, as if he were going on a pleasure cruise and not, as he thought of it, pursuing his education.

How Ellen knew the Jewish publicist in New York he never thought to ask, assuming that rich people everywhere know each other, but the invitation included the poet's wife to stay at Mr. Sonnenberg's house in Gramercy Park as his guests, and meet certain bankers and brokers who were concerned with the arts and contributed large sums to their support by way of purchases and donations to institutions, etc.

It was now late summer and the Salzburg journey would not be until the end of the year. One day at his house the poet received a strange unsigned postcard with a Chicago postmark. It had no signature and it said unsettling things, such as that he should stay where he was and no harm would come to him, and it mentioned a piece of furniture in his apartment which nobody could have mentioned who hadn't seen it. It was a hollowed-out log of a large oak tree, at least a hundred years old by its girth, which someone had made into a chair. The back was part of the trunk and the whole chair was of a piece, except for the seat which had been set in the circle of the hollow. It was terribly heavy and ugly but the poet, who had seen it at an antique or junk shop, had bought it long ago. The writer of the postcard had probably sat in the uncomfortable thing and was telling him something by mentioning it.

He kept the card. The next day he had another and the day after. Each day a new one came, always from a different post office area of the city, and they all contained the same nebulous threat and frequently mentioned still another article of furniture in the apartment. They were handwritten in a clear hand, whether male or female he wasn't able to decide. The poet began to be apprehensive and mentioned the cards laughingly in the office, and everyone seemed concerned about the nuisance. A stack of cards began to mount and he kept them together with a rubberband in his bureau drawer. In the fall one of the cards said that if he went to Europe he would not come back, and he found this one alarming. Someone knew he was going to Europe and was telling him to beware, and he began to speculate seriously who this mysterious enemy might be.

He had two suspects, one a mental case who lived across the courtyard on the third floor like him, and whose living room looked into his where the curious chair was visible. The poet didn't know this man but had spoken to him a few times when he was sunning himself in the garden and had received stares in reply, and he had seen him removed one evening from an ambulance by two hospital attendants.

The poet decided to buy a pair of binoculars and went to a shop that sold such things, and was asked what he wanted them for and would he give his name. He thought nervously that there must be some law about selling binoculars in Chicago, and he gave his name and said that he watched boats on the Lake and was sold the big glasses in an imitation leather case. At night he took to watching the apartment across the courtyard to see if the mental case was watching him, but no matter how often he fixed his glasses on the opposite dwelling he could never detect anything to confirm his suspicions, though he could see the man eating and reading and talking to his mother.

His other "suspect" was even more far-fetched: the Communist who had wanted him to write an attack on the Library of Congress and "the fascist plot on Capitol Hill." The poet had sponsored the publication of a pamphlet attacking the *Saturday Review of Literature* for its attack on the Library, and perhaps the Communist was out to get him. The poet didn't really believe this, but he was prepared to believe anything. The McCarthy-Anti-American-Activities-Committee was in full swing, and maybe he was being singled out in secret by the Communist who had come to enlist him in their cause and whom he had double-crossed. But it didn't make sense.

He made an appointment with the Postmaster of Cook County and went to an old spacious office in the Loop, where a guard with a pistol in his holster let him in. The Postmaster told him he had dozens of such cases a day and that he would have to wait his turn, and thought from what the poet said that it wasn't much more than a threat and that he would do better to hire a private eye to spy on his acquaintances. The poet took the postcards and thanked the Postmaster and left.

4.

It was too close to Christmas for the gigantic ship to be filled or even populous but it still held to its midnight sailing date, and the poet was escorted to the pier by his wife's three girlfriends, who were very gay and thrilly about what they conceived to be a romantic voyage such as one always saw in the movies, with everyone in evening gowns and tuxedoes, and champagne bottles in napkins in enormous staterooms and flowers on all the tables and apparently no bed. They strode up the gangplank onto a deck and were then pointed down a large staircase, which the poet thought he perhaps remembered from troopship days, and went along an endless curving corridor to his room where four other men were already occupying bunks. His suitcase was already in the room on a bunk, and he made his hellos and the poet and the three women went back up on deck and said goodbye with jokes and hugs. Descending again he decided he didn't recognize the interior of the ship after all, and it looked so empty he almost missed the sight of soldiers.

He knew about the North Atlantic in winter but he wasn't prepared for the storm ahead, even aboard the largest ship in the world. Two of the men in the cabin were surly and never spoke to anyone, and one was too talkative and was avoided, so the poet fell into conversation with the remaining man, a young German businessman named Heinz who had been a ski-trooper under Hitler and was in New York opening an office for ski equipment. The Jew and the ex-Nazi immediately became friends of a sort. Heinz always carried a slide rule in a fine case in his breast pocket and whenever they went on deck, mostly on the glassed-in promenade deck because of the weather, he would take out his slide rule and measure or try to measure the speed of the *Queen*, and at the end of day would check the postings in the lounge that gave the day's mileage per knots. Heinz was fascinated by the poet's accounts of the *Mary* as a troopship running away from Nazi wolf packs. He invited the poet to his home in Munich to meet his family, and the poet said yes, he would come, and he was quite serious.

The storm grew fiercer and the ship seemed stalled on the sea. From the very high promenade deck windows which spanned a clear quarter-mile of glass on the leviathan, the sea looked like elephant hide, gray and wrinkled and barely breathing, but outside the glass the wind was at hurricane force, and now and then a wave, or what the crew called a sea, rose up to the eleven-story height of the promenade windows and smashed at the ship, making her shudder, all eighty thousand tons of her. On one afternoon the seas smashed windows and the deck was closed, and everybody who had a fascination for the storm was sent below, and Heinz closed his slide rule and complained to a deck steward.

The third class dining room was practically empty. If there was a crowd on board everyone was in his or her bed seasick. But not the poet or Heinz, who both ate heartily, tended by two lonely waiters who were excessively polite. At first the poet had been seated at a small table for two with a lady named Cohen, an Englishwoman, and he thought that the British would think it right to keep two Jews together, for reasons only the British would know. They might have thought it odd that he next sat with a German, who seemed to be a good friend. Miss Cohen had been knocked from her chair in the dining room by the force of one of the gargantuan waves and was in ship's hospital. The poet visited her and took her a box of chocolates which he purchased at the stores in the lobby of B deck; she seemed very angry at the ship, and he didn't stay long.

They anchored in the roads at Cherbourg and went ashore by lighter to board the train for Paris. The poet had no idea where to go or what to do in Paris, but he and Heinz registered at a hotel near the St.-Lazaire Station and then started to walk. Heinz wanted to see the bicycle district where the bicycle shops were congregated; his company was going to export bicycles to New York from France. They walked up and down the bicycle district, had dinner in a modest restaurant and went back to the hotel to sleep. The next day the poet went to a travel agency in the Place de l'Opéra and bought a train ticket for Salzburg. His friend was taking the same train and they booked tickets together.

The train left in the afternoon and the poet leaned out of the window of the car and bought a bottle of wine and some small cakes. The compartment was crowded and convivial with skiers and their cumbersome equipment, and everyone shared the wine and brought out their own, along with redolent cheeses and skinny loaves of bread. It was a merry trip and they reached the Rhine and crossed at Strasbourg. Across the Rhine, the poet thought, and he would be in Germany where Grandpa came from, the grandpa he never knew and who was seldom spoken of in his family. The train clicked slowly across the bridge and came to a stop in Köln, and everyone sat while green-uniformed train officers came down the corridor opening one compartment at a time to look at passports. They would scan one and hand it back, scan another and hand it back, until they came to the poet. They motioned him to get up. He got up and they motioned him into the corridor. He followed them into the corridor, handing his wine bottle to Heinz.

You have no visa to enter Germany, they told him, and then stopped speaking English and motioned him to get down off the train. The poet was terrified. In the middle of the night in an empty railroad station in Germany, a Jew "out of uniform" crossed his mind. Pale, he went back into the compartment and dragged his suitcase down from the rack, while everyone stared at him. He shook hands with Heinz and went out of the train and made his way to the empty lighted stationmaster's office.

The stationmaster looked at his passport, handed it back with a regretful smile, and said in English that there would be a train in the morning to take him back to France across the bridge, and that he would find a train for Basel and go through Switzerland because he could not enter Germany without a visa. I am forbidden to go through Germany, he thought, and was beset with a thousand ironies all at once, like a swarm of bees, Jew, grandfather, the War, Yank, poet, editor, professor, OSS, the Golden Albatross, his name that he changed from Carl to Karl when he was a child because he liked K's and because it was more German. The stationmaster said he could remain in his office, but the poet thanked him and sat outside on a bench with his suitcase. There was enough light from the stationmaster's window to read by, and he took a paperback Wallace Stevens book from his overcoat pocket and found himself reading

> Now, the wry Rosenbloom is dead
> And his finical carriers tread
> On a hundred legs, the tread
> Of the dead.
> Rosenbloom is dead.

and he thought of the saying that when Americans die they go to France. And so I, Rosenbloom, am dead and am being shipped back to France. But he was sorry he had missed the chance to go to Munich with Heinz, and of course he didn't even have his address.

The train ride down the Rhone Valley was dreamy, or he was very tired as he stared out the window at the half-frozen river and the naked plane and poplar trees and the village steeples, and wondered where he was and why he had come, and he had a sudden pang of homesickness for—Chicago! But at Basel he revived in the station restaurant, which he thought palatial, or at least the food seemed palatial, for the waiter suggested venison, which cannot be had on an American menu, and he ate the flesh of deer and it was as delicious as a deer, smoky and sweetish and toothsome. He was gradually overcome with a sense of gentility and the rightness of things, not because of the meal and the pilsner, but because he was getting within range of friends and friendly people who wouldn't kick him around like a G.I. Yankee Heeb who was only interested in rape and cameras and whiskey. He booked a first class ticket with a private sleeping room and entered a small cabinet fit for a prince, he thought, with everything sparkling silver and flowing golden woodwork and velvet seats that swallowed you up, and he slept in a fragrant feathery bed as they climbed the Alps in hushed snowdrifts all through the night.

He walked out at the Salzburg station with his suitcase and looked for a way to telephone to the *Schloss*, but then a man in a kind of uniform came to him and asked if he was Professor Shapiro, and picked up his bag and walked him to a small bus and put him in. When it stopped at the ground floor entrance the poet thought, Mozart came in that door a hundred times with music under his arm.

He must have been expected but he couldn't imagine how, because he was both early and late—early for the winter session which wouldn't begin until after New Year's and it was still December, and late because of his detrainment at the Rhine station. The Director's wife met him in the vast marble vestibule and shook his hands warmly while a small maid grabbed his suitcase and disappeared. The poet and the Director's wife started to climb marble staircases which grew wider and wider as they ascended, with glimpses of baroque ceilings and halls and brown and gilt and blue and white sworls and loops on wainscoting and ceilings with cherubs and flowers, and everywhere the glint of gold and crystal. For the castle or palace or *Schloss*—the poet was never sure of the distinctions —had been owned by Max Reinhardt, the great drama producer who had staged *A Midsummer Night's Dream* and *Faust* and *The Lower Depths* and *Oedipus Rex* and God knows what, and this was his home and showplace. His real name of course was Goldmann, the poet remembered with satisfaction.

They climbed to the top of the pile, about five or six stories, and went down an uneven wood corridor and into his little two-room apartment, a small sitting room and an adjoining bedroom, very modestly furnished but cozy and very bright facing the sky and the lake below and the snowy jagged mountains. The Director's wife Esmee took him to the window and pointed up toward a high mountain and said, up there is Berchtesgaden. He stared at the mountain.

He was the first arrival and was alone with his hosts and the servants in the *Schloss.* The Director was a New England Brahmin of some kind, quiet, shy, who shambled slightly when he walked, out of excessive modesty perhaps. He was called Shep for Sheppard. Esmee was clean-looking and bone-faced and had prominent breasts, happy eyes and a voice seasoned by practicality and friendly give-and-take. They were social people who ran out-of-the-ordinary, even extraordinary institutions like the Seminar and were good at it. They could make the subtle distinctions between function and privacy, and knew exactly when to turn aside, so that all problems such as occur in a place where a hundred eager and egoistical foreigners from all countries are met to live together and study together were either solved in the process or never developed into "incidents." Theirs was not so much expertise as the air of relaxation and acceptance and pride in what they were doing, and the poet took to them at once.

The poet and Esmee crunched through the dry, clean snow of the gardens and around the statuary of the porticoes facing the lake, and climbed up to the city monasteries, and visited a dozen baroque churches looking like boudoirs inside with their fleshly paintings on the blue and white ceilings, and along the river of salt which

Stendhal had turned into a love-bath with his metaphor of crystallization, and they sipped chocolates in the coffee shops. He toured the castle on his own and wondered at the massive, swelling tile stoves which acted as eighteenth-century radiators and were stoked with peat moss, blocks of which were stacked outside all the rooms upstairs and which gave off a pleasant manure smell. He fell in love with the library with its balconies in curves. Everything curved and billowed and flowed, and there were no right angles as in modern architecture, though all the books were modern and up-to-date, with the latest works in poetry and drama and fiction and economics and philosophy and history in all the modern languages. A room called the Venetian Room was like a cave of ice, all Venetian crystal properly restored by Max Reinhardt, but it was not heated and no seminars would be held there in winter.

He examined the chapel, which curiously opened into the huge dining room, two stories high with fireplaces at either side big enough to drive a carriage through, and as the chapel was not used in twentieth-century times he thought of asking for it as a place to write, but quickly dismissed the idea. But in the dining room the Director's treasurer, a young Harvard economist, had set up good phonograph equipment and sounds of Pergolesi and Bach and *Don Giovanni* floated through the air from time to time, and the poet began to feel at home in a heavenly place. Two tiny middle-aged men came one evening in battered top hats and with smudges on their faces and sat with the trio for cake and wine, and were given gifts, these chimneysweeps of old, and the poet felt warmed.

The students drifted in in bunches, from Italy, from Germany, from England and Ireland, from Yugoslavia and Greece and France, from everywhere except Russia and Spain, of all ages from twenty to sixty and all occupations, editors, professors, poets and novelists all of them spoke better English than the poet, he believed, and they were distributed between the men's and the women's dormitories on the same top floor where the little faculty would take up quarters. The poet had been given the little apartment which faced the mountains and Hitler's eyrie, which he secretly thought of as a dubious compliment or perhaps a pretext for inspiration; the drama professor was next door to him, and the novelist was down the hall at the head of the staircase. The apartments of the Director and his wife were directly across the hall from the poet, and they were large and well-furnished, like an apartment in Boston or New York or Chicago, with big worn comfortable chairs and walls of pictures and books.

After the first general meeting of students and teachers, which the Director orchestrated beautifully in his gentle low-key American manner, there were individual sessions on succeeding nights, with the poet first giving a poetry reading. Poets are always first on the program, the poet had long since noted, and always wondered whether it was an act of homage to the art or a device for getting them out of the way of the real business of literature. The novelist was next, and spoke about the novel in modern America, the discovery of Melville and James, the Twenties and the Depression, the War and the present. Everything was informal and interruptible, almost an attempt to make the Europeans relax, the way Americans try to disarm the Europeans by refusing to play along with their codes of manners and get them to loosen their ties. The dramatist was pedantic and got lost in details but he spoke with his arm in a cast; he had slipped on the ice in his driveway on the way to the ship, and he was forgiven for being uncoordinated.

The subject lectures were daily, and the poet had made his usual mistake of writing his lectures out, not having gained the confidence of the seasoned teacher who appears without books or notes and speaks or orates at will like a god, and sometimes does nothing at all but stare and deliver occasional thunderbolts. He would learn that later.

The poet had never been around so many civilized people, as he thought of the students, and it made him self-conscious, until he reminded himself that he couldn't be like them even if he tried to fake it. They seemed to know all sorts of strange things, such as how to walk and how to eat with a knife and fork without changing utensils from one hand to the other. For a while he believed that all of them spoke all languages, because he heard an English girl babbling in French and an Italian journalist arguing and gesticulating in German with a Dutch poet, and a German girl running on in Italian as if that was the only language she knew. All of them knew everything about American jazz and asked him questions that he couldn't answer, and they were following the presidential election like hawks. Their education staggered him. The Dutch poet was an editor of a literary magazine like him, but he was also a lawyer and a psychiatrist! He told the poet that he had married a Jewess —a funny word the poet thought—during the Nazi occupation and that she had escaped detection and was now the mother of their two children. They became friends and the poet was invited to Holland to stay with them.

He walked warily but happily with them, and went on excursions into town and in the countryside. One night an enormous sleigh had been hired, and two gigantic horses pulled the crowd of about fifty students over the blue snow to a tavern on the other side of the lake. They sat by a tempestuous fireplace and drank slivovitz. The poet had never had this potent distillation of plums that looked like thick water, and he got drunk and talkative.

An Iceland writer was also drunk and talked about unhitching the giant horses and the poet said, I'll do it. He went out to the sleigh. He had never been within twenty feet of a horse in his life. He crawled under one of the massive animals and started to unbuckle buckles. The animals stood still. One lift of a hoof and he would be crushed like a worm. Then the driver came out of the tavern and spoke softly to the animals and stroked their muzzles, and bent down to the poet and said *Out, out, slow* in English, and when the poet was on his feet let fly a stream of curses at him, which brought the students to the door and they all went back in and drank slivovitz. A group of them, the poet among them, decided to walk back to the *Schloss* over the frozen lake. They were in the middle when they heard the ice cracking and they all started to run as the cracks followed them and water appeared through the cracks that spread in front of them, but they all made it to shore with wet feet and were suddenly sobered up.

One of the excursions was to Vienna, but the poet would not go, pleading inspiration when actually he was writing nothing and could not write anything. In later years he would say that when he went to Europe he could not even write a postcard, which was essentially true, as if he had lost the knack, and he wondered at this paralysis. He confided his secret reason for avoiding Vienna to an Italian girl he took to lunch in the city, and told her he was afraid of being kidnapped by the Russians. It sounded self-important and paranoid, but he meant it, and he told her about the postcards and the peculiar threats he had had about going to Europe. He stayed in his apartment and tried to write lying down on his bed, but nothing would come. His mind felt like a blank movie screen when the lights go up between features, a foggy blur that you face but that has nothing on it, a sudden death of the imagination. He began to feel physically weakened by something. It was cold in the bedroom and he stood against the tile stove in the other room and tried to hug up against it and took a sip of Stock brandy, cheap brandy that he had bought for a dollar in town and which warmed his insides. He had heard about a kind of sirocco called a *Foehn* which made everyone ill for no reason, but he wasn't sure this was the season for it. He lay down on the couch in the warmish room and there was a knock at the door.

An English girl with a hyphenated last name came in the room, a pretty, stern-looking person with tight hair. The poet disliked tight hair, it made him nervous. She had brought some of her poems and wanted his opinion. Ordinarily he would ask someone who handed him poems to wait a day or so until he could give them some time, and the idea of having the author sit by watching and waiting for an immediate verdict was something he couldn't handle and interfered with his concentration. To say something off the top of your head about a person's writing could be the worst possible thing to say, and might result in a hurt that the author would remember all her life. But he took the poems and lay down on the couch while she studied a copy of the *Partisan Review* which the poet handed her, with one of his poems in it.

There is a kind of poem, which the poet was already familiar with from teaching and editing, about which there is nothing to say. He knew what was wrong with these poems but could not discuss them, because it was not a question of the writing or the talent and skill— these might be considerable—but about concealment. The authors of these poems, by far the majority of young talents, feared clarification and directness of feeling; they used the poem as a veil or a membrane through which contours and shadows could be seen but nothing else. In clumsy critical language he would sometimes try to talk to these writers about focus, and quote Shelley's poem about the moon which transformed cloudiness into brilliant and frightening imagery, but mostly he would cop out in bewilderment and pick a line or a figure of speech which he said was successful. He hated this vagueness in his advice, and would begin to perspire.

He finished the poems and leafed through them again, trying to think of something equally kind and honest and helpful to say, but couldn't, and she sat with the magazine in her lap and looked at him. He sat up and said, "I know you have been published in impressive journals but I'm afraid I find these rather difficult, I don't mean what they call obscure but perhaps not substantive enough. They slip away from me." She frowned and then smiled and said they slip away from her, too, but that they were just early drafts, and she asked if he would look at revisions. He said he would be happy to and hoped she would tell him which of the poems were related, to give him an idea of her thematic drift, and he might be able to help her that way.

She thanked him and did not get up and they talked about the other students who were poets, and she began to remark on which girl was pairing off with which man and why. The prettiest girl of all was Pia, who was from Trieste and who was constantly in the company of a German writer who was also a ski instructor at one of the nearby mountain resorts, and he was giving her ski lessons. Two of the girls were in love with the American novelist, and one of them might have spent a night with him at the other end of the hall. The drama professor had seen her leave the novelist's room at four o'clock in the morning when he had gone to the hall bathroom, and had the miserable taste to say so to the Director and his wife. The wife was outraged at this confidence and childishness, as if it was any of his affair, and found it hard to speak to him after that. News of the telltale dramatist with his arm in a sling got around and he was politely ostracized.

Two nights later, as the poet was getting ready for bed, there was a soft knock at his door and he opened it to find about ten of the girls in their pajamas who asked to come in. They crowded into the room and sat squeezed on the couch and on the floor, and one brought pillows for his bed and said this was a pajama party. The poet took out his bottle of Stock and the two glasses, and they sat and joked and sang folk songs, which seemed bawdy by the laughter though the poet was at a loss in the languages. The merriment rose and the bottle emptied, and two of the girls danced while the others clapped rhythmically, when there was another knock on the door. The Finnish girl tipsily admitted the Director, who said shyly that he would like to join the party, and he sat down on the sofa. But the party was quenched by his entrance, and one by one the girls said good night and slipped out. The English girl of the poems had not come.

He knew he was staying in his room too much, but the inertia had grown heavier and it was all he could do to go to the library and chat with a student or two, or read in the sunny music room where most of the people congregated to relax. He still could not write, and he began to think of an attractive German girl from Munich who sat in his class but was seldom seen in the dining room or anywhere else in the building. She was a journalist and apparently was still on assignment in the area. He had spoken to her a few times, and she said she was being sent to the States for the election and would be in Chicago for a few days, and could she come to see him? It was enough to stir his imagination. Her English was excellent, like everyone else's except the Americans', and it had the slight German intonation which thrilled him as no other language did, he was not sure why. He had no such response when he heard the French accent or the Italian, and British English in the mouth of an Englishwoman repelled him slightly, but the slight German accent made his blood race. There was something magical about it, somehow more oral, more vocal, like a form of singing. It puzzled him.

The days wore on and he fell into a reclusiveness which became noticeable. The Director asked him one day if he would like to go to Italy with them as their guest after the session and he immediately declined, saying he had to get back to his job in Chicago, and was sorry ever after.

One of the directors of the Seminar was a youngish American who was writing a book on literary censorship, a subject that interested and concerned the poet. He lived with his wife and two small children on the top floor with the rest of the permanent residents, but was in the midst of a divorce-on-the-spot somehow, nobody knew quite how. The wife, who looked stricken, lived there too, though she was about to leave. One day the poet wandered to their side of the building and went in and sat on the floor with the children and played with them. When the husband came in with guests or friends who were touring the *Schloss*, the poet heard the father remark with a laugh, as he was leaving with his friends, that that was the place for the poet.

The night of the end of the session there was a grand party in the great dining room, with both majestic fireplaces blazing and Mozart playing through the loudspeakers and candles on all the tables, and the first good meal of the Seminar, with wines and toasts and jokes and the usual warm familiarities of a social breakup. The poet sat next to the Munich girl at a huge round table and, voluble with wine, asked her, by candlelight, to follow him to his room after dinner, and she made a slight nod. As people started to stand and leave he went out to a more or less secret stairway behind the chapel and started upstairs, wondering if she was behind him and not turning around lest he should find she had disappeared. When he opened his door she was beside him and he locked the door and they fell on the bed. He was kissing her when they heard voices, then knocks on the door, then laughter, then pounding, and their names being called, and they lay very still till the voices receded down the hall. The poet tried to make love to her but couldn't and had a weak ejaculation, and they both lay very silent and cooling, and she rose quietly and straightened her clothes and left.

He was alone again in the palace with his hosts. The students had returned to their own worlds, and except for him the little faculty had dispersed. He had gone with the Director and his wife to see the novelist off on his train. As the train started to slide noiselessly away from the station, the novelist leaned from the train window and tore a paper into confetti-sized bits and dropped them, leaving a trail of fluttering paper flakes in the air. As the train moved faster he dropped another handful, and then another. What beautiful timing, Esmee said, and they walked back to the car.

Two days later he said his goodbyes to his hosts, who still pressed him to go with them to Italy, which he still refused, and took the train to Paris, this time with the proper stamps in his passport and via Germany. He stared at town after town still raising itself from the rubble of war, sometimes with only facades along the street side, newly constructed but with nothing behind, like stage sets. He had no feelings at all about the destruction or the reconstruction, and passed through the country as in a boring dream.

He had had a lot of correspondence with his "foreign" contributing editor Wallace Fowlie, but had never met him. It was Fowlie who suggested that the poet stay at his Paris hotel on a quiet Left Bank street across from a nunnery and half a block from St. Sulpice, where there were Delacroix murals, and a short walk to St. Germain des Prés and the Deux Magots and such renowned places. The poet, knowing nothing about Paris, stayed there. For one thing, Rilke had lived at this hotel, and that was good enough for the poet. Fowlie was entertaining a young editor who had bought a small publishing company called Grove Press and who was going to publish avant-garde books, most from the French writers, and Fowlie was being the adviser and mentor.

It was cold and it snowed. He had never thought of snow in Paris. It didn't go with the popular songs and the poetry he had read in college, though he remembered a story by Daudet in which snow was the important image and cones of snow sat on little trees outside a house where a woman lay dying and scratching the sheets of her bed with her fingernails. He walked through the snow, just a token snow after all, and bought Blue Gauloise cigarettes, which he loved and which turned his fingers a bright yellow like the color he had been when he took Atabrine during the War for malaria. He found a small family restaurant nearby and ate there twice a day and drank milky coffee out of bucket-sized cups. He walked all day over the city, back and forth across the bridges, in and out of museums and up and down the medieval streets with their hundreds of bookshops, and he was neither happy nor unhappy, just coasting home, coasting to nowhere.

He met with the one oriental student who had been at the seminar in Salzburg, a Japanese who was studying French literature at the Sorbonne, and they took each other to restaurants. The Japanese, whom he called Riku, took him to the Comédie Française and they sat so high in the balcony the poet could hear little and understand less of the classical French piece. He went to a get-together at the Brasserie Lipp's with French writers, but nobody spoke more than a few lines of English for politeness, and he could only examine faces and expressions. The Japanese took him to a French poet's house for an evening and there was a black girl from Martinique who spoke very fluent English and who went back with them on the subway and asked the poet to come home with her, which he wanted to do but thought it would be offensive to his Japanese friend who had arranged the evening, and so didn't.

He met with an ex-student from Hopkins, a poet, homosexual, rich, who took him to a nightclub for dinner, and it was stupid and pointless. He met with a Jesuit literary critic from Loyola in Chicago and they dined at an expensive restaurant near the Madeleine and walked to the streets where the prostitutes were penned, for there was at the time a law against their promenading. They walked through a mob of hundreds upon hundreds of prostitutes, who were calling out to them and taking their lapels, and then they walked back through the mob again, with one of them planting herself in front of the obvious Americans saying, Hey, G.I., I fuck you, you fuck me, okay? and they walked away from her and went to the Jesuit's hotel lobby and talked about Chicago.

He had a note from Alice B. Toklas, who asked him to come see her, as he had been writing her about the poet for whose work Gertrude Stein had written an introduction. He had written her from Salzburg giving his hotel address in Paris. He told Wallace Fowlie about the invitation and Fowlie asked him to ask her if he could come, and she said no. The poet decided not to go, either.

He went to the Louvre with Fowlie and the young avant-garde publisher to see one picture only, as Fowlie was instructing the young man in museum manners. They passed the Victory of

Samothrace standing headless at the top of the stairs and the poet didn't want to go any farther, but accompanied them to the Mona Lisa which to the poet looked like a small green postage stamp after the Nike standing at the top of the stairs in the place of honor in the Louvre. They went to St. Sulpice and saw the enormous Delacroix in the dark church, some massacre or other, of course, as befitted the painter and the Christian religion, the poet thought.

In such a city he had nothing to do and wanted to get back to the only thing he knew, poems written by Americans, poems full of rubber tires and rusted tin and condoms and cottonwood trees and rattlesnakes and old war medals, and people who had forgotten who their grandfathers were and who lived on hotdogs and Coca-Colas and bourbon. He belonged to the redskins, even the redskins of the upper class, all barbarians like him.

He crossed back on the *Queen Mary* again as if it was his private ship, in a February storm this time with only a few people in the vast dining room, and him amongst them. He sat with a young Jewish student from New York who was having a life and death battle with his parents because he wanted to be an artist, which is why he had gone to Paris until his money ran out and he had to go home and engage in battle again. The poet said he would talk to the father on the telephone when they got to New York, and he did and the father was first angry and obscene, and then conciliatory and even amiable by the time he hung up. The poet felt like a diplomat and said goodbye to the young artist, and exhausted, went to the train to go home to what Sandburg had called the city of the big shoulders and the hog butcher for the world.

5.

He walked up and down Michigan Boulevard near the poetry office and wondered at the scarcity of people. In Paris, even in Salzburg, the sidewalks were crowded. Here the wide walks were practically empty, although the stores and restaurants were full, but the streets were bumper-to-bumper with internal combustion engines. Everybody was on wheels, and suddenly he missed the walkers, people going from place to place on foot to pause and enter and leave and say *Grüss Gott* and wrap packages by hand in little bundles with string. He was developing a European infection of a kind.

Worse than that, his long, almost monastic continence was at the boiling point and he started to look at women with one thought only —the nuns in his class at Loyola, the females in the office, Ellen, the Brahmin, the models passing his door at the office, neighbors in the apartment. He started to have proofreading groups at his office at night, the most convenient time for everyone concerned, and he brought beer to assist in the work, though beer is no assist for proofreading, and they read and reread the galleys until they were thought fit to send back to the Polish printer who could barely read English but who was all they could afford.

It was as if his little absence caused him and the magazine to fall. It wasn't simply his trip to Salzburg; it was his departure from the scene, the physical absence of the one for whom the little palace of art had been built. And it was not only that he had absconded, leaving his volunteers as well as his actual family to float on their own, not simply that he had asserted his neutrality toward Ellen. There was more. He had been met with rumors of scheming, plots to take over the magazine by Ellen's business manager, now the purser of the Art Center and her closest adviser and confidant. The magazine had not paid its bills, the manager said, and could be thrown into receivership and turned over to some executor, perhaps to be made the personal property of the owner of the mansion. The poet spoke to a couple of the Board, lawyers who watched the city from office towers, lawyers with eagle vision, who weren't about to let their pet Pegasus be led off by a horse thief.

Lawyers love paper. They eat, sleep and dream paper. They turn paper into gold, and their files are colorful and their language neoclassical and calligraphically bewigged. They hang onto the language of the eighteenth century, not solely for reasons of obfuscation but out of poetic nostalgia for the decorous and the stately. They live by the motto "Put It in Writing," and the piece of paper is waved in court like a flag. Their briefcases bulge, their offices are lined with orange-colored books stamped on the spine with black dates. But in matters of decision they are succinct and to the point, knowing full well the irreversibility of acts. Their work begins with the act and they are concerned only with consequences. They play their games with consequences and are interested neither in truth nor justice, and are the first to tell you so.

Send telegrams, the lawyer on the Board said to the poet on the phone; one line only, calling a meeting at your office, to every member except Ellen. Yellow paper with black block-print strips pasted on, the poet saw in a sudden image. To snow we added footprints, he quoted to himself from a poem he loved. He would perform the act and the palace of art would come tumbling down, and he was ready and glad and sent the telegrams himself instead of letting the secretary or one of the volunteers do it. It was for a moment still a secret between the poet and the lawyer.

[96]

Ellen had seemed distracted since his return from Europe, and he thought of it as estranged, although she had more on her mind than the house and the poetry magazine. There was now something in the paper about her every day, and photographers lurked at the entrances of the house to catch her coming and going. Anonymous letters and phone calls were now frequent, and a neighborhood association was telling the newspapers that she was running a bar in a zone-restricted fashionable neighborhood. The handsome writers-and-poets bistro was of course private, but that didn't matter to the people who lived in their townhouses along the side streets and who wanted the whole Art Center shut down. The poet was up in arms, but there was nothing he could do. It was all right to let gunmen and prostitutes rent rooms in the mansion, but taboo to have a poetry magazine, a ballet school, a "good music station," et cetera. More serious were the threats that sounded quasi-political, with obscenities to her about deserting her husband, who was going to be the next President, they said, and her defection was the main threat to his election. Her eyes sometimes looked wild when she stopped by for a moment to chat, trying to keep her equanimity and joking about the threats. She started to carry a small pistol in her pocketbook, and showed it to the poet, who hadn't touched a firearm since he had to carry a forty-five in New Guinea to protect himself against Japs who would dress in G.I. fatigues and join the long chowlines. He knew she was a crack shot; the rich know how to handle guns, he thought, but he was afraid for her. Somebody who wanted to get Stevenson might get her instead and the scandal would be too much for the American people, who shied away from blood anywhere near the Commander-in-Chief. She told him that all the phone messages were taped and that a Secret Service agent was on her payroll, or an ex-Secret Service agent, and the Post Office was tracking down the anonymous letter-writers but there was nothing she could do to keep the reporters and photographers away. But he didn't tell her about the telegrams for the meeting, and his and her impending doom as far as the magazine was concerned, and his heart ached with his hypocrisy.

As with all decisions of any moment, the outcome had been decided in advance. These seasoned businessmen and bankers and lawyers and third generation meatpackers knew with their eyes closed how to take up shock like the most expensive shock-absorbers. The magazine would move to the attic of the Newberry Library rent-free, the editor would continue to produce the publication from there, the printer and paper company would be paid —no bills had been paid for six months in order, as one of the lawyers put it, to throw the magazine into receivership and make it Ellen's personal property, and they spoke of her business manager as her lover. The poet could decide whether to keep the book collection with the magazine, or deposit it with the University of Chicago in the Founder's Room, or to have it assimilated into one of the Newberry collections. The old files of correspondence and manuscripts were also in demand, and money could be raised by having them catalogued and assessed by librarians, scholars and manuscript dealers. Everything had been thought of, and the meeting ended, duly recorded by a secretary of one of the Board, and everyone quietly dispersed.

Ellen did not appear again in her house, and the poet and his volunteers started packing the books and files. It was during this operation that one of the assistant editors called out, and the poet and the volunteers went to the bookshelf he had just emptied. An electric wire ran from a hole in the wall adjoining the baroness's apartment, at the end of the wire a small microphone. The assistant editor, who had been a chief electrician's mate in the Navy, said that that was the most sensitive microphone money could buy, and the poet knew that the meeting of the Board had been taped, along with God knows what else, maybe the giggles of the Irish proofreader rolling around on the floor with the poet. The poet called the lawyer, who made his usual noncommital remark that he would take care of it. But he cautioned the poet to tell the others to say nothing about the bugging device; it would be bad for the magazine.

It was winter and freezing in the attic of the Newberry. The only heat came from exposed pipes and the warm air of the stairways that led to the marble floors below, but the open space in the one room was a full city-block long, and the chill of the Chicago wind filled the air.

He made friends with a musicologist who worked in his cubbyhole on a half-floor below transcribing what he said was ancient Greek music he had smuggled out of Macedonia. He was a Russian refugee with a tremendous basso voice who had escaped from Russia, deserting his country and its ideology, disguised as a Greek Orthodox monk, and in fact was taken into a very ancient order in the mountains of Greece and allowed to copy what he liked in their library, staying until the Nazis came and he decided to risk an escape to the West, for the Nazis would surely shoot a Russian deserter on sight. He cut up his music transcriptions into strips and rolled them into balls about an inch thick and covered them with varnish and glue and strung them onto belts to wear around his waist. He had at least six of these belts and swam rivers with them, often shot at by both Nazis and Greek partisans, and succeeded after months in making his way to the Allied lines, where he was taken by the British, interrogated, and run through to one of the holding camps for the displaced. He contacted musicologists and curators of music libraries in Paris who had heard of him and his father, who had been a court conductor under the czars, and one correspondence led to another and he was offered a fellowship at the Newberry Library in Chicago if he could get there. He got there and never told the poet by what means, but was living penuriously in a tiny apartment near the Library with his wife, whom he had sent for and somehow got.

Yury, as the poet soon called him, was soaking the music balls in vodka, or so he informed his volunteers in the attic, and the composer was half-tipsy all the time from inhaling the fumes. The poet sat in his cubicle with him and watched the process and sipped the vodka. The poet got the notion of keeping a quart of the potent fluid in the poetry filing cabinet, under V, and the staff were told to help themselves when it got too cold in the makeshift office. The faint potato smell of the vodka soon mixed with the cold currents of the attic air. The Attic air, the Attic air, the poet intoned, where burning Sappho loved and sung. The winter turned pleasant at the magazine.

And now he received an offer to teach again. He had tried teaching at Iowa City, a fourth job, what with his editorship and teaching at Loyola and editing the Newberry Library *Journal of Acquisitions*, and he knew he was restless to wander forth in the vastness of America and try his fortunes, although he had no goal in leaving and wandering other than to write poems. But he felt he had had enough of the poetry magazine and all that went with it. The Iowa teaching was only one day a week and it proved abortive. He would take the train to cross Illinois and the Mississippi River and get down at the little station and go to a little empty hotel where he thought he was the only guest except for a student desk clerk. In his room lay a great coil of rope tied to the radiator, in case of fire and in lieu of a fire escape; he was on the third floor. The class he taught was large and dangerous, charged with fierce backbiting and critical competition, and the students were from all over the States, mostly New York, hating Iowa City. It would become a tradition to write an "exposé" of Iowa by its graduates from the writing seminars, and hating each other, the poet thought nervously. But they all had talent, and each and every one would publish a book before long.

He found himself caught in the mesh of the New Criticism, in which they were all indoctrinated, and he fought it in his lectures, substituting Longinus for T. E. Hulme and Eliot, and lashing out at the function of criticism according to the soi-disant arbiters of taste.

He argued in defense of Whitman and Williams and Cummings and Dylan Thomas against the eggheads. He hated the idea of the poem in vacuo and the contempt for the biographical and the historical, and he grew exasperated and advised one poet to get out of there and go to California, which was tempting him. Finally he went to the Director of the Writing Program and said he was going to quit and was sorry to break his contract, but if he heard one more *explication de texte* of a poem by John Ransom he was going to dive into the Mississippi. The Director was furious and said he would summon Robert Lowell from Italy to finish out the course, and the poet left.

The way he shed jobs, like a poodle shaking off bath water, astonished his friends: the Associate Professorship at Hopkins, the editorship of *Poetry*, the Newberry Library, Loyola and now the famous writing workshops at Iowa, all for a semester teaching stint at Berkeley, a campus known only as a backwater even in the middle Fifties, just before it made itself famous by espousing revolutions, any and all revolutions. He would not regret leaving *Poetry* and would always feel he still had a hand in it even when he had stopped reading it. And such was his confidence in himself and his future that he never looked back, even though in later years he sometimes experienced a kind of shudder at what he considered his part in the wrecking of the Art Center, the palace of art which Ellen had so set her heart on.

BOOK II

Poet in the Academy

6.

The poet had said yes to a rather casual and temporary invitation to California and decided to buy a car to drive his little tribe to the Promised Land. A friend of his wife's from childhood, a kindly tough Southern meatpacker, found a beautiful secondhand Ford station wagon, all wood, a "woodie," and the poet drove it around and bought it "on time" from the friend, for there was never any money at hand.

They had rented a furnished house in Berkeley but it was dark and moldy in a moist and moldy climate, and worse, it had no view. He had convinced himself that the main reason for moving to California was the View of the Bay, the beautiful bridges, the sight of white San Francisco across the water, the islands. The entire town of Berkeley sat on the shoulder of a high longitudinous hill and all of the view could be seen from everywhere, except from this dark and moldy house. He found another, much more to his longing, not even on a street but on a flowery path, whose over-decorated living room opened out to the visual rewards he thought he deserved. The garden, or rather gardens, were elaborate. The professor who was leasing the house was a botanist, and a Japanese gardener came twice a week and tended the roses and trees and lawns and poisoned the millions of snails in the ivy and raked up their shells after the arsenic had done its job.

He lectured on modern poetry again, this time tackling the real meat of the subject, but walking carefully because of his uncertainty about his background and his inexperience in handling students. A well-known professor-critic came to his Gerard Manley Hopkins lecture, and although the poet loved Hopkins and thought he could discuss him, Duns Scotus and all, inside out, he was a nervous wreck, because he knew that the professor had come to see if the poet was worth hiring permanently. The poet before long was dying to be asked to stay and stare across the water at Angel Island where he had been quarantined for fighting for his country, and at the Golden Gate bridge and the thousands of sails on the beautiful Bay. He lectured badly, he thought. The time at Berkeley was all too short and the wandering would start up soon again.

But that summer he was sent around the world by the State Department. And eleven weeks later he came back to California, to Davis in the Sacramento Valley, in a state of emotional and cultural shock, out of India, like a Conrad character, a shambles. Women love to nurse these invalids from the tropics, he quoted from Rimbaud. Two days after his return a woman phoned from San Francisco and asked to speak to him. "She says she has just come from Madura," his wife reported with the telephone in her hand. "Tell her I don't want to speak to anyone from India," he said.

He had been finishing his semester teaching at Berkeley when the invitation came from the State Department. He was then still the editor of *Poetry* in Chicago, and they wanted a poet to carry the message of Walt Whitman around the world. It was 1955, the hundredth birthday of Whitman's *Leaves of Grass*, and though he would have preferred to stay in California, which he had fallen for, he agreed to go, not just to India but to several other countries beginning with I—Ireland, Italy, Israel. He wondered what kind of bureaucratic idiocy this could be. Were they working on the letter I at the State Department? Why not Belgium, Brazil, Bolivia and Borneo? He was boning up on Absurdism at the time and getting a new appreciation of the nonsensical. And of course he wouldn't be able to land in Israel at all, because his itinerary would land him in Beirut, and planes from Israel were not allowed to land there. He didn't interfere or even ask questions. His plane would go from Rome to Beirut to Karachi, a fine way to treat a Jew, he thought, and he would never see the land of his ancestors.

He went to a designated hospital for shots, more shots than he had received in four years in the Army, six at a time, that put him to bed for four days with his mind fuzzy and blurred.

He went to the designated travel agency for his bulky ticket, an inch thick, which made the agent's eyes bulge. First class around the world, he said, looking at the poet. The poet remembered something Robert Frost had said to him once when he took the old poet to the train in Chicago: poets always go first class.

He wrote his lecture on Whitman and called it, on a clue from Lawrence, "The First White Aboriginal." He talked about Whitman's sensuality, his mysticism, but mainly his Americanness. He was the first American, the poet argued, the first one fully conscious of his and our newness and uniqueness. He talked about his unpopularity, especially among poets, and his vast influence beyond the traditional. He skipped the homosexuality and the foxing of pronouns and the central Calamus poems, lest the State Department yank the red carpet right out from under him.

The poet always gave himself more work than he was asked for. In his last stint as editor of *Poetry* he decided to do an Indian issue, to collect poems in English in India or to have translations made. The State Department would notify the USIA people in Delhi and the word would get around. How fast and how well it got around, the poet could not know until it was too late. A million doors flew open and a million poets poured out. In India, he would discover, everyone is a poet, regardless of age or caste or knowledge of language, any language. He would discover something he called Anglo-English in which nearly all these poems were written, and he would all but suffocate under the tonnage of paper. An error of appreciation if there ever was one.

He flew to Washington and met an aristocratic Hungarian gentleman at State who had issued the poet the invitation. He flew to New York and met an exotic poet from Ceylon, another poetry editor, who gave him the names of poets in the subcontinent. The Ceylon poet wore a long brocaded tunic adazzle with gold and velvet, and his black hair hung below his shoulders, and the hostile waiter at the airport bar asked if he was the elephant boy at the circus. The exotic poet gave him a smile. He flew into Ireland and landed at Limerick and had a drink in the hotel bar, where a priest turned to him heartily and asked whether the Yank was a Protestant or a Catholic. "Neither, father," said the poet, "I'm a Jew," and the priest put down his drink and scurried out. He walked into the city and gave a poor lady in black with a large black shawl covering her baby all the change in his pockets, and she thanked him and uncovered the baby and the poet saw it was a doll.

He flew into Dublin for his first lecture.

From now on he would be in tow wherever he went. A young lady from the American embassy picked him up in her little car and took him to his hotel. They had dinner together and she explained to the poet about the lecture the following night.

"You will be introduced by the poet Austin Clark," she said, "who will give a long introduction. After your lecture you will remain on the podium and Mr. Clark will ask for questions. Then the fun will begin."

The poet looked at her.

"It won't have anything to do with you," she said, "and you mustn't think you had anything to do with it. The poets will start attacking each other. That's what they come for."

He was glad to be prepared and actually enjoyed the miniature Donnybrook. The Irish poet thanked him for the lecture about Whitman, about the only time Whitman's name was mentioned, and then three members of the audience leapt to their feet and started shouting criticism, ad hominem barbs, imprecations, derision, indignation, blustering, all having to do with poetry somehow, and suddenly everyone else joined in and bedlam broke loose, though there were no fisticuffs. After a long round of this the young lady gave the poet a nudge and a nod, and they got up and left without even being noticed.

She drove him to the Prime Minister's house where he was expected for a nightcap, and she couldn't come in, she said, and left him to ring the doorbell.

Inside was the opposite of the poets' brawl, a silky decorum pervading the rooms, people quietly conversing, "where all's accustomed, ceremonious," the poet thought, as befits the ones who know they are in charge. He conveyed greetings to the Prime Minister from the red-haired Boston Brahmin who was his first reader at the poetry magazine, as they had once been lovers. The Prime Minister thanked him politely as he sat by the side of his wife.

In Rome there was no fuss. Whitman in Italy would be child's play, the body, homosexuality, democracy—the Greeks and Romans had done all that. Who was this fat pink barbarian who spread himself around like butter from a spilled vat? But the simpatico Italians would never offend and said all the right things. The poet thought to himself, damn, the *beati innocenti*, that's us. That's what James Joyce called William Carlos Williams and wife after he met them.

In India, however, Whitman was a smoking pistol.

The poet sat in his first class seat on the Air India plane for Karachi, the sole passenger. He would be on lots of Air India planes as sole passenger, feeling alternately like a rajah and a criminal meant for isolation. The stewardess would bring him beer as he sat in shirtsleeves, and there was no talk between them. He gazed down upon a desert where he thought Mohenjo-Daro was supposed to have been. The poet loved prehistoric civilizations, the lost worlds that never made it into the history books. Cities before writing! What a thrilling world that must have been, and he tried to conjure up their life.

He was nursing his beer when they landed at Delhi, and he ambled down the aluminum gangway, when he was called by name and was escorted into a large waiting room marked V.I.P. where sat about fifty newspaper reporters pen in hand and pads on their laps. An American functionary shook his hand and said he was going to be interviewed by the Indian press and announced in a loud voice —NO POLITICS!—and sat down on the far side of the room.

The beery poet was thunderstruck. Couldn't these sons-of-bitches have warned him that he was going to be confronted with a coven of newspapermen sent to get a headline on the visiting American poet who was going to give them the low-down on Walt Whitman? NO POLITICS! the functionary of State had yelled, as if Whitman had never heard of politics, and the poet had a flashback to his debacle at the university, which had let him out because a professor had decreed that he was Too Bitter Against Big Business.

He was answering their questions dutifully when the stewardess rushed in to say to the poet that he hadn't paid for the beer, and the American host paid it and a fury began to build inside the poet's insides. So he was going to be watchdogged up and down India, and was going to be a monkey on a stick for these bureaucrats. The reporters departed and the poet was driven to his hotel and lay down in sweaty air-conditioning and fumed. The host called to take him to dinner and the poet thanked him and said yes, and they went to a posh restaurant where the poet ordered the hottest curry on the menu, which he was warned against, one that would melt forks, and they talked about Adlai Stevenson and his wife. But the poet was very careful what he said, and wondered how many of these ferrets would nose him through the subcontinent and make his life miserable. He was informed that after his grand tour he would return to New Delhi for a gala farewell, a triumph. The poet wondered about that.

He started in Bombay in style, in his spacious and even luxurious room at the Taj Mahal Hotel, with his balcony looking out upon the Arabian Sea through the marble arch that the British had built to designate the gateway to India. He looked down on the street below always mobbed with rivers of pedestrians, all dressed in white it seemed, a dark people addicted to white, except for the women in their silken saris of colors that would make a rainbow blush. There was a strange, not unpleasant smell in the air, which he would later identify as cow dung used as fuel, mixed with sea odors and car exhaust and incense, he thought. The nose comes awake in the tropics. He had laid two garlands of jasmine and frangipani and godknowswhat flowers on the bed, necklaces of overpowering scents which would be hung around his neck wherever he went. The drowsy syrups of the East, he thought, that had led Columbus in the wrong direction. India, it began to dawn on him, was a world destination, the alpha and omega of history. Coming in from the airport the taxi drove through miles of hovels, tin and paper shacks in seas of mud, not fit for pigs. Men, women and children were all over the place like droppings—refugees of the civil war, the religious war, refuse of history. What was going to happen to them? Like every other writer who had ever set foot in India he would try to delineate the contrasts. In a poem he described something:

> A crow came to my window by the sea
> At four o'clock in the Taj Mahal Hotel;
> He cocked his eye and when I turned my back
> Flew to my tea tray with a hideous clack
> Of beak and claws, turning over the tea
> And making off with the cake. The crow did well,
> For down below me, where the street was black
> With white-clad Hindus, what was there to take?

The poet was glad that his guide from the USIA office was a Hindu, albeit with an Old Testament name. "How is it your name is Ezekiel?" he asked the Hindu. The Hindu replied that he was a Jew, that his people had been in India since the Romans had destroyed Jerusalem in A.D. 70. He said it as if it were yesterday.

He gave his lecture and he read American poetry at universities and ashrams and at literary clubs, poets handing him manuscripts which he took to his hotel and groaned over. He dined with writers and editors and visited with international types on Malabar Hill, a surprising number of Americans among them. Were we now the Western Raj? At night he stared at the huge electric sign seemingly standing in the Arabian Sea and reading Standard Oil. It made him feel foolishly at home.

A woman with poems came to his room one night. Her name was Lalage and the poet was fascinated, more by the name than the woman. The only Lalage there was, he thought, was the one in Horace's poem where she was *dulce ridentem, dulce loquentem,* sweetly laughing, sweetly talking. They discussed the Latin poem a bit and he looked at hers. She said her chauffeur was waiting for her but made no sign of leaving; she sat down in front of the large vanity mirror and began to apply makeup as if they were married. He put his hands on her shoulders and she shrugged them off. She went out on the balcony and stared into the night and he followed her. She wouldn't be touched and went back in the room and sat on the bed. He came toward her and she said, "I am Moslem. I have a silver dagger in my purse," and she took it out and handed it to him. "It's pretty," he said idiotically and handed it back. "Thank you for reading my poems," she said. "I hope to see you in Delhi." She left.

The poet liked Ezekiel, who was himself a poet, a good one in true English, and they became friends. Ezekiel was assigned to escort the American to his next stop, Ahmadabad, but here the friendship came to an abrupt halt.

On the plane the visitor mentioned a poet he intended to meet in Ahmadabad, a woman whose work had been well received in England and which he hoped to include in his Indian issue of the poetry magazine. Ezekiel said he hoped he would not, and the American expressed his astonishment.

"What is it," he asked. "Is she a Communist, or worse?" Ezekiel answered with a non sequitur that she lived in a palace, alone except for a young daughter and over a hundred servants. He begged the American's confidence and told him that he had been sent along with him to dissuade him from seeing this woman. Nothing could have convinced the poet more that it was his duty, his obligation, his right and a test of his character to pay a visit to this lady. He was not told the reason why she was supposed to be off-limits to the American; Ezekiel said he didn't know, only that her brother, a nuclear physicist at Oxbridge, was somehow involved in politics. They spent the rest of the flight arguing about the intended visit, Ezekiel pleading that it would mean endless trouble to him and maybe even dismissal. Everything he said increased the poet's resolve. Whenever he felt himself falling into a trap he would resort to quips, and he believed that that was the origin of poetry. To trick one's way out of a word-trap was a serious form of survival.

He said to Ezekiel, "If you are a Jew and you are not paranoid, you're crazy," and then he proceeded to tell him about his own long bourgeois history of insult and slight and recrimination, beginning with the history professor who wiped him out of the university for sounding like a Marxist—"for Marxist read Jew" he said—to the accusation of the Second Lieutenant in the Army to the raid on the barracks and the quick shipment overseas and the banishment to the desert and to the jungle, to the accusation of the foul-mouthed Librarian of Congress of not only Communism but fellatio.

"But it hardly sounds like *Kristallnacht* or Auschwitz," said Ezekiel, "and after all you *were* the Poetry Consultant at the Library of Congress, and you *were* a professor at the same university that dropped you, and you *are* being sent around the world as the choice of the State Department to celebrate Walt Whitman. Your complaints are rather distant echoes, don't you think?"

The American poet had nothing to reply. In Ahmadabad he phoned from the hotel and made his appointment with the off-limits lady.

His was not really a hotel, though it had most of the characteristics of one. It was a series of dust and rain-stained barrackslike buildings along a dry riverbed. In the thick heat the poet lay down under his mosquito net and tried to nap before dinner. He was hungry. He crossed a party of young Californians, big bronze boys and girls, and chatted and joked with them. They all complained about intestinal earthquakes and mudslides, and the poet said he didn't have any such curses.

For dinner he ordered a hot curry and the waiter, splendid in his high turban and gleaming uniform but barefooted, tried to talk him out of it. "Very, very hot," he said, "not for Europeans. I will bring you the Irish stew." The poet convinced him he wanted the very very hot curry and he sat back and waited, looking around at the diners, all white, mostly American. Then his eye fell on something moving under a table on the far side of the room and identified a rat. He drew his legs back under his table a little. He glanced to the other wall on his right and spotted another rat, big, just lying there. He counted five in all and didn't dare look behind him. He wanted to get up and leave but he was too hungry, and let his lower body turn paralyzed while the waiter served him the golden fiery meat and rice. He ate every gram and wiped up the gravy with the *papadams* and walked slowly out of the dining room, glancing at the quiescent and well-mannered rats, and thought, they are probably overfed.

He gave his lecture and read American modern poets and visited a Gandhi ashram and conversed with the disciples of the great man and felt moved and slightly shaken, for Gandhi had lived here and a cobra had crawled over his body while he slept, the poet had read, and the venomous animal had not struck him. About Gandhi he believed the whole myth.

There was an out-of-doors reception for the poet in a kind of park, eating sweet cakes and drinking sweet fruit juices and the poet was dying for a drink. India was locked into prohibition and only "Europeans" could enter a bar, taboo to the natives. In hotels, the poet would enter one of these vast mahogany drinking places and be the only customer. Having a glass of something would evoke guilt and nostalgia and a sense of being posthumous. In India one is liable to feel posthumous, so much humanity has flowed over the dam. It was like their architecture of the temples, that made you feel drunk and lecherous and holier-than-thou simultaneously. It was a womb and a grave where birth and death were synonymous.

A limousine drove up and the driver asked for the American. He thanked his hosts and waved to Ezekiel and got in.

It was an actual palace he was driven to, yellowish marble, about five stories high, maybe a block square. The chauffeur ushered him into a small vestibule where a gilt elevator waited, and he was taken up a few stories and let out onto a marble gallery. The poet looked down the gallery. Shoulder to shoulder leaning against the wall were white-clad servants with apparently nothing to do. He walked to the end and knocked at a lighted door and the poet of the palace let him in. The room was air-conditioned! A little girl of about eight was introduced, their chaperon. A bottle of bourbon sat on the table and two glasses.

They talked about poetry and poets in England and in America, and sipped bourbon and water while the little girl leafed through magazines. The Hindu lady handed him a sheaf of her poems to pick from. They had no points of reference in common, really, except the craft of the poem. That was enough. What were those zombies at the State Department so worried about? Of course he knew. Could there be any method of codification safer than the poem? His mind flickered: the physicist at Oxbridge—it was the period of traitors—was passing secrets to his sister in Ahmadabad, who would codify them in poems, and the American visitor would print them in his Chicago magazine which the Kremlin had a subscription to. Ergo Ezekiel bird-dogging him: *don't go to see that woman!* It was all too funny and all too conceivable.

They shook hands and said goodbye and burst out laughing, in-

cluding the child. They were all in on the idiocy. The chauffeur
drove him back to his rat-infested hotel and the poet lay awake
with the lady's poems and a small flask of bourbon she had given
him for a nightcap. Her poems were okay, better than Lalage's anyhow. Lalage was missing that last ounce of spice which converts a
common dish into a tasty morsel.

A little sad at losing Ezekiel, he flew to Hyderabad alone, once
more in an empty plane with a lone stewardess bringing him his
beer, with a nuance of disapproval. Hyderabad was Moslem country, and prohibition was part and parcel of their religion. The
Hindu prohibition was mostly an anti-British spinoff or a Gandhian
piety. Drugs were okay with them. On every street corner every
Hindu purchased a fresh green leaf into which was rolled betel
and spices, which even the most resplendent and beautifully saried
ladies chewed and spat out red. The sidewalks were red with spit
from this national high. Daintily the elegant women daubed at their
red leaking lips. The poet had tried the concoction, but the spices
made him queasy, and he smoked his American cigarettes with
menthol and went to the ghostly bars and had a whiskey or two.

As they were coming into Hyderabad the stewardess came and
sat down beside him and buckled her belt, and the poet buckled
his.

"We have a practice pilot," she said. "We will land four times."
The poet thought she was joking and looked out as the plane was
about to touch the runway, when suddenly the motors gunned and
roared and they swooped up into the sky. They made a slow circle
over the white marble city and came in for the second landing. This
time the plane hit the concrete hard and bounced hard and one
wing scraped the speeding surface, but the plane coasted again and
picked up speed and took off a second time. The poet looked at the
stewardess who seemed nervous and he thought maybe he should
be nervous, while he sipped his beer. Eventually they landed and
he was met by his expected American and driven to what was called

a hotel, but was really a summer palace of one of the sons of the Nizam, the local ruler who was in the process of being bought out by the Nehru government. All the local princes and rajahs were being pensioned off by the new democracy, if it was a democracy, and the palaces were taking on the impersonality of museums.

His was now a hotel. In fact, he had a separate little palace of his own, a small white marble edifice set off a little from the main building, a guest house perhaps in better days for some visiting prince or princess. It consisted of one palatial living or bedroom, black and white marble with one wall of marble tracery or lacework more or less exposing the bath chamber—it was too regal to be called a bathroom—and he had the sudden impression that it had been for the harem or a portion of it. But what astonished him most was the strange plumbing. When he got up from the white American toilet, Kohler & Kohler, and flushed it he saw the water and its contents pour into a white marble gutter which ran around the base of the walls and disappear into a hole on the far side. The poet's literary interests did not extend to scatology, and he accepted this phenomenon as merely another detail in the cyclorama of India. After all, he had been in the lobby of a modern glass building in Bombay during a sudden downpour and stood next to a white cow which had also come in out of the rain. This dirty cow is a god, he told himself, when a Hindu gentleman gave it a whack on its rump and sent it outside.

He visited the Nizam's private, now public, museum and had a new astonishment. The one room was two to three stories high, also white marble, everything was white marble, and looked like a secondhand junk shop. Pictures from Italy hung twenty or thirty feet off the floor alongside overstuffed chairs, blunderbusses, friezes from Greece, and bicycles. It was pre-museum, an eighteenth-century atelier of a rich man, a storehouse mixing treasures and trash.

He gave his lecture in the Nizam's marbly university and read

modern poems to the handsomely dressed audience, and pro-
pounded William Carlos Williams as the best modern American
poet to the very skeptical Moslems and Hindus. The ones who had
attended American schools were slightly more sympathetic than the
ones who had attended English schools, and there was a tug-of-war
going on between the English-trained and the American-trained
about educational theory and everything else. There was a strong
nostalgia for the British raj in spite of the old hatreds; the stamp of
English rule had struck deep.

He was now taking trains to places where there were no airports,
into jungles and over the flooded state of Orissa, in the general direction of Calcutta. Everywhere he had been he carried the large
cardboard photo of Walt Whitman, bearded and mysterious-eyed,
a Hindu if there ever was one. One night as he sat in his first-class
wooden stall, like the inside of a red packing case, he decided to
say goodbye to Walt and opened the window of his cabin and let
the picture slide out into the dark jungle. He was certain it would
end up in a temple, where it would be set up in style among swimming carvings. Worshippers would lay rice and fruit and garlands
of dense-smelling flowers in front of it, and the poet of Camden
would be very pleased with his passage to India.

In Calcutta he was met by a Hindu goddess in a blue sari which
exposed her midriff and outlined her liberal bosom and buttocks.
She informed the poet in British English that she was to take charge
of him, see him to his hotel and his lectures, conduct him on
sight-seeing tours, introduce him to poets and entertain him. Jesus,
thought the poet. But somehow, driving into the city through the
staggering slums she mentioned to him, apropos of nothing, that
she was a Christian. The poet didn't know how to field that one
and wondered if the announcement was some kind of admonition.
Or it could even be a proposal of some kind. India was turning his
mind to mush and was beginning to resemble one of those moun-
tainous temple sculptures where the holy and the erotic climbed all
over each other into the sky. Well, if he had to have a watchdog,

this beautiful blue Hindu Christian would be just fine. He told her that he was looking forward to visiting Dakshineshwar, that he was practically a disciple of Ramakrishna, that an American convert had sent him Sri Ramakrishna's bible, if you could call it that, and that he could understand India better for having read him. She gave him a neutral smile and he noticed something about her mouth, which was forbidding and would never be a target for a kiss, not his anyway.

She was a marvel of companionship at that, and would stay with him for hours in his hotel room sipping tea or lemonade while he laced his tea with Dixie Belle gin, which he bought in the bar and which had the horrible aftertaste of fusel oil.

Why she accompanied him to the Hindu temple where Ramakrishna had held forth he never knew. Of course it was her assignment and she stuck to him like glue. He would rather have been alone on the banks of the Hooghly, which Kipling had described as a river of filth, the river into which Ramakrishna had waded to his drowning. They took a taxi—the poet always took taxis—and got out in a large stony courtyard where clusters of beggars eyed them silently and without moving. Better to wait until they emerge from the shrine, in a giving mood.

The spoiled rice, the rotting fruit, the browning flowers were piled at the feet of the gods and goddesses and monsters, and the poet stayed longest under the blank and hideous Kali with her necklace of skulls, in one of her four hands holding a severed human head. She had three eyes, she stood on Siva, who lies supine on the thousand-petaled silver lotus. He would write a poem about it. Kali was the saint's darling.

"If you compare that Mother with the Christian Mother of God," the poet said to his companion, "you can see that the Indians have more imagination."

"A rather bloody imagination, don't you think?" she answered him.

"But Ramakrishna was a man of peace, at least as much as

Jesus, or more so. He had been a Moslem, he had been a Christian, he wanted to unify all the religions so they would stop killing each other off. Don't you know that the fundamental basis of war is religion? Marx was a surface-skater. All he could think of was goods and services. He even thought you could erase religions with a stroke of the pen. You can't erase religion because man is half-god, half-animal. There's your god-animal," he said, pointing to the black basalt Kali. "That's no sickly Raphael sugar-coated valentine. That's a killer."

"You've read too much Hemingway," said the Hindu Christian.

When they were passing back to the courtyard she said, "You must not give the beggars any money or even make the suggestion of a gesture," and he said nothing. They moved toward the taxi which he had told to wait as the clusters of men, women and children moved toward them. He dug into his pocket and pulled out a handful of what he felt were worthless annas made of cheap alloys. One of them knocked his hand up and the coins flew everywhere. He pulled out more coins and the same thing happened. And now the Donnybrook, as the Hindus rolled in the dust and mud puddles fighting each other over the annas, screaming and punching. They made their way to the cab and forced their way in, hands thrusting through the windows and he dug out more coins and even rupees, while the woman sat beside him stony-faced. Driving back, he turned to her and said, "One of Ramakrishna's gems was his answer to a disciple who asked him why, if God was so benevolent and loving, there was so much evil in the world. And Ramakrishna laughed, he was always laughing in these sessions and answered, 'To thicken the plot.'"

At the hotel the American said he wanted to rest before his lecture and he went to his room quaking. He stared out of his window onto an endless street with iron overhangs fronting the shops. Under these awnings families lived, people were born there on the sidewalks, grew up, married, died there. He had been told that some of these people would never see the inside of a house as long as they lived. They were sidewalk people. In the early morning he would see them move from the awning shelter to the street with their begging bowls and squat down, projecting their bowls to passersby. They were clean, they were immaculate, and they washed and bathed under the street-corner tap, modestly somehow, with no show of limbs. Some of them were mutilates whose arms had been taken off deliberately, at birth, to make them members of the begging caste. Many of the women wore nose rings, a small spot of gold or two or three hanging down from a nostril. It was their wealth.

He saw old women working like drayhorses, four of them pushing a grand piano up a hill, the cords standing out on their black necks and glistening with sweat. Elegant rectilinear modern buildings were going up, covered with a scabrous, crooked scaffolding of bamboo, and hundreds of workers filing up and down ramps like an ant army. He was told that there were a hundred and fifty thousand prostitutes in Calcutta, that suttee was still practiced, that nobody could break the caste system. Visiting a professor's house he saw a beautiful housemaid, a harijan, who fled at the sight of him as if he had been a monster. She was an untouchable and would eat in a corner with her face to the wall. The poet thought bitterly, what had Gandhi done but gotten himself killed. He couldn't wait to get out of this hell. Simultaneously he felt a welling up of love and wonder at the teeming horror and intensity of it all, everything living and crawling and procreating. It was the primal ooze, pure spontaneous generation, the life-in-death of the oldest civilization, the meaning of the wheel of life from which there was no escape.

The poets and poems were becoming more numerous and he cursed the day he thought of publishing an Indian number of his magazine. The watchful Hindu-Christian told him that he needed a secretary and said she would get him one. She sent a young girl who took shorthand expertly and typed his notes of rejection or encouragement or, rarely, acceptance. Like a true Yank he asked her why she didn't go to America. Her answer shouldn't have surprised him. "In American they will think I am a Negro."

On his last day he visited a poet and his wife at their house, a modest bungalow hidden behind bushes of jasmine. While they talked poetry, birds flew in and out of the living room, to the visitor's astonishment. They had actually nested in a bookcase, with the consent of the owners of course, who told him to peek at the chicks. Such a touch almost compensated for the horrors. Besides, this was a good poet, and the two discussed which of his poems he would print in the India number.

He took leave of his guide, who would have accompanied him on the rest of the trip if he had wanted. It was evidently part of her job and Uncle Sam would pay for her. But he decided not to ask.

He went to Poona, he went to Bangalore, to Pondicherry which has its own special vultures. Vultures are a necessity in an overpopulated country. A delicate Parsee woman in one of the cities pointed out a very tall structure which she said was the Tower of Silence—quite an irony, the poet thought, since they laid their dead on top for the vultures to eat. He liked vultures and thought them superior to most beautiful birds, looking like broken umbrellas or prime ministers. He wanted to make a side trip to Goa but was not allowed. Thousands of Gandhians were marching on Goa to try by Gandhian means to force out the Portuguese after four hundred years of colonial rule at its vilest. It was the last stronghold of the barbarians, a Hindu professor put it. The poet knew that if he went he would end up with the marchers and have his picture in all the Indian newspapers, and not only Indian. *No politics* echoed in the poet's head, just lectures on Walt Whitman, the father of political and homosexual poetry in America. The State Department must have juggled Whitman like a hot coal before they decided to celebrate the birthday of his book.

He never saw Goa. Instead he went to Madura, which though he didn't know it was to be his last stop in India. Stendhal says in his autobiography that he *fell* with Napoleon. The poet would say in later years when he spoke of India that he *fell* in Madura. His trip was canceled, he never knew why, the newspapers lied that he had amoebic dysentery, which the poet didn't mind having an imaginary case of. He was exhausted and wanted to sleep for a month.

Curiously, there were no lectures there. He was only to meet with American officials and be entertained. It was a kind of rest stop before the final leg of the journey south and the return to New Delhi for the finale.

He checked into his hotel and was handed a small sack of mail, more poems in Anglo-English, he thought, and saw that he had an invitation to dinner at the house of the American Consul. He rested a while and got dressed.

There was nobody home, he was told by a servant when he got to the house, a large place in the middle of the city, with an enormous garden behind a white stone wall. He asked if he might leave a note of apology, saying he had to leave early in the morning for Mysore. The hosts drove up the curved drive as he was leaving and they introduced themselves and he decided to stay.

Whether he would stay a weekend or a week or a month or a year, he never bothered to decide. All he remembered was the beginning. He was the first guest that evening and was served pink gin, which is to say gin and bitters, which the Yanks had learned from the Brits, a deafening sort of martini. Guests began to arrive and regular martinis appeared. Dinner appeared, for about twenty brightly laughing, brightly chatting Americans, and the focus was on the new arrivals who would become part of the Madura contingency, happy worried young wives with children and strange houses and turbaned servants and tropical gardens and even poison snakes, pure poison in India, and the caste system and the politics —but that was the husbands' business—and the food the opposite of American or European, and all such things to learn and become adept at and sophisticated about, except the languages, of course. They would not learn the languages, any more than the British did.

It seemed a wonderful dinner, with multi-colored curries and chutneys and dripping sweets, although garnished with wines and the servants silent and shadowy and silken-dressed, and the new Americans going off in gales of laughter about their adventure.

There was a double staircase off the dining room and the poet remembered people in ones or twos floating up and floating down the staircases, and the gaiety increased and the host, very much in charge, informing and instructing and encouraging—a regular tour guide, it seemed. He certainly understood the apprehension of the Americans about hauling off to India. The poet himself felt like an old Kipling type who knew it all, though he didn't know anything, but at least had had a blueprint that he had traced.

He went to the Consul's office once, by request, to discuss his itinerary, which had ceased to exist, and the poet, who was never completely fogged out, saw that the stoppage of his grand tour of the subcontinent was being arranged by the Consul. He would never know why and didn't care, except in an abstract kind of way, like finishing a crossword puzzle. The Consul would finish his crossword puzzle for him. He even decided that there was some kind of altercation going on between the Consul and the embassy at Delhi and that he was being used as a little pawn to make a point of some kind. He didn't care about that, either.

He was sent home to the U.S.A. via Calcutta, via Bangkok, and he wondered why it didn't sound exotic or even interesting. He was fed up with the magic of the East.

In Calcutta he discovered that the only money he had was rupees and he went to change them into dollars. But the Indians weren't going to give up an American nickel or dime, much less a dollar. The bank told him to go to the central Bank of India. He went to the central Bank of India, a two-block-long shed with white-dhotied clerks sitting on tall stools side by side. He spent the afternoon there, going from one clerk to another, gradually getting to bureaucrats in black coats instead of white cotton, eventually being ushered into the office of the Vice President of the Bank of India himself, who consented to change his rupees, which were a pitiful few, into American. His exhaustion by then had turned to fury. He wished the English, French, the Portuguese would come back, and a few other vultures. He flew out of Calcutta almost with a cheer. He never wanted to see the famous subcontinent again.

He still wasn't home free. They glided in over the golden nipples of Bangkok and landed noiselessly and changed planes. A small, handsome and authoritative American came up to him in the airport and introduced himself, saying he was the American Consul at Bangkok and was happy to meet the poet and would like to hear about his trip to India. They would be both in first class, of course.

"Of course," said the poet. "The bastards," he thought, "they're going to watchdog me all the way to Yolo County."

In San Francisco the diplomat shook hands and said goodbye. The poet said to him, "You people work so hard," and they both laughed. Kafka, the poet remembered, said Americans were always laughing.

A poet from Berkeley picked him up to drive him to Davis on a heavenly winding country road—it was just before the birth of Freeways. The poet looked at Berkeley enviously; he had wanted to be kept there but hadn't been asked. He didn't know anything about the university, which hadn't yet been made famous by the street revolutionaries but was about to be. He wanted to stay in Berkeley for the View.

He had boned up hard on his modern poetry course at Berkeley and thought he knew all there was to know, and had the paradigm in his head and most of the poems at his fingertips and could cite the big-gun critics, but knew he lacked ease, that particular insouciance which makes a professor tenable. He recalled the friendly professor who had come to audit his lecture. The friendly professor was a crypto-Jew, or a Jew who pretended he wasn't. His name sounded German, he didn't look what is called Semitic. He wrote for the far left New York journals which ignored ancestry and nationality. He was a quiet big shot. he came into the poet's lecture in a huge shadowy auditorium with twenty students and the poet on a stage. The poet did his thing for the inspector and knew he had flunked.

Well, he figured, English Departments can't stand more than one or two Jews, and this big shot wasn't about to take on another member of the tribe, who didn't even have any degrees. Discretion is the better part of Humanism, and in fact he sympathized with the crypto-Jewish English Professor, as for a person with a secret disease. What effort it must take to be someone you aren't, to feel constantly put to the test and never to relax into yourself.

In a few years all that would change and the nineteenth-century English Department would turn "Jewish," the tight curriculum would burst open like a seed pod, the curtain was coming down on Wasp gentility. The attributive "great" would be applied to Berkeley because it was soon to be trashed, incinerated, helicoptered. In America, he thought, it's the desecration of institutions that confers honor upon them. Martyrdom as a badge of respect. And he recalled his hometown anthem which contained the hilarious and bloodthirsty couplet

> Avenge the patriotic gore
> That flecked the streets of Baltimore!

to the tune of "Tannenbaum, O Tannenbaum."

In the pretty rented house in Davis the children climbed all over him, his wife beaming solicitude. He brought out silks from India and spices in gold-medallioned tins and miniature bronzes of Kali and the elephant god. And he wrote what he called his India poem.

The year at Davis was not an idyll, no year was, but it was as close as he would ever come to a place of his desire. What was it he desired of a place? He doubted if he knew, was it simply the absence of snow? he loved snow. Was it the distance from the Atlantic coast? that was more like it. He loved the idea of the un-passable mountain range hanging above the valley where hundreds, thousands had died trying to cross in the early years, where trains clung to the edges of the high canyons like spiders, where even now the highways were perilous. The valley, the valley, that was it. To be sheltered in this long, green, fertile, rich, sensual, four-hundred-mile-long slit, cradled by the coastal hills on one side and the Unpassables on the other, even closed off at the top by the Siskiyous and at the bottom by the Tehachapis, sealing him off from Los Angeles and all that. Though there was nothing in the little town or even the campus that would have made such demands on him, it was the wombness of this far world, cool saturating rains, flowers bursting at Christmas, oranges and lemons decorating the trees everywhere, so many that nobody seemed to pick them, the olives dripping off the trees, and covering the ground, the high palm trees leaning this way and that in the wind, the eucalyptus reminding him of Australia. Half the time he thought he was back in Australia in a war zone without a war, as it had been there, as in some sense it was here, after India.

But the year had no resonance and almost no imagery, so that when he tried to recall it he only had the sensation of looking at postcards of the place, all too bright and with a Sunday deadness, with that emptiness of postcards which sets them apart even from photography. He was holding himself in, he felt; he was "behaving," working hard, being the father-husband-poet, on trial perhaps in this easy-going intimate place which might offer him a job. He would take it if they did, but the Department was too small and there would be no openings at the top. He must start at the top.

7.

Around Christmas he wrote a dozen letters to universities announcing that he was available for a full professorship (with tenure) and waited for the replies. He had read at Seattle at their university and the poet Roethke, who said he was going on sabbatical for a year, asked if he would like his job for a fill-in, but he declined. He had met Roethke before on their travels, liked his poetry, liked and wondered at him, a huge flat-footed giant, always gently drunk, dribbling obscenities in a kind of almost charming manner, watched over skillfully by his Bennington wife, as Bennington wives, the poet thought, are trained for just such missions in the world. When the visiting poet came into the party following his lecture Roethke, surrounded by admirers, said in a booming voice, Well, if it isn't the bourgeois poet, and he immediately adopted that name for himself, christened as it were.

A beautiful young woman stood in the group, looking like a model, and Roethke said, grabbing her arm, this cunt writes good poetry, and the poet's bourgeois mind reeled.

It was too misty in Seattle and the jagged snow-glittering Cascades too close, menacing. The city was full of lakes, beautiful, but he was already homesick for California where boughs of oranges bent to the grass and roses went riot in February and camellias swam down the street gutters and the students were dusted with sun even in what they called winter. He thought his heart would break if he had to leave California, and his time was running short.

He had taught well, he was a smash, and the locals wondered what such a famous poet was doing in this Aggie college at Davis, but he didn't know he was considered a great something or other. The neighbors saw him as a nice youngish academic with a good-looking wife and good-looking children and a normal station wagon and a normal rented house. He had no "side," as the English call it, and he kept his suffering, if any, to himself. In fact he was deeply unhappy but refused to think about it and was not interested in his internal emotional disorders. He detested people who let their internal disorders surface, though he remembered with heartache the raving and catatonic soldiers on the ghoul-ship of returning troops, but marveled at what he thought of his own insensitivity. He could only stare at them in memory, yet he thought of them often, wondering at the fragility of the mind which in a split second can cross over into disorder. Would they ever recover? That Marine he saw coming up the beach with his platoon, who fell into convulsions and had to be tied in a straitjacket—what ever happened to him?

There was a girl in his class, pretty, rather wispy, California golden as in the ads, with a Buick convertible. She was married and they caught each other's eye, but he did nothing. Not here. He wasn't going to be a traveling salesman, like his father. He waited.

Answers came to his self-advertisement. He had not written any schools east of the Missouri, wanting to stay as far west as possible. The university at Boulder offered him an Associate Professorship with tenure and he carefully declined. The University of Nebraska offered him what he wanted and he took it. Interviews were not necessary. He had lectured there for a week while he was editor at *Poetry* in Chicago, and they wanted him and needed him. The editor of their regionally famous literary magazine was retiring and the poet was exactly their man. It was West enough but, oh God, two thousand miles from the oranges and the sun-dusted girls and boys. He prepared his wife and children for the drive in the summer. Simultaneously he accepted a summer job at the Kenyon School of Letters in southern Indiana. The family would live at a beach in Michigan while he commuted on weekends, a straight drive of three hundred miles down the Wabash, the poet drinking beer out of cans all the way and passing lines of cars at twice the speed limit and feeling immune from accidents.

He sat with the wispy blond student on the lawn under a steel umbrella at the Memorial Union, sipping Coca-Colas and without making arrangements made arrangements. She would come to Lincoln, Nebraska, as soon as he got there and put up at the Cornhusker Hotel, where he would visit her. Her husband would probably divorce her, her father would say she was acting like a "back-alley nigger." Yes, he said, come.

Leaving California was an almost physical wrench, an amputation for the poet, and he was horrified at his mindless love for the place. There was nothing here but climate. Why did he love it so?

There are almost no exits and entrances to California. That is part of its magic. There are about two and a half seaports from the Pacific and about two and a half passages across the mountains, one in the center of the state where the crossers once ended up eating each other from starvation, one in the south through the desert where other horrors have been transmogrified into movie gold. One can drive down from the north where the Oregon Trail ended, but that is a slightly epical drive which took the aboriginal Asiatics perhaps a hundred thousand years to accomplish. The poet and family took the southern route, flanking the Pacific on which the poet's eyes lingered achingly, until whenever it went out of sight. In Southern California they turned east to the Mojave Desert. In the desert he immediately readjusted his psyche as if it were a radio dial and let his California consciousness sink little by little into shadow like a September, beautiful and dying. They came to Needles.

Only a poet could have thought of a name like that. Needles sits at the bitten edge of the state on the Colorado River. Cross it and you are out of California, into Arizona, expelled from Eden. From there on it's petrified forests and yucca and cowboys and Indians, the bad movie, the crippled mythopoeia of America. At the motel the poet and his family sat around the swimming pool in a Bessemer heat; he sat there while they went into the room to cool. Across the pool he watched a muscular slinky man and an even slinkier bikini woman smolder together, take a swim, snatch their towels and fade into their room. He could have died there and then. Hail and farewell, reptilian California!

It wasn't until they had negotiated all the Southwest and the dry ocean of Texas and came up into Oklahoma and entered the fertile Kansas womb that he knew he was entering his new home. By now he was gathering the Middle West to his bosom, and began to sniff deeply the wheat dust and the cornflower and gaze at the endless cathedrals of grain, white phalli bursting with the fertility of farms, the copulation of steel plow and wet black earth. He began to lust for the place and for the wispy California wife who was coming to have him at the Cornhusker Hotel, like a corny ballad nasally twanged out in a Fort Worth bar in the slaughtering district. And his heart ached for California like a Hallmark card.

The poet and his wife stood on a green and windy hill and picked out a site for their house, for they were going to build one, split-level and overlooking the rolling farm below and the Georgian Veterans Hospital in the distance with its white lantern tower, all in all a very pleasing prospect. He wondered why people said that Nebraska was flat, for there was nothing flat about it anywhere. What people meant, he decided, was that there was no limit to the view, no mountains where the eye could stop, no limitation of shore. In the Sacramento Valley he had left, flatness was all, but one didn't notice it because there were the low coastal mountains on one side and the High Sierras on the other, and the pool-table flatness and greenness never impinged on the consciousness because one felt enclosed, framed. Without these frames man becomes vertiginous, seasick, and the poet, who had never been seasick, "because he didn't believe in it," held that seasickness was terror of landlessness. When people began to fly, there was airsickness, but that had stopped as planes became more and more like living rooms or theaters.

Hardly anyone ever looked outside except on takeoffs and landings. It was all a pretense of standing still, and passengers could actually complain of the quality of the food! The idea that people sitting seven miles up in the sky in a comfortable chair could complain about sky food struck the poet as both touching and disgusting, touching in its simplicity and selfishness, and disgusting for its lack of imagination and ecstasy. It was this same simplicity that drove people to say that Nebraska was flat, when all they were saying was that too much sky made them dizzy.

They drove to their rented beach house in the Indiana dunes and the children gleaned crinoids from the pretty beach, petrified spinal segments of ancient sea lilies, delicately hued, which the Indians had strung into necklaces. The little house sat on a dune a hundred feet high and a flight of wooden stairs went frightingly straight down to the beach. He would stay aloft much of the time, writing or doing his lectures which he had to telescope for the School of Letters, and gaze over the ocean-sized Lake Michigan or down where the children were bobbling in the waves and his wife lay reading on the sand. His feeling was that he had nothing to look forward to, that he had landed on a kind of plateau where he didn't want to be. He didn't know where he wanted to be, and even California was only a palliative that cloaked some unknown longing, some love he had lost or never had and probably couldn't attain. He wished he could break out of himself, he wished he could be a drunk like Roethke and have nervous breakdowns and be nursed by worshipful professors and a curvy Bennington Florence Nightingale, but he could never be a drunk or a psychiatric number. Drunks disgusted him, as did psychiatrists, those vultures of the towers of silence of the mind. He felt frigidly alone. Well, the California blonde was coming to sleep with him in September but he knew there was no point in it, no exit, only an entrance, a calling card, almost a point of etiquette.

Certain evenings he would make a pretext of going to the village store in order to phone her long distance in the Sacramento Valley and make sure of her visit, and there was no doubt about it. He would make the hotel reservation as soon as he got to Lincoln. She insisted on paying her own way.

He couldn't wait for the weekends to end and Sunday to come, when he would get in his car and kiss the children and his wife, drive a few miles to the Michigan line and buy his beer at a point where three states intersected—Michigan was the one where you could buy beer on Sunday—and settle back for the long straight two-hundred-mile drive, with all the windows open and the wind pouring hot air over him and the radio playing "Standin' On the Corner" and "Oh Glendora, I Wanna See Mora You." He coasted happily through the little Indiana towns, all looking more or less alike, smug and pretty and no friend to poets. One was where Ezra Pound was kicked out of the local college for housing a burlesque girl one night; was that the origin of his righteousness and wrath? the poet wondered. He savored the swift murky Wabash River he crossed and recrossed down the state, a drowning-river he knew that had swallowed many a murder and suicide. And in Blooming-ton he would go to his hotel room in the gasping heat and lie on his bed naked and brooding, trying to write, keeping the jazz on the room radio, sometimes awash in tears, until he slept. He had standing invitations to professors' houses these nights, but seldom left his room except to meet his classes or for the colloquies with the others of the faculty.

The seminars were successful, they must have been successful on his part, for he was invited back again and again. But he could never remember anything about them except that certain famous people were there and one or two students remained his friends for life.

They headed back to Nebraska, across the Mississippi, across the Missouri, now song names with an incipient history, mostly invented but not all, for the poets had done something about De Soto's bones and Indiana was full of French names like Boise and Terre Haute, and Germans in Nebraska still spoke Frisian dialects which had disappeared in Germany. All the peasantries of Europe had sprouted seed in these places and made it rich and redolent of distorted memory, and prejudice, and racial collective unconscious, and utopian idealism, and insanity such as can only spring up in a new world. The university he was going to in Lincoln was ugly; most American universities were ugly, except Jefferson's, and that too would be uglified in the nineteenth and twentieth centuries. But these huge Midwestern universities were all like neo-colonial gyms or warehouses, and wherever there was an oldish baroque or Byzantine structure ornamented in the Sullivan style with dreamlike columns or architraves it was slated to be torn down to be replaced by a glass and steel chicken coop for dark-suited bureaucrats. All the state universities were being transformed into what a California sociologist-educationalist called the Multiversity, and were swallowing up the small colleges and seminaries and turning education into business and government, and the poet thought that the corporate state was just around the corner.

He was called to the last of the Byzantine-Sullivanesque buildings at eleven o'clock one morning, in a roundabout way. He was in bed with the California girl at the Cornhusker Hotel, having told his wife that he would be at the university library most of the day, libraries being the last best refuge of the academic philanderer, and to cover his tracks had phoned his new chairman that he would be there too. But the chairman had said that the Chancellor and the Vice Chancellor would like to meet their new poet, that morning in fact, at the Byzantine building, and would he please? The

poet said, of course, naked and drinking Scotch in bed in the Cornhusker Hotel at 10:00 A.M. stroking the behind of his ex-student.
He went, reeking of Scotch.

It was only three short blocks to the squat, imposing building
that housed the top brass, Chancellor, Vice Chancellors, Deans,
and he exhaled deeply as he walked, thinking he was expelling
dragon fumes of alcohol as he went. He had read that the Chancellor was about to be made the Secretary of Agriculture of the United
States. He felt a certain awe and a twinge of fear, remembering his
first encounter with the Librarian of Congress. These high officials
frightened him; why did they have to see what you looked like?
What kind of image was he supposed to measure up to? He didn't
want to start off on the wrong footing again, and when he entered
the building he found the men's room and looked in the mirror and
combed his hair.

The Chancellor was about the poet's height and very handsome,
with beautiful wavy graying hair and prize teeth. He put the poet at
ease by talking about the Sacramento Valley and asking about his
friend who was the Chancellor at Davis and a scientist in the same
agricultural field. He called in his aide, a short bustling fellow with
prominent blue eyes, and it crossed the poet's mind that this Vice
Chancellor would never make it as Chancellor because he was too
short. Politicians need a certain height, and these chiefs had to
go before state legislatures and plead for money. The Vice Chancellor asked about his writing and said he had read all the poet's
books and was very happy he had joined the faculty. The secretary
brought coffee, they chatted about the famous football team, shook
hands and parted. The poet fairly skipped back to the hotel; he had
got that over with and would have a solid alibi about his doings this
day when he got home.

The Californian stayed about a week, mostly in bed, for there
was nothing else to do in a town where there was no museum except for dinosaur bones, no theater, only a couple of movies. Or

she sat in the little beer joint across the street talking to students who sat down with her, taking her for a student. They made love mechanically, drily, for there was little love in it, only the yearning to cross a void in their lives. They were like two mountain climbers spanning a crevasse, handling each other's rope, looking for safe purchase, cold and excited, staring at dangerous emptiness.

He was on the rise, pushing away at her with her legs over his shoulders, when she said to him in a calm voice, "Allen Ginsberg says you can't write for shit." His erection immediately shrank and his penis fell out.

He lay for a moment paralyzed at the brutality of the remark. Ginsberg had become famous overnight and was in the process of fathering what was to be known as the Cock and Balls school of poetry. The poem *Howl*, the ban on the book, the trial, the powerful publicity which the participants dramatized to the full, capitalized on, battened on righteously, gaily, demonically, turned rapidly from a literary to a social cause, soon to be called a revolution, which in fact it presaged. There was no denying it, however much one detested the means. The bourgeois literary applecart was about to be upended and with it all the outer accoutrements of the balanced society, clothes, underclothes, hair, especially hair, language, especially tasteful language, property, government, religion, especially Saturday and Sunday religion, stimulants—no more booze, "Scotch is for fathers"—unless used with mushrooms and LSD, marriage, sex, especially sex which was now free for the asking in the socialist-anarchist Land of Fuck with its capital in San Francisco, food—it was the apotheosis of the alfalfa sprout—education, especially the university, the tool of the military-industrial complex, racial gradation by skin color. For the blacks were coming, the barbarians were coming, and poets named Mal Content and Missa Genation were mounting the platforms before screaming audiences of thousands, and the Beat, Beatific, Beatitudes surrealistically metamorphosed into the Beatles who were at this moment being admitted to the presence of royalty in Buckingham Palace.

[136]

Yes, he thought, pulling on his shorts without drying himself, it is the time of the Ginsbergs, and he said to the naked Californian lying there, "Do you remember when Eberhart brought Allen to Davis? He hadn't published anything and was as unknown as a clam. His hair was short, he wore a three-piece suit and horn-rimmed glasses and he was silent, subdued. Eberhart brought him to my house and said this is the new Hebrew Walt Whitman. Him? I thought." The girl replied, "His hair is long, his foot is light and his eyes are wild."

But one of the first things the poet did when he started his new editorship was to print an editorial called "Romanticism Comes Home," in which he defended Ginsberg and his Bay Area bacchantes. Yes, he would aid and abet, contribute to and fondle the Revolution and never be a part of it. He hated concerted behavior with a passion and would remain an outsider above all. He wondered if there was something cynical in his attitude. No, not cynical he decided, only—Virginian. Virginia, something spoke in his ear, was named for the virgin queen. Virgin, queen, what was the matter with him. He was dressed and went over to the Californian and took her foot in his hand and kissed it and left.

They had parted pleasantly enough and he saw her off at the airport, with a slight fear of being recognized. The professors were beginning to return from their vacations and the airport was crowded. He knew enough people in his department from his weeklong lecture visit a few years back; his picture had been in the local papers as the winner of the Golden Albatross and new poet-in-residence—which he wasn't, but newspapers always called him that as part of their shorthand. But he didn't see anybody he knew and didn't have to introduce the girl. They exchanged a few letters in the months to come and then it was over.

India too faded from his mind, and he thought he would be content to sit on the great plains and build his house and write his poems and edit his magazine, but suddenly there came another invitation to travel east, this time to Japan. He had been chosen by the PEN Club to be the poet in the American delegation to the big convention in Tokyo. His was an impressive delegation with John Steinbeck, John Hersey, John Dos Passos—all Johns?—Jon Brooks, and would he accept? He would.

His plane would leave from San Francisco, and he immediately had the idea of spending his San Francisco time with the Bennington girl who had worked for him briefly at *Poetry* in Chicago on her work-study program. She had been writing him at his office, not at home, and their letters were becoming intimate. Bennington, as the poet called her, would stroll on the beach in the morning, she wrote, and now and then pick up a stranger and take him to her house. Yes, she loved her husband very much and she loved these adventures too. With the poet she felt a different adventure coming on; she loved the poet in him, she said, but she didn't exclude the Muse Erato from her mind and sent him the pornographic poems of Verlaine in French, which she had copied out by hand at school. They were not yet translated into English, as far as she knew. The poet plowed into these poems the likes of which he had never seen, true pornographic poems by a true poet. A third of the vocabulary of course was not in his dictionaries and he had to guess at cognates from Latin, driving himself into a kind of verbal-erotic frenzy.

One day he received an envelope that rattled. In it were some exquisite tiny bones, vertebrae, that he poured into the palm of his hand. The note said, "Last year we were living in Laurel Canyon. I killed this rattler by my pool. Part of his backbone. Love. Benny."

She was discreet and exercised a certain degree of fidelity, namely secrecy from her husband, and had told him that she was going to visit her sister who was teaching in San Francisco. But when she came to his hotel room she was cool and seemingly untouchable. Damn, he thought, like Lalage with the silver dagger in the Taj Mahal Hotel; foiled again, he thought, with a kind of cartoon humor. But why did you come? he asked, and she stood slowly —all of her movements were slow, as if practiced—and began to unbutton her dress, a taffeta dress that rustled with a sound that only taffeta can make.

The afternoon was happy. After they dressed they took a cab to the Marina where she wanted to see the yachts; they were thinking of getting one, she and her husband, and possibly living on it in southern California. They ate at a Japanese restaurant sitting on the floor and she told him what to order. They went to the airport together and he took her to her plane for Los Angeles and when they said goodbye he saw that she was crying and he knew that he had failed at something, but wasn't sure what. All he knew was that there was a certain finality in the goodbye. She had been tender and satisfied with the lovemaking, he thought, and she had moaned. He had never heard a woman moan before, and knew it was a kind of higher music that came perhaps with a Bennington education. But she had gone away in a cloud of sadness and he blamed himself.

It was dark when he boarded the big Pan Am and he took his seat. He saw large men working their way down the aisle and recognized some of the anthology. That's John Hersey, that's Ralph Ellison, there's Steinbeck. Steinbeck was the star and was going to give the American speech at the convention. Everyone was rather subdued, tired like the poet. There is something exhausting about being in San Francisco even for a day. The city is an energy sponge that sops up your vitality, like Naples, like all cities that live on the lip of disaster, coastal earthquake cities swarming with beautiful people and rats, exciting cities bordering on hysteria, cities full of extremists and cosmopolitan restaurants. They took off with a murmuring roar, slowly it seemed. It was a piston plane and the wing lights glowed on the silver circles of the propellers which you could see through while they were still over the lights of the city. Then the wing lights went off and all was soft blackness around and the cabin lights dimmed and he dozed. He felt pleasantly benumbed and nowhere.

This kind of airplane had to make stops to refresh itself, and he was awakened by an announcement that they were coming into Wake Island to refuel and that the passengers could walk around for an hour. There they mixed and introduced themselves and ate breakfast or lunch, as time was going backwards, as they were back into a world older than Europe. In the plane he went downstairs with Steinbeck, for the bar on this Jules Verne airplane was separate and hung below the plane with windows all around so that you gazed down into the sea. The stewardess had given the key to the cabinets to the writers and told them to help themselves, for apparently the whole plane was filled with writers going to the convention, and the poet and the novelist sat and talked, not about literature, which writers avoid as conversation, but about California.

An ex-soldier returning to the country of an ex-enemy has a mixture of emotions, all contradictory, all thesis and antithesis and no probability of a synthesis. This makes the visit doubly exciting. The poet now had "Japanese" friends at home in his new university town, Nisei, the husband a professor of modern Eastern history, the wife a soft-voiced intelligent knowledgeable woman, perfect hostess, cooking genius, but with that acceptance of pure femininity or wifeliness that marked her off from her more brash American sisters. She had one physical defect, a deep, very deep scar that ran from her scalp, if not under her scalp, all the way down her cheek, just missing the eye, to the chin. This she tried to cover unsuccessfully by a curving lock of black hair, and curiously, the poet observed, this disfigurement didn't seem to damage her looks. He was thinking of them as the plane lowered for a landing in Tokyo, and the long conversations he had had with them about postwar Japan, the red-faced Yankee barbarians, as the early Japanese had called the invaders, and the attitudes of the hosts who were now rolling out red carpets all over the place for the foreigners honoring them with their presence. That was what the poet thought the Japanese thought, in a manner of speaking.

A remark of an American occupation general popped into his mind. Not long after the American victors had made themselves at home in the ex-empire an order came down from the top, from MacArthur himself, which said, Any American who slaps a Japanese will be given five years at hard labor in the penitentiary. And a Japanese general wrote in his diary, *It was then I knew that we had lost the war.*

Watch what happens when the plane stops, said Steinbeck to the poet, his seatmate. What? asked the poet. Ladders, he answered, photographers leaning against the windows up here. For you? the poet asked. For Hersey, said the novelist, he's the hero in this country, he's almost as much a god as MacArthur. Faces began to appear at the little plexiglass windows and lights flashed as the passengers got up for departure.

He was greeted by a rather stout Japanese gentleman who sat with him while they waited for the luggage. He spoke excellent English and it gradually began to dawn on the poet that this was someone he knew, that it was the Salzburg student and friend, and the poet burst out with astonishment and having made an ass of himself this far, went further and exclaimed about his friend's corpulence. In Salzburg and in Paris where they met after the seminars he had been thin as a match, hollow-cheeked. Now he was an established professor, if not as stout as a sumo wrestler at least a sleek cat with authority on his side. They began to exchange reminiscences. Professor Fukuda saw him to his hotel, friend and personal envoy.

It wasn't an ideological decision he had made, the poet thought to himself as he began to feel a kind of giddiness about his presence in Tokyo at this august meeting. And it *was* august, with hundreds of famous writers from every country except Russia. It was simply the fact that he was himself, with his deficiency of establishmentarian dignity. He just couldn't take the goddam thing seriously. He couldn't take any official function seriously, especially if it had anything to do with poetry. Poetry defuses, he believed. It also detonates. But this didn't look like any detonation operation and he got ready to coast.

He went to the opening meetings, he went to the smaller meetings, he spoke to Japanese poetry groups, had lunches and dinners with the people he was supposed to, but he cut it to a minimum. Not that he had any plan, he never had any plans. It was that he simply couldn't feel impressed by the self-conscious pomp and circumstance of these things, and couldn't distinguish a convention of international writers from a convention of tire salesmen. He was constantly turning down invitations which others would kill for. The Navy Department had asked him to fly to Antarctica in a plane full of high brass, admirals and so on, to talk to the frozen soldiers about poetry. The poet asked if the plane would stop in Australia, and when they said no he declined. The new Air Force Academy in Colorado asked him to come and read poems and he asked what they would pay. He decided that the pay was too much below scale and declined, though it was another one of the things he would always regret.

Not that he felt he deserved these lavish gifts, but only that he didn't believe in the seriousness, having become indoctrinated with the faddish philosophy of "the absurdity of the Serious World." It fitted in with his teaching of Modern Poetry, which is a minuscule history of the assault upon the Serious Mountain, a tireless exercise in improvisations, in irony, a fake-out really, one of those clever evasions of artists which prevent them from being caught up while coyly enticing all the art lovers and hangers-on. But this esthetic maneuver works only when the actor is unconscious of motive. Otherwise he is quickly spotted as a con man. The poet had never conned anybody, though he had conned a few poems, and the eagle-eyed and beady-eyed poetry competitors had immediately drawn a bead on him and were beginning to pepper him. He was aware of the sniping and put it down as another version of the ascent of the Serious Mountain, and felt that it was good to be out in the open, naked and defenseless and thumbing his nose at all the honor grubbers who would have given their right arm to be invited to the Antarctic with admirals or to the Air Force Academy or to Japan as the official American poet. He did his minimum best and went off into the night.

He wasn't interested in sexual expeditions, the usual culmination of night-prowling, but more like sight-seeing in the dark, more like a "shade" on a conducted tour through forbidden places, a kind of Dantesque all-paid tour. A man had appeared at the door of his hotel room, an American poet who worked for the State Department in Tokyo, a civilian with a high military rank, for the pay scale, and not a member of the delegation, and they hit it off immediately. The visiting poet had heard of him and had even published a few of his poems in the Chicago magazine, and he knew he had been the lover of a talented and incurably drunken poet in Berkeley.

They sat in a Russian bar sipping vodka while the State Department poet, with the unusual first name of Carmen, told about his life in the conquered capital. He was living like a prince and was supporting a young Japanese college student who shared his bed and board. He had his own staff car and chauffeur, of course, and had discovered that his car was bugged, but decided to do nothing about it but instead to give his secret listeners a merry ride. Sometimes when alone in the back seat he would deliver long garbled monologues as if speaking to a confidant or accomplice, the sort of role that poets fall into without effort. Poetry is all code anyway, they agreed.

Last night, said Carmen, I was at a live show. Liveshow should be one word, synonym for fuckwatch, as my boyfriend calls it. Now that's commonplace, but what interested me was that the man, who was very powerful and muscular, too much so, was on the bottom and had his long thick thing inside the woman, whose legs were straight out at a right angle, and he lifted her up a few inches and spun her completely around like a top, first to the left and then to the right. She had eleven-teen orgasms. Would you like to watch that? Yes, said the visitor from Nebraska.

Carmen's Japanese was minimal, and he was a long time under

the street lamp trying to explain his wishes to the pimp and using elaborate gestures which made the visitor burst out laughing. Even so they made a mistake, and were conducted to a movie where students or young people sat on the floor silently watching the old spotty Parisian film of a man coupling with a smiling fat lady. The Americans exchanged remarks and were shushed by the Japanese. They returned to the street and were finally led to a brightly lit bare room and sat on the mat when two bespectacled middle-aged people, probably a husband and wife, undressed and pretended to couple, for it was obvious that they weren't interested or excited but seemed to have been routed out of their sleep for these bored Americans. Carmen paid the husband and they returned to the Russian bar.

Steinbeck was ill with a high temperature and took to his bed and couldn't deliver his speech. It was probably written out but no one read it, and Dos Passos took the podium and read about ten minutes of epigrams about writers and writing and America. The poet was relieved that the other Americans were being as hit-or-miss as he was, for the other delegations, the French for instance, delivered two-hour orations with a solemnity of heads of state announcing a grave crisis. The poet sat with Stephen Spender, who filled him in on each personage who spoke during the long session. There were headphones for translations but the poet didn't use them after a few minutes of each speech. Nearly everyone spoke platitudes about literature and international understanding, as if originality was out of order here. He understood that there is a certain amount of intentional pain inflicted in these official get-togethers; the cement of culture has to be poured, has to set itself before even a skeleton of beauty can begin to make an appearance, and they all sat patiently in their seats enduring the labor and the hod-carrying.

Chopin poured from the big windows of a music conservatory, and from another window an eighteenth-century violin cadenza and he wondered at his own reaction—why did he think it incongruous?

He didn't want to fall into the wartime cliché that the Japanese were a nation of imitators, monkeys was the more brutal term, but he could not help marveling at their adaptability to foreign forms. Even the convention to which they had been sent was a seminar on translation, for the Japanese translated everything from everywhere almost as soon as it was published. He remembered the stories about the first imitation, when the American invaders entered Edo harbor in 1853 and the Japanese immediately sketched the ships in such detail and with such statistical accuracy that it was only a moment in time before they were building identical ships, and another moment before they defeated Imperial Russia at sea and became a world naval power. Only a short generation or two before Pearl Harbor. And now, proudly arisen from what had seemed annihilation, they were again a world power, not exactly a super-power but close. Where was all this tending?

His Japanese professor friend took him from music bar to music bar, one which played only pre–World War I jazz, ragtime and buck-and-wing, one which played only the latest rock and roll releases, one which played only string quartets, and in all these places the young men and women sat at attention, as it were, as if they were in a learning situation. They had sat that way at the porn movie too; they were constantly absorbing knowledge, any kind of knowledge, as if starved for the experience of the outside world. After all, they had a unique history of cultural imprisonment and had lived in a feudal dream-state for centuries, until the Commodore in his black American ships edged into Edo harbor with bared black cannon mouths pointed at the dream. They had all flown into colorful confusion, like a field of butterflies invaded by a must elephant. *Must*, thought the poet, a dangerous sexual frenzy, special in elephants. Walking with his friend he felt tall, too tall, passing all these dainty people who were in the first descriptions by foreigners always compared to dolls, were called dolls, who bowed to excessive depths as only dolls can do—people who seemed in their natural element wearing silk, whose sense of beauty was so advanced that they could construct a masterpiece of a garden out of gravel, whose very fish stalls were breathtaking in the arrangement of their catch. He could feel himself falling in love with these people, and hadn't every other writer and artist? Their art had transformed the world. It took the French to see it first, but there it was. Painting could never be the same after the forcing of Japan. Thank you, Commodore Perry. Back at the hotel he ran into the American novelist Ellison and said to him, I think I'm getting Jap-happy. He was, and it would stick. How could one reconcile this sense of beauty with the savagery of their soldiers? But of course they were still feudal people and had only exchanged the crossbow for the hand grenade. Things like Geneva Conventions made no sense to them, who had never even been told that Switzerland existed. War was part of the landscape: cunning, defense and the fountains of blood. Why would the Americans show indignation at the capture of the soldiers at Bataan? Of course it was a death march, and what do the defeated expect?

They went to the grandest parties and receptions the poet had ever seen, at the embassies, at the governor's (Governor of Tokyo —they were still having nomenclature problems), at robber barons' mansions, red carpet all the way. They all entrained to Kyoto, put up in style, wined and dined like the conquerors they were, cajoled in the Japanese manner with their pretty cry of *aidez-moi*, in return for doses of beauty which melted the bones of these writers. Who could resist them?

The poet went to the monastery at Ryoanji-ki to find the American poet Gary Snyder, but nobody understood him; Snyder was probably using a Japanese monkish name. He sat and marveled at the sand and boulder garden, long famous. He could understand the nature of this kind of beauty, mysterious and as offside as constellations, the mystic genius of an exiled island people like the English, people with a deep-rooted desire for conquest, permanently feared throughout history.

He was having a drink before dinner at the very comfortable "Western-style hotel" with the editor of a famous American avant-garde quarterly who said, I know a restaurant where the waitresses are all completely naked down to the soles of their feet. Let's go, said the poet.

They couldn't find it, of course, and went from bar to bar drinking Amerigo-Nipponese–style alcoholic beverages, taking taxis from this place to that, and getting stupefied, talking about poetry and more or less forgetting their mission, just Yanks on a junket. But there was a duty to get laid, they thought, as their minds sank into the quicksand of nocturnal necessity. In one rather low establishment where G.I.'s were standing at the bar, they sat down and had a drink and spotted two women sitting alone. The editor said they look good. The poet, who would never have done any such thing alone, said I'll ask them, and got up. Simultaneously the G.I.'s at the bar turned and looked at the Yankee civilians, put down their drinks, paid and left.

The girls, women, who spoke a kind of G.I. transactional English, escorted them to expensive restaurants with well-dressed hostesses who had had their eyes fixed and did not bow, an officers' kind of world, and they ate and drank and absconded to a railroad hotel. Hotels beside railroad stations are bad news. The poet discovered that he had spent all his money and the editor vouched for him. The couples separated and went to their beds.

At four o'clock in the morning the poet suddenly decided to leave and dressed violently. In his pockets he found an American ten-dollar bill, and he gave it to the astonished woman. She studied it. It was barely a tip from a rich American civilian.

He had a vague idea where to walk to his hotel, up a steep hill between stone walls, and he reached the place but the doors were locked and lightless, and he knocked and banged until he was admitted and apologized to the porter.

He visited the temples that tourists visit, the wooden palaces, the one where the Emperors had been under house arrest for generations while the feudal Tokugawa family ran the closed world. He walked on the "nightingale floors," floors made to squeak at every step to warn the Emperor of creeping assassins, and the delicacy of emptiness began to hypnotize him, the soft tatami mats, the translucent sliding walls like theater properties, for it all seemed theater, real theater where real love was made and real blood shed. The people were bamboo people, very strong, unbreakable, but graceful and held-in, casting small sharp shadows, practically silent, like silk, yielding and close-textured.

Back in Tokyo he refused to go to see Kamakura, where the giant Buddha was. He disliked the giant Buddha, and remembered that when he was a child every other house in Norfolk, Virginia, had a miniature of it and they burned incense in its lap for the scent and the pretty purple plume of smoke. But he went to the Noh plays, put on out of season just for the visiting writers.

It would be a long time before the plays traveled, because the very construction of the theater prohibited it, the use of certain woods, the layout of the stage and the necessary wooden bridge, the symbolic painting of the pine, the weird musical instruments, the special masks, the costumes, the actors themselves trained for life to talk-sing in unnatural and eerie tones and move to the dance. Every step, every lift of the hand or turn of the head was ordained by tradition, sometimes five hundred years old, much of the symbolism so tenuous and deep-rooted that even the experts and the Zen priests could not fathom it. They were spirit-plays, ghost plays in which the shades of ancient lovers, unfulfilled in their lives, would return to their significant place and sing and dance their loss or their tragedy. All of the actors were men, and behind the white-faced princess mask with amazingly beautiful black teeth one could discern the swarthy jaw of a big male actor. The silks were dreams, the animal masks astounding in their golds and reds and manes of white. The poet could hear the playwright Rice explaining to a novelist the parallel with the Greek drama. Could Sophocles have

At Johns Hopkins University, Baltimore, 1947.

With T. S. Eliot at party, *Poetry* offices, Chicago.—*James A. Mitchell*

Top: Karl and Evalyn Shapiro, at *Poetry*.
Bottom: trustees of *Poetry*, Newberry Library, Chicago.

W. H. Auden, *center*, with Henry Rago, *left*, and Karl Shapiro, *right*, at *Poetry* offices.

With Dylan Thomas, Chicago.—*James A. Mitchell*

Housecleaning, with Joan Farwell, at 232 E. Erie Street
before move to new *Poetry* offices.

At Ellen Borden Stevenson's Art Center building, 1955.

Top: conducting seminar at University of Cincinnati.
Bottom: en route to Italy, aboard ship,
left to right, Evalyn, Elizabeth, Karl, John Jacob, Kathy.

Top: lecturing in Berlin.
Bottom: with students, Nebraska, 1960s. At left is poet Ted Koozer.

At home, Davis.

Top: with William Stafford, Davis, California.
Bottom: Karl and Sophie Shapiro, Davis.

In Washington for assembly of past consultants in poetry at
Library of Congress.—*Helen Whittemore*

made his way to Cipangu in one of those unrecorded voyages of antiquity? How much did these mysterious people know?

Much more intelligible was the *kyogen*, a kind of palate cleanser, a brief dance-play exhibiting a noetic humor, probably Zen, such as the Owl Play they were watching. A man possessed by an owl, so that he can only warble and hoot like an owl, comes to a monk to be cured. The monk sings and dances around the victim trying to exorcise the owl and expel it from the possessed, but as the dance increases in intensity it becomes plain that the owl has decided to lodge itself in the monk.

The poet went with his Japanese friend to buy an authentic princess mask. He would keep it all his life and carry it from place to place in his endless moves.

They went to a Japanese restaurant where non-Japanese were never seen, a place frequented by professors from the various universities, took off their shoes and slipped into straw sandals and sat on the floor. Kimono-clad girls with swoopingly high black hair moved around the room on their knees. As the poet started to light a cigarette one of them glided over to him on her knees and lit it for him. He stared at her in astonishment. His friend suddenly relaxed —collapsed into relaxation, he thought of it afterwards, as did the other professors at their squat table. It was as if all the stiffness and starch, all the formality and muscle armor had been removed by an invisible hand and they were as boneless as rag dolls. Their conversation underwent the same metamorphosis, politeness giving way to ribbing and jokes and loud laughter. The poet drank unnumbered sakis from thimble-sized cups, for he had already acquired a taste for this warm, slightly pungent rice wine. It was clearly a man's place, a man's world. Back home the women would look at him reproachfully as he raved about the beautiful attendants in their magnificent kimonos serving him on their knees.

It was all over in less than two weeks. He said goodbye to his State Department friend, went to the farewell reception at the

American embassy, and enplaned for home via Honolulu. Pearl Harbor, he thought; the war was only twelve short years ago and now he was a lifelong convert to Japan. Two days later when he debarked at Lincoln, Nebraska, and was met by his wife and the resident Japanese history professor and his wife, he overflowed, he erupted and spouted like a Roman candle about the glories of the Japanese, their art, their architecture, their clothes, their fish, their women on their knees, even their religion, if Zen was a religion.

Three days later, to his horror, he discovered a chancre on the head of his penis. He stayed in the bathroom a long time, frozen. He had slept with his wife the night before. He went to his office as soon as possible. Of course he hadn't said anything to her, though at breakfast he spilled his coffee and his wife said laughingly that he was homesick for Tokyo. Kyoto, he amended to himself, where he and the American editor had picked up the prostitutes. Oh my God, he remembered, the things I did with that woman, and he turned away his mouth when the children kissed him goodbye.

He locked the door of his office, the first time he had ever done that in working hours, and turned to the physician section of the phonebook, not sure what he was looking for. Urologist, that must be it, and he telephoned for an appointment, an emergency he decided to say, and got an appointment for 2:00 p.m.

The doctor, placid and businesslike enough, took a smear from his infected member, drew a blood sample, looked his body over, and said the test results would take ten days. No sex, he said, until we know. The poet instructed him to call him at his office only and the doctor answered, of course.

Walking back to the campus his mind reeled. Baudelaire, he kept saying to himself like a mantra, while his memory recited *le mal sacré, le mal sacré, dementia praecox*, Baudelaire raving in his syphilitic insanity. He managed to work through the day, opening manuscripts that had come in and stacking them neatly without reading any. Luckily it was not a teaching day. Now and then he would take out his penis and stare at the sore. He thought he had never seen anything so ugly or frightening, and it was his, his very own secret, his unmentionable, threatening, even life-threatening disease, his syphilis. He was beginning to feel proprietary about it.

Getting through the next ten days took more control than he thought he had. The strain of talking about Japan, which everyone wanted to hear stories of, was almost as bad as getting into bed with his wife, bad as pretending he had strained his back hauling his heavy suitcase, giving a significant wince once in a while and saying he was making an appointment with the orthopedist who took care of the football team. Not that his wife made any sexual demands; she was having problems herself and talked about her tipped womb. Ten days seemed ten years, ten centuries.

The call came from the doctor's secretary, and when he appeared in her reception room he studied her expression for some news but could find nothing. She knew what he had, she typed the reports. He spotted the manila envelope with his name on it.

Negative, said the doctor, but the poet was bewildered, feverish, and asked if negative meant what he thought it meant. You do not have syphilis, the doctor said, or anything else but a surface irritation. The sore should be gone by now. But it was not gone and the urologist gave him a prescription for a salve, shook hands and said goodbye.

As he walked out of the building onto the street he felt—disappointed! He paraphrased or redacted or distorted Stendhal's remark, one of the poet's favorite quotations in which the French novelist shows amazement at his experience of war, his experience of love: *What, is it nothing but that!* And he almost understood Baudelaire's lust for Hell.

Things tapered off, he slid into his new duties swimmingly, fawned over, feted. The new house was rising, and although he sometimes ached for California he was happy, his wife was happy, even the children were, visiting their future home half-built, watching their father jump down in the still excavated parts looking at he knew not what.

They visited old friends in Iowa at one of those expensive colleges for rich children of the hinterland who would go on to Eastern universities and Eastern or Parisian marriages, scions of corn and pig fortunes. The wife had been the teacher of the poet's eldest at a private school in Baltimore, the husband had been a journalist for *Time* and was now teaching journalism and English at Grinnell, as the place was named. The visit turned sour. The journalist, a handsome, small, very wiry, almost acrobatic man, had fallen in love with a winsome, small, very wiry, almost acrobatic teacher of ballet at the college, and they were preparing divorces on both sides. The wife of the journalist was in shock and her pretty children clung sometimes to her, sometimes to the father, everyone slightly hysterical, on the verge of tears.

One afternoon the about-to-be abandoned wife was driving the poet and his family into the country—it was all country out of town in any direction—to see a little farm they thought they were going to buy before the ballet dancer, for she was still hoping that the affair would end and life would go back to where it was before. They were parallelling the railroad tracks through the cornfields, and could hear the musical song of the train intoning at all the innumerable crossings which had no liftgates or warning lights but only white X-signs saying R.R. At one of the crossings she slowed down, then stopped, on the railroad tracks. Had the motor choked? The poet screamed at her and she seemed to wake up from a trance and slowly drove off the tracks as the train thundered past them by a few feet. In the car were the driver, the poet and his wife and their three children, said a kind of headline in the poet's head.

When they said goodbye next day and the hosts and their brood gathered around the station wagon to wave them on their way, the host put up his hand to halt them. The poet kept his foot on the brake and the host at a standstill put his hands on his hips, leaped up in the air from a standstill, and landed on the hood of the car and bowed. Then he leaped down and laughed and let them go. His wife stood by with a drawn face, waving her hand.

8.

A phrase had stuck in his craw and gave him a throat tickle that wouldn't go away, a kind of permanent reminder of something really vital. He had been pinked, as fencers say, but not with a rapier, and it wasn't quite a wound, more of an accolade, an embrace, a promotion, if he chose. It was hard to know how to take it, especially considering the source, the gigantic flatfooted highly talented lush poet of Seattle, Washington, who had invited him to take his place for a year, and who had bellowed out: "Well, if it isn't the bourgeois poet!" and given him a bear hug. Right, he thought, or as T. S. Eliot would say, precisely. He said nothing but carried the phrase back to his motel room and mulled over it, and made it his own: it gave him definition, purpose, a sense of his place, a fulcrum, a lever, a book to write. He was going to name a book *Poems of a Jew* in order to exorcise the fear of the word, Jew, with its jagged edges that cut both ways, the fear that had once almost caused him to change his name. The same impulse to reinstate a slandered, misused, abused word, a word used as a slur, even a curse, drove him to write his *The Bourgeois Poet*. Wasn't Everyman in America middle class or bourgeois? Bourgeois was no longer what Baudelaire meant, what the political leftists meant. They were talking about money, convention, propriety. He was talking about the American word *relax*, take it easy, no problem, about a problem-solving people, a culture of middle-class hedonists, pragmatists who rejected mystery. There was a hitch; art is mystery. The bourgeois poet would have to guard the mystery, stand inside and outside his situation at once, not easy to do. Their poet, he would say, he had from the beginning called himself their enemy, their poet. But he was one of them.

A poet is his own enemy, of course. People were always saying to him, You are your own worst enemy, because he didn't go for the gold, he refused to ferret for honors or preferment or money. If he absolutely needed it he would ask for it; if it wasn't forthcoming he would tighten his belt. He had no material desires, ate what was in front of him, wore what was in the closet, drove junkers, ridiculous cars that made his neighbors laugh, a three-cylinder Saab that farted at stoplights, a tiny Fiat once, so small that when he was stuck in a snowbank in the university parking lot, a Japanese psychologist who had been a kamikaze pilot lifted it out of the snowbank with his bare hands. All this was more or less acceptable to his bourgeois neighbors, after all, he was a professor and on top of that a poet, and on top of that a Jew. What could you expect? And if he split wood in his driveway in the winter barefooted, what could you expect? And he achieved a kind of mascot status in the split-level neighborhood.

They accepted him pretty well, although one summer night the dentist who lived next door mowed his lawn after dark and the poet rushed out and chased him off. He liked long grass. The neighbors hated long grass with a passion. His unwashed collie dog liked long grass, too, and he would roll in the grass with the dog sometimes. And one day in the fall when the pheasant season was on, someone gave him two fat pheasants just shot, and he didn't know what to do with them. His Italian friend, the contessa, said, hang them up on the clothesline until the feathers fall off. The dentist saw the hanging birds and rushed over and said, don't eat those, I'll give you some of mine. And he took down the hanging pheasants and rushed off and returned with two neatly frozen pheasants which he had in his coffinlike freezer in his basement. He had thrown the real pheasants away; dentists like to throw things away, especially unsanitary things dripping blood in the long grass.

He had just received a Guggenheim and they were going to Italy for a year, the three little ones and wife and big yellow secondhand station wagon. He had never bought a new car in his life. They had rented an eighteenth-century villa high up above Chiavari, Chiavari where Ezra Pound had been arrested by the American Army, Chiavari where Nietzsche had thrown his arms around a horse in his madness and was taken away. The ad in the *Saturday Review of Literature* put there by a young Harvard student and his wife who were themselves subletting it and couldn't pay the rent, said: Eighteenth-century villa with view of the Mediterranean. Now he drove the long yellow Ford station wagon onto the grass when a peasant rushed up and waved them off, making wild gesticulations at the car and the ground. The car was sitting atop the cistern and would crash through the turf and everybody would drown, and he backed the car off and the peasant wiped his brow.

The villa was barely furnished but clean, the light at night almost nonexistent, a couple of forty-watt bulbs in twelve or fifteen rooms, depending on what counted as rooms, no refrigerator, only a food chest that would keep the cheese from the rats, no view of the Mediterranean except from the second-floor window in one room, the sea about twenty miles away and far down. The place was pretty, picturesque, not really a villa. He wasn't sure what a villa was, but this was no mansion and he had to drive down the mountain to the grocery stores on a one-lane road, and if the bus happened to be coming up he would have to reverse the big car and back up until he found a passing place. It was totally isolated, and they were worried about the children getting lost in the mountains or falling off a cliff. There was nothing to do for anybody but the poet, and he couldn't write, especially at night under the weak bulb, and after a couple of weeks they went to Chiavari and telephoned the contessa, who was also visiting Italy with her husband, a Siena scholar from the University of Nebraska, and she said she would come up and see if they could break the lease they had signed in Nebraska.

The Harvard couple was angry and apparently desperate. All they had to live on was their rent from the villa, they said. The young blonde woman sat out on the slope of the hill with the poet, letting her white dress creep up her thigh and laying her hand on top of his, and he was uncertain what to do. He had already heard that the couple had earned some kind of reputation in town. The young husband hung around the bars in the mornings and drank *grappa*, a dynamite potion, the dregs of the dregs of the wine barrel scraped out and further fermented, distilled—he wasn't sure how they did it, but it was almost a joke word. Anybody who drank *grappa* was on the way out. The Italians didn't like drunks; those G.I.'s with their blind staggers had shocked them worse than the Germans. The G.I.'s went for *grappa*, and here was this handsome young blond American knocking back *grappa* at ten o'clock in the morning, and as if that wasn't enough there were hints of his wife visiting the hotels with Italian businessmen, picking up lira in the time-honored way. Maybe she was trying to get the poet to stay in the villa in the time-honored way.

Their friend the contessa had arrived and met with the owners of the villa in town who had rented the place to the Harvard couple, and they were the origin of the rumors. The negotiations proceeded, the poet driving the contessa into Chiavari to meet with the owners, the wife going to market while he bought the children ice creams and Cokes. They had lunch in a hotel dining room and coming out through the lobby he was shocked to see a tense crowd of Italians huddled around the television watching "Gunsmoke" in Italian, the Harvard woman among them, brushing up on her Italian, perhaps. At night the children huddled in one large bed; they had heard the rats in the walls but hadn't seen them, so far, and everyone was sleepless and couldn't wait to get out of the beautiful eighteenth-century villa and find a twentieth-century one maybe on a beach.

A couple of months' rent settled the negotiations with the Harvard couple and the owners in town accepted the settlement. As long as they were getting their share from the lessees up on the mountain it was all they could do. The poet and family and the contessa piled into the yellow station wagon and started south, to Livorno where Shelley had set out in the storm to be drowned. Further down you could see Elba and the poet recited the palindrome for the children ABLE WAS I ERE I SAW ELBA and told them about Napoleon. Everything seemed beautiful even when it wasn't.

In one town where they stopped for lunch, the poet took the station wagon to a garage to have the oil changed. He made his request more or less intelligible by pointing and gesturing, delighting the Italian mechanics with his pantomime. When one of the mechanics pulled out the dipstick, they had never seen a dipstick that long. It seemed endless; they all gathered round, roaring with laughter at the length of the dip stick, and examining the interior of the Ford Fairlane with awe at the amplitude of the American machine. They had seen plenty of American G.I. vehicles but nothing like this living room on wheels, bright yellow outside with chrome bands and an assortment of front and rear lights and the luggage racks on top. The contessa had decided on Grosseto. Its marina had good beaches and comfortable modern houses. The new bourgeoisie now had beach properties, and she would find the place. They went to a real estate agency and an appointment was made with the young good-looking Italian businessman landlord and they all met at the beach house—not exactly on the beach but set back in a pine forest in the sand, lovely and cool with the high pines in a constant whisper overhead, the house all stone and marble, travertine and tile, spanking new and neatly furnished and five minutes from the sparkly Mediterranean. This was more like it, thought the bourgeois poet; he could settle down here and write his book.

The combination of insouciance and willful ignorance does not make for good management, especially in money affairs. He was not sure how far the Guggenheim stipend would stretch. He had already used up several more months of rent to buy out of the mountain villa than he thought he had. His wife was no better manager than he, the pair of them babes in the financial woods, always in debt, and he had a vague theory that everybody is in debt though some hide it better than others. He remembered his father's big Victorian house and the live-in maid and other servants and two cars and in fact no money but his salary. The middle class lived well because that was their style. Money had little to do with it. It was a credit economy and people gave him money to write poetry or to talk about it. That was why he was in Italy. Of course, with his family along and the long yellow Fairlane he was considered by the Italians as a typical rich American. There was no question about the rent and the deposits, and he wrote another big check having a vague feeling that he was using up the money too fast, and it crossed his mind that they didn't have a round-trip ticket home. Their plans had been open-ended and the return tickets were not part of the plan. They decided on the house at once and the owner brought out the papers for signatures and they had a glass of wine. The poet produced a bottle of Poggibonsi from the car and they had a toast and the young bourgeois pronounced the poet simpatico with a sincere smile. People were always saying he was simpatico and it puzzled him; he was even suspicious of the compliment. They all shook hands and the owner left.

It should have been ideal for his writing, the children at the beach with their mother, the murmuring pines, the cool tile house, the peace. But something paralyzed him. He couldn't write a word. He paced around and around and wound up at the beach sunning himself. He was a sun freak and only went in the water to cool off. He discovered how to have the beach to himself, the Italians would all go at the same time, to be together it seemed, all go to their two-hour siestas at the same time, and he would go to the beach alone and have it all to himself except for two gargantuan German women a few feet away from him under their umbrella. He could hardly believe their proportions, their world-size breasts, their thighs like the piers of triumphal arches. One day he dozed and opened his eyes in a shadow. One of them was standing over him, a white titan, and he sat up. She asked him in German what time it was and pointed to her wrist, and he told her by holding up two fingers. She thanked him and he watched her stride back through the sand, his eyes glued to the rise and fall of her fabulous hams.

It pleased him to be in a place where nobody spoke English except one man who had come up to him, a schoolteacher who taught English in Grosseto. He should have made friends with this Italian but he preferred to be alone with his locked-in English. The children quickly made friends and were already chattering in Italian. They made a happy game of it and had no inhibitions about languages as he did. He was terrified of making mistakes and confined himself to a few words of greeting, the hails and farewells and *grazies* and *scusis*. Though one day to his surprise an American sergeant in uniform sauntered up to him and sat down to talk. He was the general's driver, he said, and they were finally shipping home. His staff car had six extra gas tanks under the floor in case of emergency, extra batteries, food supplies, medicines, lots of booze, a machine gun, grenades. Why was the sergeant telling him all this? In case of atomic attack, he said. He loved the Italian wine, he said and had become a wino. His Italian wife was very unhappy and wanted to get to America where he could be cured of drinking. He got a glimpse of the staff car, which looked ordinary enough except for the fender flags with two stars. He just wanted to talk to a fellow American, and he gave a mock salute.

A sinister man on a bicycle came to the tile house in the pines and spoke at length in Italian about protecting the house, with elaborate gestures and demonstrations. He seemed to be explaining that he would protect the house from burglars for some hundreds of lira a month, and the poet shook his head. The man went away and came back daily and could be seen pedaling his bicycle through the pines, eyeing the house. The poet and his wife were worried and went to the police station and spent an entire afternoon with an interpreter and a fancy-dress carabiniere who took pages and pages of notes. Yes, they knew the man, they would make him stop annoying the Americans. No, there was no danger at the marina from burglars, nobody locked their doors, and after a few more surveillances the cyclist disappeared.

Still the poet could not write. He took his notebook to the beach and took it back again. He decided that you can't write in transit, life in flux. He tried a journal and nothing came. It seemed wooden and pointless. He couldn't even write a letter or a postcard. He drove into the town and visited the Etruscan museum. This was the land of the mysterious Etruscans, of Tarquin, of the rape of Lucrece. The museum was all funerary, strange as Easter Island images. Nobody really understood these people who had disappeared, who predated the Romans, who had been conquered by Aeneas's soldiers. He liked the way the Etruscan women did their hair, *simplex munditiis*. Lawrence would have it of course that they were obliterated because of their love of the phallus, the phalli all over the tombs, and the Romans wouldn't have that kind of life-worshiping symbol all over the lot. Of course this was not one of the best museums and the best of the antiquities had wound up in the Vatican museums without the phalli probably. But the beautiful Italians lolling on the sand were sure to be Etruscans. He hoped they were, buxom handsome women, said Lawrence, who loved Frieda's breasts and made them immortal.

But something within him insisted that writing was out of the question here in this place that seemed perfection to the poet— the lovely house, villa the natives called it (all individual houses were called villas), the ancient and gentle pines shaped at the top like umbrellas, the peaceful Mediterranean, the land of the Etruscans, the wine—everyone was happy but him. He was blocked, and he had never suffered from what writers' conferences called writer's block. He had always avoided writers' colonies, mansions where writers were sequestered and taken out of the mainstream in order to create. He thought those places artificial, a mockery of "the poetry of situation," his made-up name for his poetic.

He had always refused Yaddo, for instance, one of the famous writers' colonies. He had been practically begged to attend and live in one of their cottages, where lunch is discreetly served by an attendant who leaves the tray of food on your doorstep so as not to disturb the creativity within. Only at dinner would all the writers meet and get drunk. Most of the tales were of drunkenness and fights and assignations. He wanted nothing to do with those places, so artificial and imprisoning, he said. He had written all the time, in the army, in the war, in barracks and tents, on trains and ships amidst unbelievable din and disorder. What did he need with a cottage with an invisible Do Not Disturb sign on the door? Yet here in the pine forest near the sea, Our Sea, *Mare Nostrum*, he could do nothing. It was something like a writers' colony, and it blocked him.

One day a workman had come to fix the shower which wouldn't quite turn off, the front door stood open. There was no screen, there were no screens in all of Italy, and as the man was leaving the poet came to pay him in the tiled living room, the workman's face suddenly took on a frightened look and he pointed to the middle of the tile floor. An almost transparent light-green spider, the size of a man's hand, stood on the floor on pointed legs. Spiders with pointed legs are poisonous, the poet thought. He had a big book in his hand. He walked over to the spider without thinking and simply dropped the book and flattened the arachnid. The workman's face relaxed. It was a kind of omen, the poet thought, maybe even a warning. We've got to go home, he thought, and as was his wont his mind immediately began to make plans for the departure. The children want hamburgers and French fries and ketchup. I'll take what's left of the Guggenheim money and build a study.

Immediately he planned the study. The kitchen had a door to the garage, the garage was big enough for two cars. He would have the study at the rear half of the garage with a picture window and an oak floor, bookcases to the ceiling on all available wall space. What's more, he would have a deck built off the study. There were no decks in Nebraska. He believed he would have the first one and could sun himself in the sunny months. He had to have his sun and called himself a desert rat. The deck would remind him of California, where everybody had decks or patios. His mind was halfway across the ocean in a second, and he knew without any doubt whatever that he would write his book the minute the study and the deck were done. He had this way of planning things in an instant and getting them done with a wave of his hand. Money didn't enter into it; time didn't enter into it. He had made his decision and his wife hadn't even been told. He hoped she had had enough travel for the time being. The children probably wouldn't object, and the first step was to get tickets.

The young woman at the travel agency in Grosseto was delighted to use her English and to deal with the American, a family of five and a station wagon from Naples to New York via the Straits of Gibraltar. The *Statendam* would be sailing from Naples. Dutch ships were excellent. She itemized the fare in dollars; too many dollars, the poet thought. Did he have enough? His university salary was being deposited at home. It would take a long time to withdraw that much money. The Guggenheim was in monthly installments. There wasn't enough for the ticket, though there was plenty for motels and gas and food when they got to New York. He drove back to the marina dejected. There had to be a way to get the tickets. Now he was in a hurry to get going and build his study and write his book. He sat around the beach for a couple of days fretting. He couldn't concentrate on what he was reading. Writing was out of the question. One night at dinner, the children were already talking about hamburgers and French fries, it flashed into his mind; of course! They could cable the travel agency in Lincoln, Nebraska, where they had started out. They would arrange for the tickets and would simply bill him. Why hadn't the Italian agent thought of that? He drove into the city the next morning. The manager understood and said of course he would arrange for passage, car and all, and for the hotel in Naples, and even for a visit to Pompeii across from Naples. The children would love that; he would too. Mostly he wanted to see the wall paintings. The contessa and her husband came from Sienna to say goodbye, the car was loaded again, and they were off in a week with boat tickets in hand.

Around the corner from the baroque luxury hotel with its armies of uniformed servants was a sidewalk cafe run by a Neopolitan who had worked in the G.I. kitchens in the war and whose exotic specialty was hamburgers and French fries, which they all ate reverently, patriotically, while the famous street urchins of Naples watched and begged for money. He gave them money and more urchins appeared. There was a Yank emptying his pockets. The waiter, who had a pocketful of corks, began with great dexterity to bounce the corks off the urchins' heads to chase them off, though it was like chasing a swarm of flies off a side of beef.

They drove with a guide around the beautiful Bay and up the shoulder of the volcano. The driver insisted on stopping at a cameo factory where innumerable children sat and worked the pink shell into delicate profiles. But they didn't buy any of the baubles, and went on to the ruins, and walked the streets and entered the roofless houses, and the children pocketed tiny square tiles from the floors. The tourists were stripping Pompeii and nobody stopped them. The poet wanted to see the erotic paintings in the forbidden places, but didn't want to make an issue of it. Children were not allowed to see such things. He had seen them in the books and they didn't seem all that erotic to him—more ecclesiastical if anything, holy sex if anything, not salacious or dirty. (Not that the Romans didn't have plenty of that, too.) He watched a group of archaeologists sifting new rubble. The digging of Pompeii could go on forever. It was a playground for historians, a playground for children. The whole modern world was on a treasure hunt in the bowels of the earth and now in the heavens, probing and digging in every dimension, turning time inside out. Driving down the mountain he thought he spotted their ship in the harbor. He was in a hurry to board her and head west through the Gates of Hercules.

The return was smooth enough, uneventful like most modern voyages, except for the last night. He was sitting with his wife and some shipboard friends, chatting and sipping, when an acquaintance, a young Italian physicist came up to them and in an agitated manner said that their daughter was in the ship's hospital. The Dutch bartender had sold the fifteen-year-old and a friend a quart of whiskey. The two children had drunk most of it. They were unconscious, very white, lying in the beds. The doctor said they would be weak when they landed and would have to be helped off the ship. The poet ran to the fancy mirrored bar and demanded to know who had sold the children a quart of whiskey, but nobody took credit for the sale. He thought of going to the ship's captain but everybody was merrymaking. There was nothing to be done; it was just a mark of punctuation to a failed trip abroad.

They moved the tenants out of their house without trouble, students who had done considerable damage with their partying; no contest. He went to the construction company and told them about the study and the deck. He knew precisely what he wanted and where, and they started breaking out the brick wall the next day. He watched the whole operation day after day, the flooring, one bright oak strip after another, grain this way and that; the wiring, the glazier, the carpenter building his library shelves, the painters. It was a big secluded room, with the heat and the cold air for summer piped from the main furnace, and one day it was all finished and he started moving the books in from the living room, all the poetry books—most of his books were poetry, dictionaries, encyclopedias.

He made a desk by buying a hollow-core door and iron legs, and screwed them on himself. The desk stood under the big picture window which looked down on the sloping backyard and across the roofs of the houses lower down, across a farm of sorghum to the big Georgian Veterans Hospital with its white lantern, a passable view on the whole. He started his book: The bourgeois poet closes the door of his study and lights his pipe. Why am I in this box, he says to himself (although it is exactly as he planned). The bourgeois poet sits down at his inoffensive desk—a door with legs, a door turned table—and almost approves the careful disarray of books, papers, magazines, and such artifacts as thumbtacks. The bourgeois poet is already out of matches and gets up. It is too early in the morning for any definite emotion, and the B.P. smokes. It is beautiful in the midlands: green fields and tawny fields, sorghum the color of red morocco bindings, distant new neighborhoods, clean and treeless, and the Veterans Hospital fronted with a shimmering Indian Summer tree. The Beep feels seasonal, placid as a melon, neat as a child's football lying under the tree, waiting for whose hand to pick it up.

This is a poem, he thought; this is the way to go. From his window he saw the world organizing itself like patterns in a kaleidoscope, the bits of colored glass endlessly rotating, forming, reforming, the colors extremely important, pure or refracted but in relation, if not consanguineous at least mutually magnetic. It didn't matter where you started or where you ended. What is the relation of the child's football lying under a tree to the Georgian tower of the Veterans Hospital? Everything, nothing. It is the random disarray of experience that the words organize. Williams knew that, every poet knows that. The question of what they call form is one of magnetism, what is attracted to what, what repelled. It is all done if not with mirrors, at least with the energy of the invisible. Rhythm is the energy. The poem is surrounded with a field of force, the rhythmus, and sometimes you can make it visible by what they call versification, meters, but these are only structural devices and bear as much relation to the poem as a blueprint does to a house. To write the poem without that visible scaffolding was the challenge.

He couldn't be tied down to feet with this kind of work; too slow, hobbled. Use feet if you want to, but not systematically, use rhyme if it crops up, not purposefully but by chance. The accidental acquires power of its own, the haphazard drop of paint can recenter the whole landscape. He wasn't talking about automatic writing. He didn't believe in losing all control. Somebody has got to fly the poem, keep it aloft, circle it, land it. About that time his son was flying his kite out in the street. He was good at it, but a gust of wind made it nose-dive into the high tension wires, and all the power in the neighborhood was killed for a mile around. It was a miracle the boy wasn't hurt. Luckily the nylon string didn't conduct those thousands of volts. He became something of a hero among the other boys for having plunged the neighborhood into the pre-electrical age, for a few hours at least.

If a poem makes a direct contact like that kite you get a blackout; the killing-effect comes into play. That's the problem with most love poems. They give the reader a jolt, an electric shock that blots you out. The poem needs insulators, which is why they look the way most poems do: surrounded with white space, lying in patterns, sounding in patterns. Typography is serious business, margins and indentations like silk and rubber wrappings, like skin and flesh that cradle veins and let them do their job.

Why am I in this box, he says to himself can be read as what they call iambic pentameter, including the eleventh syllable, but that's the way this language works, this English, queen of poetries. It's the steady rise of the voice from low stress to high stress. He was aware that his prose poems, which were beginning to flow, used the entire iambic pentameter line as a "foot," opening the rhythms wide. It was right and inevitable to use the decasyllabic standard as a unit, where the voice felt it naturally. There is no preconceived schema to this kind of poem except the logic of rhythm, the music of statement, the diagram of color. You feel your way along the line. There are no signs posted.

It's the difference between an English garden and a French or an American one. In the French garden everything is laid out to perfection in a worship of geometry, angles and parabolas, distancing of fountains. In the English garden the tendency is toward the field, except of course for the palaces. The garden shades into field or countryside. It's nature without corsets, bustles, makeup, not the beautifully crippled trees or topiary grotesques of eighteenth-century France. Why should a boxwood hedge look like a man on horseback? And the American garden, if there is such a thing, is more field than anything else. So with classical French prosody, the looser, more natural English, and the wild American.

It had to be done in the vastness. Whitman grasped it, took the bull by the horns and threw it down, a Paul Bunyan type of operation, absolutely necessary if there was to be an American garden of poetry—did it singlehanded while the New Englanders were still being Englanders at bottom. Even Emerson, though the only one to see what Walt had up his sleeve, greeted him for midwifing American poetry. It would take a century more or less before Whitman's rhythms were heard. They were too big to hear; you can't hear a whole ocean at once. Pound heard it in part, Williams in part. Mostly it went unheeded. Sandburg heard it in part, heard the recession of the wave rather than the crash upon the shore and against the rocks. Eliot wouldn't hear it and was afraid of it; unsuitable he said of Whitman, not for him with his masterly Websterian modernizations, his Laforguean hems and haws.

But in spite of the French topiary prosody, the French heaved their way out with a mighty heave into what is awkwardly called the prose poem, and this clumsy name was descriptive, after all, because of the looks. It looked like prose, even read like prose, but not really. It was poetry but not pitched as high, more like recitative before the singing resumes. It was in the age of the smokestack, more down to earth, more street-wise. Like all the arts it opened a window on the street. It started at about the same time as the camera, in the same country, France, and didn't spread across the ocean for a hundred years or so, never spread to England at all. He had picked it up from Baudelaire during the war and wrote several, one of them, his best of the genre, called "The Dirty Word," and satisfied with the experiment dropped it and returned to his more settled ways of writing.

He was not ready to commit himself to the prose thing as a method. He hadn't enough life experience under his belt, in spite of the War. War is not exactly life experience but a parody of it. He would have to wait twenty years before he sat down in his study and wrote, almost at a sitting, so to speak, the whole *Bourgeois Poet*. You needed a stationary vantage point to do that, to pick up the kaleidoscope and start turning the bits of imagery in your mind's eye. He could see plainly that he had a start, with clear sailing ahead and he could now concentrate on the form, first the typographic form, paragraph form but with the indentation reversed, the margins justified but the first line or any further paragraphing of a first line jutting to the left and the rest of the paragraph indented, roughly in the shape of the state of Oklahoma with its panhandle sticking out on the left and the body hanging from this stem. That was a simple problem solved.

Length was something else; what are the limits of the poem? Of the book itself? When the manuscript was completed he sent it to the editor, who had never seen such a thing as this peculiar book of "poems," and said drily that the only limit to the manuscript seemed to be physiological. He was right in a sense that he didn't know, that the size and shape of the poem depended on the size and shape of the piece of paper in the typewriter! A discovery, he believed, a secret, a key to prosody, the proportion 8½" × 11", the ever-mysterious rectangle that painters had always used without saying why, the shape of books, in varying sizes but always with the same ratio.

He had never before written poems on a typewriter, and abhorred the idea while recognizing that Williams and Cummings did it well. They used the typewriter as a painter uses a palette. There was something in it after all. It wasn't that he needed to justify the shape and size of a sheet of typewriter paper with, "In the beginning there was typewriter paper, and the typewriter paper was eight-and-a-half by eleven, and he saw that it was good, and he called the size of the sheet a member of the family of golden numbers in the Fibonacci sequence, and all these sheets are golden sections, and one sheet is a rectangle of the whirling squares which can be divided into the logarithmic spiral out of which spiral are formed the horns of mountain goats and the tusks of elephants and the claws of a cat and the tail of a monkey and the lovely fall of a lock of hair." Of course these scientific or quasi-scientific analogies were consolatory and exciting but mostly they were just kibbitzing the Muse, exercises to keep students awake.

Nevertheless he felt at home with the shape of the page in the typewriting machine and began to write these block-shaped poems, adjusting his ideas almost immediately and unconsciously to the shape of the page. When he was about a third of the way down, after the initial theme had been stated and developed just enough, he would perform the *volta*, the turn, the turn of thought, sometimes a contradiction of the theme above, sometimes a reprise with a different twist but a turnabout, the conjunction *but* the pivot, as in sonnets. Theoretically in all sonnets which are built upon theme, counter-theme and resolution, the structure of the sonata itself is a very musical way of thinking, feeling.

These were prose sonnets on the whole, with the advantage that the prose door admitted many more characters than the poetry entryway. All kinds of quotidian colloquials crowded in—street signs, lids of trash cans, the ears of coffee cups, condoms, doggerel, typewriters, dates from newspapers and encyclopedias. The problem was what to keep out. Yes, the limits of such a book are mainly physiological, as the sardonic editor said. He would have to impose some outer limits on the work, define an edge.

He wrote a poem every day, or part of a poem, or sometimes two. He didn't like to write more than a single poem a day. He was superstitious about that, thinking one poem might muddy the other. The poem had to be alone by itself for a while, like him in his study. He wasn't in a monkish solitary mood, that was not it, but now he felt at home in this new kind of poem and understood that it was a poem of immediacy, even if he was writing about the Parthenon or some incident out of his childhood. In this kind of poem what was happening at the moment was germane to the theme somehow. Though he could not do that in Italy, he could write about Italy now that he was out of it. He couldn't do it while he was there. Most of the time he stayed at home. He was still on his sabbatical and his fellowship, but would visit the university library for books or the tobacco shop downtown or the liquor store where the Jewish proprietor had been taught by the salesmen to say *bon appétit* to every customer after a sale. Things like that, not normally the stuff of poetry, got into these poems.

He began to see Lincoln, Nebraska, allegorically. Everyone was taking part in a play he was writing. He was the stage manager, director, author and actor, too. The most commonplace things took on a lively significance. There was no such thing as a negligible detail—the day's weather, the dog barking—and most of all there was a sense of the presentness of the past. It was hard to distinguish the past even from what was happening under his nose. He enjoyed this feeling of hyper-reality, the sensation he had had when he first wore eyeglasses and a new and sudden clarity burst into view. Poetry was a way of re-seeing; that's what seer meant. It was a state bordering on hallucination, but he was afraid of hallucinating and avoided what some called surrealism. Rather he reveled in those odd angles of vision which certain new artists were playing with, optical art, pop, the abstractionists. He loved abstract painting but not abstract poetry. Poetry can't be abstract, he said. He discovered Satie and got books on primitive and naive art from the library. He wanted to be an artist.

Between poems he would go out on the deck where he had put up a large easel and painted. He painted on odds and ends of wooden leftovers, the panels of drawers from broken bureaus, rectangles of masonite. He kept only a few of these artifacts as he called them, sometimes painting over them a dozen times. If someone asked for one he would give it to them. Juxtaposition was what fascinated him, the effect one color had on another next to it, the infinitude of shape. Modern art, he believed, aspired to unknown shapes, not just impressions and the metamorphoses of light. The beauty of discarded things fascinated him. He would pick up a flattened beer can in the street, one that had been mashed by a thousand cars, the rust, the distortion of the printing, the broken colors. He decided to take a class in welding in the fall. He wanted to handle acetylene and oxygen torches and melt iron and steel into new forms. He began to see, or imagined he saw, the "primitive" in the most finished masterpieces of old. He couldn't dissociate these interests of the eye from the prose poems.

Of course he couldn't prevent himself from being oracular, bigmouth; it was a fault he had to live with, part of his style. But he hoped for the best outcome in the poems. He recorded memories of smells. What better way to find your road back to the past than to evoke the odors of the past? The nose is much neglected in sensory literature, he thought; almost everything in poetry is visual. What did a Roman street smell like in the time of Catullus? Auden says that Shakespeare probably stank. What kinds of perfumes did the Dark Lady use? All the voyagers had sung the praises of the fragrances of the trade winds. Huysmans had started a vocabulary of scents from flowers. There was something decadent about this passion for the primitive.

He was interested in the decadent, the dying of old days and
forms. He had met Mario Praz in Rome, Praz living in his two-
thousand-year-old apartment in the Teatro Marcello, the ruins of
the ancient theater, a beautiful apartment decorated with a sixteen-
year-old mistress, a sarcophagus in the foyer, Napoleon's cradle
hanging from the ceiling. He adored Praz's *The Romantic Agony*,
read and reread it, taught from it. Under the great rock of Romanticism crawled all those horrors. He was hypnotized by the monsters
and vampires and dybbuks, sadists and sex fiends and poisoners.
He loved Praz and his famous book, felt himself decadent with the
new American decadence of tin and tinsel and the smoking Saturday night special, rape in the used-car lot, the worship of gangsters,
the whores draped in the flag, a seething cauldron of the ultimate
vulgarities in his beloved sweetheart of America.

Sexual obscenity had begun to attract him seriously. He was wor-
shipping at the shrine of Henry Miller. Maybe he was getting old.
He never thought of age, and hardly even knew his birthday. He
loathed birthdays, not because he didn't want to advance in years,
he didn't care one way or the other. What if people reached a certain age, say thirty-nine, and then started to grow backwards? Your
next birthday would be your thirty-eighth and so on. He didn't see
what difference it would make. He thought he was forty-nine, on
the cusp of the magical number fifty. He looked in the mirror and
couldn't see anything that looked like fifty—what does fifty look like
anyhow?—though he suspected a certain retro-purpose in writing
these prose poems. He was picking up the pieces, and besides,
he was having sexual irritations and exacerbations which lead to
trouble, shivering the timbers of the ship of domestic tranquillity.
Not that he was on the prowl, but something worse. He began to
feel about this book that it was a Rubicon, and if he crossed this
river he might land in the land of Praz, where the horrors were
waiting under the stone slab.

There was already friction about the new poems, the use of raw
language, the general departure from the kinds of recognizable work

that had made his reputation, got him jobs and prizes. The *New Yorker* would never print this sort of thing, not even *Poetry* magazine probably. He was out in the open, defenseless. He was riding for a fall. His wife had grave misgivings about the work. She had seen nearly all his earlier poems through publication. This was definitely not her dish. He wanted it that way, he knew. He was creating a firebreak to stop the original fire by setting a back-fire; that was his way. It was a somewhat dangerous stratagem, which would get worse. He was bored. He was setting all his old bridges off with this new torch, pulling the plug.

He plowed on day after day with the new poems and liked the lack of encouragement. It gave him a free hand. Nobody could nod happily at these things or say a polite not-quite. They didn't have a measuring stick for this, only he did. He began to drink sherry, the old ladies' drink which is at once socially acceptable and dynamite to the corpus and the brain. He bought cheap California sherry at the *bon appétit* shop and hid it from his wife in the woodpile just back of his biggest wall bookcase, and when she was out he would slip into the garage and take a swig or two merrily. He could hear her drive into the garage through the wall of books, and go to help her in with the groceries. But one afternoon he went to the glass door too eagerly in a sherry-like haste and missed the door latch and put his hand through the glass. It was a deep puncture wound and lots of blood. He held a towel over his hand while she drove him to the hospital. He grabbed his Ezra Pound *Cantos* on the way out to read in the hospital. He had severed a tendon of the ring finger of his left hand, the wedding ring finger or perhaps the widower finger of that hand. The surgeon didn't do a good job; he would be left with a defective finger for life. But it made no difference. You're not a watch-maker or a pianist, said the surgeon, and let it go at that.

The blood-letting and the hospitalization—of course he wrote a prose poem about it—had some kind of climactic-atmospheric effect on him. He still believed that isolated individual acts with sufficient energy produce a chain reaction and set events going in a new direction. His putting his hand through the door glass meant going out the hard way. He was home nursing his wrist and typing when the phone rang. Nobody would bother him on his sabbatical unless it was important. He was told that one of his graduate students had been killed while on a job interview in Arizona, a car wreck, and would he come to the funeral at the Lutheran church.

He went there and watched the young mother, the very young child in her arms, with its beautiful golden hair hanging down from the stunned widow's arms, the cold sermon, the chill of the death of the bright young husband. Afterwards, out on the sidewalk in the sharp western light, he spoke to a woman he'd hoped he had forgotten and went home with her after they first paid their respects to the family at the widow's small apartment, went to her basement apartment where they copulated like a couple of seals, and it broke the rectangles of his poems or at least opened them up. For they like all forms had begun to close tight, to become comfortable, a law unto themselves. This time they made a louder sound, something between a paean and a scream. The rectangle had developed spirals, and spirals have to go someplace, even as the nebulae.

He noticed he started to use the holy O, the call, the vocative. Once you start using the O you might as well be saying Thou, you are either praying or moaning or howling—the poem *Howl* had already swept the land—unless the O is that reverential French Academic O, which is a bow to the holiness of things and used wrongly can sound as phony as, say, Alas. In fact, when the poem was published a fellow poet-critic he respected made fun of his O's, as in his lines O pickpock moon, subject of all lost poems, birthplace of tides et cetera, true bottom of the sea et cetera, O wallsocket. I know, he thought, pickpock is sort of phony, but it clamps on to wallsocket; the pocked moon was a Laforguean invention. We now knew that the beautiful lady had a smallpox face. He wasn't quite sure how wallsocket got in there—"for the rhyme" he joked, for the shock, sticking his finger up the Muse's ass. For the passage had begun, *Sunburn. Happy the widow with a hard white ass and a willow tree. O pickpock moon, subject of all lost poems, et cetera.*

The widow's ass was important. Where he sat in his garage-turned-studio gazing down on the backyard next door, the youngish widow of an airforce pilot—who was flying atomic SAC flights from the Nebraska base to who knows where and crashed the great plane over Minnesota, dead, all of the crew dead and no atomic explosion over Minnesota—paraded herself in her white, tight bathing suit in the backyard and could see him staring at her bug-eyed. He couldn't resist marching her into the poem, *Widow-woman, why on Memorial Day, you who love white, did your bathing suit turn black? Woman in naked white and black. He dove down the billion dollar plane, hands at the jukebox switches.*

He didn't think he was overdoing the O, used it rather sparingly in fact. In Lincoln, Nebraska, the main street through town is named O Street. It was one of those American alphabetical towns, and O cut the city in half. The famous author of *Howl* had come to Lincoln, partly at the instigation of the poet. He had helped set up publicity feats for Ginsberg, who had renamed O Street Zero Street. Damn, thought the poet who didn't want Ginsberg invading his territory, poetically that is. He enjoyed the wild and revolutionary antics of the guru with his busload of originals and freaks and pot, apostle of blue jeans and buggery and beards. What did he know about Lincoln or Nebraska or the U.S.A. to call O Street Zero? It was the street of the whole western migration, of Willa Cather and the soddies and the tragic Indians who had tried to hold back a locomotive with their bare hands. It was the street of dinosaurs, more dinosaurs' bones than any place in the world, that was more of an O than a Zero. Of course that wasn't what Ginzy, as he called him, was talking about; he was on a socio-political trip that meant business.

The BP would write a novel about Lincoln himself and fit the Beat invasion into it, make it central, show how the bourgeois poet could see beyond the fringes of the revolution. It was a revolution for sure, that was standing everybody on their heads. Hair would never be the same, clothes would never be the same, language would hit the fan, custom would go down the tube, plans, credit and the Muse would all go to hell, Tohu-vah-Bohu Chaos and Void come again to stay. He was reading Ortega on love; man is a victim of *naufragio*, shipwreck. The good man must be solitary, not in a revolutionary busload. Ortega was correcting Stendhal on love. He quoted Ortega in his poem at the end and used O for O Street, Lincoln, Nebraska, and for the Spanish philosopher. Love is the exact reverse of desire. O. A quote from Ortega.

In the act of love the person goes out of himself. O. It goes forth towards the object; it is continuous; it is fluid. O. He mixed this in with O Street. Down O Street came the big moving vans with letters high as windmills. There were always Brothers in the name of the company, abbreviated to Bros, pronounced brose. Who was moving, what woman but the woman of the poem? He didn't know what attracted him to her. Unspecific attraction is fascinating, magnetic, fatal. He followed her like a dog. She treated him like one. He seemed to hanker after such treatment like a cur, and he was nearing the breaking point of marriage, and had reached the lover's leap upon which cliff one does not even think of the children anymore or perceive evil in any action, though the longish poem ended with his youngest child playing with her kitten in his study while he was writing.

He had no plans. He never planned the way rational, sensible people do, but let things happen. Inaction is just as causal as action. Doing nothing is doing something, and the nothing may turn out to be as action-packed as a major campaign. He was leafing through a magazine and his eye stopped on a full-page whiskey ad, a man and a woman holding glasses and standing in front of an alpine house, a ski lodge perhaps, what is called an A-frame house because the roof is so steep that it looks like a giant A, especially with the cross-beam through the middle. He tore the page out and his mind said build that. He would build that, when? Tomorrow. By tomorrow he meant not in the future, not when he was divorced or separated. What would a bachelor do with a big A-frame house? He meant tomorrow, say fifteen hours from now.

He would talk to a builder, and as if he were an experienced architect he quickly designed the interior in his head, almost exactly, as the architect told him when he showed him the whiskey ad next day and told him how he wanted the interior, the entire A completely glass facing the little artificial lake which he had seen outside the town with lots of for sale signs all around. All rooms would be open to the little lake with sliding shoji screens instead of walls, the first floor living room and kitchen, the second floor recessed and open like a stage, three bedrooms two baths, third floor still more recessed and open, his study, free-standing ceramic fireplaces on the first floor with a black metal round chimney shooting straight up through the center of the house like a tree, serving the second fireplace in his study. Simple.

Instead of quarreling at dinner he told his wife about their new house. She seemed delighted, relieved, the children excited. Children love nothing better than a move. It makes them part of the grown-up world, and after dinner they drove out to the artificial lake and picked out a site. All this on the verge of breaking up the family, the architect excited over the A-frame. It would be the first in town and fun to build. They discussed cost barely; that was not the point. The poet knew that the bank would give him the loan; full professors can get loans. Banks think professors are responsible citizens, and if he went into debt that would be nothing to worry about. Life was more serious than that, and he went to the basement apartment of the other woman, who was in a receptive mood, and told her about his plan for the A-frame. She thought it was crazy, on the verge of a divorce. The poet didn't see that much of a connection between the two actions except the connection of A and O, the alpha and omega of his poem.

He had come to the end of that particular poem with the Bros. departing down O Street under the pickpock moon. The woman that afternoon was very drunk and randy. She was in love, she said, with a Dutch student, but he was engaged and wouldn't sleep with her. Maybe the poet could intervene somehow, soften him up. He imagined himself in this strange role of cupid. The idea was both repulsive and interesting, and he made a kind of reluctant assent. He wondered if he carried any authority in this department, you couldn't just call a student into your office and say Wanda wants to sleep with you, or could you?

This whole area of his life was so outrageous as to be commonplace. Common was the word he had grown up with, a snob word from Virginia. He had heard a German woman say common about the people next door, and that summed it up: people who fought in public and used four-letter words on the street. He was being common and didn't care. This book was leading him into the paths of unrighteousness; he was very unhappy. When this book was finished he would have to pull back a little. It opened too many doors at once. He would lose compression if he kept going in this direction.

He didn't want to enter the surrealist jungle where anything goes, didn't want to use cut-up-method as it was being called, words at random spilled all over the page, though when he went to paginate the book he didn't want to over-organize it either, but piled the pages up haphazardly. What I did, he said, was to get a ladder and sit on the top step with the manuscript and throw it. What he picked up was the order of the book.

9.

He brooded over his broken marriage sometimes, not very often, had no plans, no future, future didn't really concern him, each day was mysterious enough, always in a constant state of wonder and acceptance. If the Nebraska police had come to the door and said you are under arrest for murder he wouldn't even have been surprised. Maybe they were right.

There are broadly speaking only two kinds of divorces, those in which there is the intervention of Another Person and those in which there is not. His was of the second kind, the kind that would now be given the abstract name of Incompatibility, the kind that leads from a long-developing disharmony to combat, the divergence of personality bases, the opposite of the original attraction between the pair, an atmosphere of anti-magnetism leading to fear, unpredictable bad behavior and unbearable recriminations and the unintentional terrorizing of children. Such a situation cannot last. Hasty and drastic steps are taken to mend the fences, but it is too late. The attempts to patch things up are only cosmetic; you can't change personalities in midstream. The rupture widens. In the middle-class world it is the wife who goes to the psychiatrist first, often to the scorn of the husband, certainly to the poet who thought of psychiatrists as quacks and con men. Most poets thought that about shrinks. Why he felt that way about an entire class of medical specialists, as they considered themselves, he couldn't say, of course he had the resentment that any artist has about Freud with his putative inside stories about Leonardo and Shakespeare. He hated wound theories of artists all the way back to the Greeks. Freud battened on those theories and myths, sexing it all up, making poetry a form of prurience, but in the provincial clime the psychiatrists gave the arts a wide berth. Whenever he met one of these people at a gathering he made a point to try to get him to talk about poetry or music or painting. They shied away from such talk with a glint of fear. Artists were the enemy, the poet thought, and now his wife had found a psychiatrist and was going frequently, he didn't know how frequently. He was a youngish thin man with that haunted look, a mixture of superiority and power with cowardice and genuine humility, always behind that mask of a gumshoe, an agent of a new and secret kind. They were a worldwide brotherhood now, a danger to civilization he thought. In this case the shrink was acting as marriage counselor; that meant involving the poet and probably the children. He didn't want anything to do with that, but not one to withstand the turn of events agreed to visit the doctor once to see what he had to say. The doctor looked him over very respectfully; after all he was a big fish in this Midwestern bowl. I would like you to visit a woman colleague of mine, he said. I belong to a group that travels through the state and assists people in situations such as yours, avoiding any direct references or terms such as marital problems. The idea of visiting a woman psychiatrist intrigued him for some reason and he agreed, agreed also to an invitation to spend New Year's Eve at the psychiatrist's house with his wife, a somewhat funereal occasion as it turned out, as the four sat stiffly in not too comfortable chairs watching the clock. The doctor wouldn't open the champagne till midnight. It could have been a Grant Wood painting or a Grandma Moses; ramrod, at midnight the champagne popped and they all toasted each other severely, after which the gloom descended again and the psychiatrist said to the poet, would you like to see my knife collection? The poet followed him upstairs to his study and thought he had entered the armory of Attila the

Hun. The walls glittered with knives of every description, scimitars, machetes, hunting knives, dirks, ivory handles, engraved blades, each with a small description neatly typed underneath. He didn't bother to ask why the psychiatrist collected lethal weapons; the question was superfluous.

At the shacky wooden county building at the edge of the town where the itinerant county psychiatry was done, he sat down with the woman doctor, a rather blowzy and friendly woman, and answered her questions ingenuously about the children and his work and sex. He forgot whom he was talking with and started to ramble, beat around the bush. She seemed genuinely rather than professionally interested and he agreed to come back next week. He went back several times and finally thought he had said everything that interested him at least, and her final suggestion took him unawares: Dr. Swanson and I think that you and your wife should visit the Menninger Clinic for a talk, if you are willing. He wasn't willing to take time to go all the way to Wichita, Kansas, and sit in waiting rooms, and said so, but his wife put it as an ultimatum: either the Menninger Clinic or divorce. So be it, he thought to himself, and agreed to go. This sort of thing does more harm than good, was his opinion. It sets final rules. We are really coming to the end of the pike.

It was a divide and rule situation, the poet to confer with one psychiatrist, another woman, he thought curiously, and the wife with a man. The sessions took hours and felt like all day, but there were breaks and they were asked if they wanted to see the psychiatric museum, a small collection of obsolete devices once used on what were called madmen, and in one room was a case with King George III's straitjacket. For some reason it struck the poet sadly. Who tied up the king? He remembered the soldiers in straitjackets coming home, staring into space, some singing, remembered them being led down the gangplank in San Francisco to be taken away to psycho wards. Was anything more tragic than madness? Of course they had to have a final talk with the famous Karl Menninger, a hulking kindly man who questioned them about their differences and lay back with his eyes closed. What was he listening for? the poet wondered. These people hear things you don't know you are saying. He seemed completely neutral, saying goodbye as if he had other bigger things on his mind.

He began to examine his bookshelves. He would take only those books he needed to teach from, the poetry, the criticism, small reference works. He began to pack in secret. When she was out he would load a box or two and leave it in the garage. There weren't many boxes and when he made a gap in the shelves he would push other books into the gap so that nothing looked disarranged. There were almost no ornaments or artifacts he cared about. Besides, he wasn't going to Timbuktu, only to a little apartment when he found one. He would see the children as much as he did before, almost; he would just be under another roof. One day when he had his notes and books in cartons he put them in his car and drove to find a professor in the art department who played around with real estate. He found huge old houses and had them divided into apartments and played landlord. The art professor took him to a couple of places and he settled for one. He didn't care for wall-to-wall carpeting, but took it anyway and moved his boxes in and one suitcase with clothes. At the grocery he stood in line; one of the English professors and his wife were also in line and they chatted. Suddenly the professor's face clouded over and he looked at his wife, who had a similar reaction. The poet was holding a new broom and mop and pail; if he had had divorce written on his forehead, it couldn't have been plainer. Everybody knew it was about to happen and here was the evidence. He watched the professor and his wife walk away rather heavily, as if the poet had transferred some burden to them.

There was no particular joy in the move, no sense of liberation or vision of a future. Rather, it was more like an army move. He had to do everything himself from top to bottom, and he liked that self-dependency and indifference of it all. He thought of King George's straitjacket. Who has the authority to bind a king, who held him when they tied him up, his arms folded across his chest? Of course he wasn't going scot-free. He told his lawyer to give her what she wants, the house, her car. They socked him with half his salary for her alimony, which he thought mistakenly was also child support. Actually it was what they called a Settlement, which is to say ransom, and it was to be paid until the day of his retirement. He didn't care whether it was fair or not; he needed to be by himself, not in the family cauldron, a poor excuse as a father, worse as a husband. The poet signed the outrageous statement without even looking, the way he had signed publishers' contracts. Money was not going to be something that kept him awake. He was highly employable and didn't mind the work, play was more like it. He wanted out, and would pay all their dues and then some: let's get it over with. She seemed satisfied. The wretchedness of divorce is one thing; compensation is something else. It confers social status to get off handsomely, fine with him to make that concession. He went back to the house every day, taught his youngest daughter to drive until she got her license. If you are an American you have to have a driver's license; it's more important than citizenship. He was making plans to go on a lecture tour to Europe in the summer for the State Department; she was planning to move to Washington to get a government job, and he wrote her good letters of recommendation to ease her way.

They had met on the sidewalk, the poet, his wife and Marya as he would call her in the novel, about to join a backyard cocktail party. She announced herself as an old admirer of his and he pretty well monopolized her in the backyard over martinis, his wife silent and motionless at his side. Later he saw her plastered against the wall of the house by a black Air Force captain, and the next morning he visited her in her baroque stone and brick house and drank beer while she played some posthumous Chopin work. She was divorcing her psychiatrist husband and would keep her four young girls, if all went to plan. They began to meet clandestinely, her husband moved to an apartment, legalizing a separation, and the poet began to write—sonnets! Coming after *The Bourgeois Poet* this took his friends and critics by surprise and occasioned not a few brickbats to which, as usual he was, or pretended to be, oblivious.

The divorce process in Nebraska was slow and they both would have to wait at least a year before tying any more knots. Marya decided to move to Omaha with her girls to be near her mother, the poet had bidden a professional farewell to the University in Lincoln and had taken an identical job in Chicago, arranged without fuss by the poet and friend John Nims. And he decided to move to Omaha himself for the summer and tried to persuade Marya to come with him to Chicago in the fall. He succeeded.

He had started what he hesitated to think was his novel in the third person and saw this was a mistake when he had finished it, when his new wife-to-be translated it all back into the first person, making it surprisingly less rather than more personal or confessional, a word he loathed. Ensconced in Chicago with a new household, he began to write it in earnest, beginning with the sentence: "Seven miles over Labrador the ice had melted in my martini." It wanted to break into a kind of poem, Labrador had melted into my martini, or like a Dylan Thomas discovery, the anchor dives through the floors of a church. But he held his ground and shut off the poetic impulse, trying to feel what it is like to write a story with characters moving around. The first thing he began to notice was that he, the teller of the tale, was both himself and somebody else, a part of himself that had never come to light, himself perhaps as others saw him, worldly, capable and weird, tender and criminally outspoken. So many poets he knew were something like that. Every time they opened their mouths a toad hopped out, if not a scorpion. He himself was a Scorpio, as people were constantly reminding him. He liked being a Scorpio, part of him did. He once tried to get an anagram out of the name, Karl Shapiro, that would yield shark. He wanted a bit of shark, but it just wouldn't work, and his anagram solved out to Hark, Sir Opal, which was funny but also revealing: his occasional knightliness and his fondness for semiprecious stones, especially opals. He had heard a snobbish novelist say that opals were vulgar. To hell with her.

He would tell his students to mine for anagrams in their names; it was important. After all, Wystan Hugh Auden had found a directive in his name which said Hug A Shady Wet Nun. That couldn't be an accident. It was a revelation, a prophecy. And Auden had found T. S. Eliot to translate into Litotes, a figure in which an affirmative is expressed by the negative of its contrary; not bad at all. Hark, Sir Opal was the reason why he clung to the spar of iambic pentameter after the whole poetic flagship had sunk beneath the watery floor. His prose poems had used the old system in a sidewise method, using the whole line as a foot. Now, writing a fiction, he was on his own and went entirely by ear. Rhythm is everything in a verbal work of art; without a rhythmus the whole thing falls apart. Arrhythmical is a description of heart trouble, fibrillation. He didn't worry about his rhythms in the novel, but by intuition kept them in hand. It was too mysterious to systematize.

The old prosodist Saintsbury had written a book about English prose rhythms with diagrams, but it was one of those post-mechanistic experiments that didn't get off the ground. What is the use of calling something dochmiac because it has x number of syllables to the phrase? You might as well call it a fried egg. All the same a rhythmus had to be there in the prose as much as in the poetry. Here, too, the mysterious voice, the verbal personality, governed the flow and the sound scale. By his age this sort of thing had become second nature. A trained musician doesn't have to count. A reader doesn't have to move his lips. Luckily there are no manuals of prose prosody. It might be better if there were none for poetry, either; the eye and the ear are books enough for the writer. He told the story of his trip abroad, of his new bachelorhood, of the woman he snuffled after, of the creative writing madness at the university, the visit of the country's foremost guru. He called him Akiba Mem, made him a cross between Ginsberg and Robert Lowell, poets who exploited political events partly for self-aggrandizement and partly because they believed what their followers wanted them to. He told about his alienation from the revolutions and thus his alienation from his colleagues, about his meeting with the woman who was to become his second wife, the burning of his office by radicals. A good invention, he thought, a wishful idea perhaps, his banishment to a campus greenhouse, ending with heterosexual intercourse in a snowstorm.

Some of the book he wrote on the beach off Tampa, Florida, with a portable typewriter on his lap. There was no effort to this writing. He was highly suspicious of this but kept going. It flowed out. It was fun. He had no plans for publication—he seldom did—but when it was done he had copies made and sent it off. His own publisher rejected it; large parts were obscene if not porn. He wanted to try his hand at that. Most porn was so wooden and lusterless, barely even exciting. An avant-garde publisher rejected it with a slur, the millionaire avant-gardist saying he was a publisher not a grocer. He gave up sending it out and forgot about it until one day someone suggested a New York publisher who had made his fortune publishing a dope and sex novel, but who also had what are called serious writers. He sent the manuscript with a xerox of his career from *Who's Who in America* and got a prompt phone call. The publisher had read two chapters and was sending a contract. Would you and your wife meet me in Las Vegas? I will be your host, he said; they went and were put up in a huge brothel-style room with a canopied bed on a dais, and more or less Roman statues life-size, a bathroom fit for a harem, Caesar's Palace in fact, and the publisher gave the poet's wife chips to play roulette and she won.

The book appeared in orange, magenta and yellow stripes like a beach awning on the Riviera, a photo of the author on the inside jacket looking like a highly successful banker. There were some reviews, not many, a couple of good ones but no blockbusters, none on the front page of the *Times* like his poetry. He wasn't too concerned; he could hardly see his mixture of sex and anti-radicalism as a dish for them, and apparently it wasn't important enough to attack.

In Lincoln, Nebraska, it caused a furor. There were attempts to ban this insult to the city which he had called Milo—wonderful choice of names, he thought. Milo is a sorghum, Nebraska was sorghum country, maybe also Venus of Milo. A full-page review appeared in the local paper trying to match the book characters with actual people, a risky proposition for the reviewer and the poet. The publisher was arranging for him to go on a nationwide tour to be on talk shows and news segments. He had called the poet to Las Vegas to look him over for the part. The poet loathed that kind of huckstering but said yes; he always said yes first and no later. One of the publisher's staff, a very expert woman publicist, would accompany the poet on his trips. All this for the paperback which was coming out shortly. They were talking to movie people about rights. Who knows where this book is headed? said the publisher. There was to be an advance of fifty thousand dollars for the paperback, not much, but the biggest money for a book that the poet had been near. Until one day he received a registered letter stating in legalese that the publisher's company was in bankruptcy and that no advances or future royalties could be paid. The poet had a curious reaction, or so his friends thought; he laughed. He was not even angry except for a slight feeling of indignation about publishers in general. How can you laugh? asked one horrified English professor, and the poet only looked at him. It was funny; that's why he laughed. Authors weren't even allowed at the bankruptcy hearing; they were not "preferred creditors." The poet thought, the Muse did it.

Quite literally the Muse had done it. You can't serve Mammon and the Muse simultaneously. They are both jealous gods and will make mincemeat out of anybody who plays a shell game with their rewards. All the mammonites can do for the musites is to buy their wares, erect mausoleums for paintings and shell out grants-in-aid, as they are called, for the indigent writers and poets. A poet who makes money is immediately blacklisted by the Muse. It's okay if he has a job that keeps his nose to the grindstone, like Williams or Stevens. It's even okay if he is born with a silver spoon in his mouth or inherits a fortune. But it is taboo for him to go for the gold, except for the wheedling and whining for grants-in-aid; the Muse forgives that.

The poet remembered how shocked he was to hear that a good poet had gone into the real estate business, of all things, and was driving his own earned Cadillac and buying and selling houses and commercial properties. He nicknamed the entrepreneur the truck driver. There was another good poet who went to Hollywood and got rich and still tried to remain a poet, but there was a blight on his name and fame that all the California suntan and blue chlorinated pool water couldn't cover up. What he would have done if his novel had made him a millionaire, he didn't know. He didn't know how corruptible he might be. But then, what would he have done with all that money? That was why he laughed. There was nothing he wanted to buy. He was living approximately where he wanted; he worked at a job he liked, sometimes even loved; his salary was deposited without his ever really knowing how much it was. He would have to ask sometimes when there was some form to fill out for insurance or the like; his wife would hand him the forms and say sign here. She had already filled in his wages. And he would sign.

10.

His politics were always "wrong." "Different" would be a better word, "contrary" better still, and he often worried that he was in a constant state of dishonesty simply because he always took the other side. Many times he had to catch himself in company when he was being addressed and when someone made an assertion he thought he heard himself beginning an answer with No. He was aware of this and began to single out people who would begin a reply with Yes even when they were in disagreement. They would hold the disagreement in abeyance, and he believed these people were superior to him because he had the automatic No response to any system of belief, like an ill-trained dog that distrusts a friendly hand. They do the civilized, polite thing of preparing for the disagreement by at least seeming to agree, and he knew he must do something about this, although it took a conscious effort on his part. He would have to rehearse to himself quickly the preamble of a reply and come up with something like, "I think I see what you mean, but," or "I have the same reaction, however." He simply had to learn to qualify his No's, to give people an out, and he had to stop wading into a little group as if they were armed to the teeth and he was going to slay them all with the jawbone of an ass.

In spite of his charm (people were constantly referring to his charm, a very suspicious compliment, he thought, bordering on hypocritical), he knew he could not really engage in conversation or any dialogue or dialectic. He was a monologist, a one-man show, and when he tried to play games he merely disrupted them. He hated and feared charades, which people were beginning to play at parties, and when he did play games he always played to lose, to get it over. Except perhaps for chess, and even then it wasn't the win that mattered to him but the gamesmanship; as in tennis which he never learned to play in style, having never had an instructor, but the rhythmic dancelike engagement of the game was more than enough for his taste.

At bottom he felt he must be what people call antisocial, even sociopathic, unable to endure crowds and nervous at gatherings, huddling with the first person he happened to sit down next to and staying put. It was just as bad at dinner parties, where he would forget that there were people on either side of him and get lost in a conversation with only one, and if someone spoke to him from two or three chairs away he would be startled as if he had been dis-covered eating potatoes with his knife. The result was that most of his answers sounded like epigrams, brief, humorous, cryptic, and this in turn made him sound evasive or gnomic. He didn't mind that assessment; poetry was something like that. He didn't under-stand people the way they presumably understood each other; he even liked people, at a distance that is, observed them with wonder and what he thought of as sympathy, no matter how boring or gross in talk or crude in apprehension or esthetically ignorant, he felt a fellow-feeling for them which made him feel not superior in any way but the opposite. He could echo the grossness and crudity and ignorance himself, though he generally refrained from coarseness except among soldiers and only when it was called for, which was almost always in the lower ranks of the Army.

He knew what he could not receive was received opinion, and some reflex in his mind acted like a hair-trigger and he would go off half-cocked at any remark that sounded dogmatic or assured and confident. Smugness was what he couldn't stand, the smug-ness of Communists, for instance, groaning and even weeping over something in the *Daily Worker* which was such a palpable lie that he would gape—Finland, lynchings, civil war in the Midwest—always of course with a grain of truth at bottom which was enough for the dogmatists. He lacked, he felt, that capacity for belief which all men seemed to be endowed with, and though he felt he understood the nature of belief better than they did, he could never hold to a structure of beliefs like the Roman Catholics or the Marxists or the Jews.

He knew that belief was possible for him by some kind of mystical act of the will, *credo quia absurdum est;* it was one of the quirks or maybe curses of the human psyche, and, yes he would say, there is nothing miraculous about miracles. The reason we have invented Positive Science is to preserve human sanity. Positive science is a tissue of fictions which veil the miraculous real from the ordinary sensual man, what Whitman called in his funny language the divine average, and even T. S. Eliot had said humankind cannot stand very much reality. Everything hinges on the contradictory meanings of reality. What is real to the biologist is not to the poet, and vice versa, and it is only on the borders of positive science that the positive begins to lose its hard edges and begins to sound like music. It was this uneasiness with positive people with positive opinions that made him burst out with his No's, and even sometimes lose his head completely and begin to rave and horrify strangers whose flags he had just ripped from the staff. He was ever after horrified at these recollections.

He was at a party in one of the hill towns above San Francisco Bay, at the house of an English professor he had befriended in Urbino the summer before. The poet had been lecturing on American poetry in Urbino and defending all the Ginsbergs and the other consciousness-raisers, as they were terming themselves. The Italian students loved it and applauded his outlandishness in praising automatic writing and the cut-up method of Burroughs and rock music and LSD, which he would never try, and maryjane, which he would never try but once or twice, and homosexuality and Buddhist anarchism and communal living and the death of all institutions. Not that he was a devotee of any of that, but he got carried away and sounded like an evangel or a medicine man for the cause, and afterwards one of the visiting faculty said to him wryly that it was sad to see a forty-five-year-old hippy. But the California professor was all for the poet, as were the students, the majority of them, locked into the ancient European system in which professors are gods and students their slaves. It was probably a breath of fresh air for them to hear this American poet smashing icons left and right, though half the students were Communists themselves but they didn't get that kind of treat from Communists who taught that all Americans were diseased and decadent remnants of capitalism in its final throes.

The poet was not happy about his performance. He had left the students with the impression that he was one of the Beat poets himself and had almost convinced himself that he was. He had got it all wrong, and there was no way to correct the impression unless they read his own poems, and even some of those sounded West-Coastnik—he had already caught the California culture virus of permission to all for everything desired. California was an endless weekend pass, its hedonism was sweeping the world; that was the real revolution of the twentieth century. The God of Misrule was in the saddle and all criteria were referred to the sensibilities of the child. Their scientists had turned the cosmos into a cosmic jungle gym. Life was a game and so forth and so on, *Om mani padme hum.* Yes the jewel is in the rose, Buddha is the second coming and the surferkinder are riding high.

It was just the usual academic dinner party, but California-style, a cross between an executive coffee break and a luau, the only person wearing a tie was a tailor-made Englishman who even had a white handkerchief in his breast pocket, not unlike the fabled Briton who dresses for dinner on a cannibal isle. They all milled around on the wide redwood deck and admired the bridges leaping the Bay in the sunset, the famous sunset over the Golden Gate, and the talk turned to Bobby Kennedy who had recently been assassinated. They had moved inside with their drinks and their talk of the Kennedys, when something snapped, as it is said, in the poet's mind like the spring of a rattrap which can break your wrist. The adulation of the Kennedys amounted to a keening, a religious service. It was like a memorial meeting with family. He gulped his martinis and held himself in. He had been as horrified, even grief-stricken at the assassinations as anyone else, the day the President was shot, the day as it was said when everyone would remember all his life where he heard the news, and he had sat in his office on the campus and for the first time in his life heard radios turned on in the university building and young instructors wandered up to him dazed and asked what to do, as if he were some kind of dean. He answered as if he had rehearsed it, tell your students to go home, and he then decided to go home himself and sit in front of the television for three days and nights.

He had heard the news of the second assassination in the lobby of the little motel in Davis, California, when he had gone downstairs for a newspaper and heard the TV playing a mass at nine o'clock in the morning, and he asked the proprietress what had happened and she looked at him wildly and began to say incoherent things about the end of the country. He recalled the third assassination, of the black leader who had won the Peace Prize and that, the poet thought, could very well mean the end of the country and the cities in flames.

He had gotten into the habit of calling himself a patriot. It was an inflammatory word to liberals, a laughable word to humanists and academics. Nobody used that word except as a provocation, and that was the way he used it, and he said he had bought a big silk American flag and staff which he hung outside his house on the proper flag days and they joked about it, the educated people who could quote the saying about patriots and scoundrels. It was enough to start an argument.

But this religious sanctimoniousness about the Kennedys made something snap in his mind and he turned on them all like a zealot or a madman and called the Kennedys shanty-Irish aristocrats, robber barons, egomaniacs who barely averted the nuclear war and would probably get it anyhow, planning their war in Indonesia, journalists, Massachusetts ward-heelers, papists, vulgarians putting on intellectual airs. The White House was better off, he said, when Eisenhower had the Marine Band play John Philip Sousa instead of the Budapest String Quartet, and without Jackie Kennedy with her interior decorating. The whole vulgar scene was on a par with Andrew Jackson with his muddy boots on his desk, only in reverse. What were they going to do with old Joe Kennedy's whiskey franchise millions but act to the manner born? The arrogance of those people, to think they could overthrow a highly organized revolution in the Caribbean with twenty-five ill-trained Boy Scouts, and the P.T. boat hero wagging his finger at the world and saying you're next. He was no different from Teddy Roosevelt, who never did charge up San Juan Hill, anyhow, but walked up it when the gunfire had stopped. An intellectual saber rattler is exactly what this country can't stand, he fumed on amidst the stunned guests of his friend of the Urbino summer, whom he would never see again. His wife stood by, also slightly pale, but said nothing, even on the long silent ride home after dinner, which they left early.

It was a time when terrorism had become a household word and nobody could feel safe anymore. No more leaving doors unlocked, no more walking through the streets at night, no more letting children play in distant neighborhoods. We were back in the Dark Ages, the Empire had fallen, and behind every tree and bush lurked the rapist and the assassin, in the smallest village as well as in New York and Chicago. He entertained a somewhat geological idea of history—seismic might be a better word, as he was living in California and there was so much talk about earthquake faults, who lived on or near which fault, what the Richter scale reading meant, which areas were sinking, what volcanoes were stirring in their sleep. He perceived social history as seismic activity, the build-up of incalculable energies along the faults where the rock-plates were locked for the time being, maybe for centuries, a moment in geologic time. One set of plates was trying to move north and the other set of plates south, until the tensions were too powerful and there was a sudden violent release with no warning, and the very landscape which might have sat still for twenty million years was a whole new landscape, and God help the people in the way. That single bullet that had shattered the President's skull was of the magnitude of seven at least on the Richter scale, and the shock waves rolled around the globe in an endless succession.

Such a bullet aimed at the Archduke Ferdinand had been the starting gun of the First World War, and now America was ready to plunge into an Asian War from which it could never extricate itself. The aftershocks would never subside. Whole cities would catch fire by spontaneous combustion, and all institutions tremble, all social structures weaken and crack, all social contracts ripped in half, history itself go into a major convulsion. Among the peaceable there was consternation and among the young great joy, the joy of children let out of school, joy of the prison break, joy of the looters after the earthquake.

The newspapers, the media, as the means of public communication were now to be called, were calendar-minded by nature and decade-minded as a cultural convenience, with each decade given a capital letter, each personified and made into a separate entity like an era, and given modifiers, as in the Gay Nineties, the Roaring Twenties, the Crew-cut Fifties, one could supply the qualifiers, but the Sixties would be in a class by itself, and everyone knew that that decade was a landmark decade, a turning point of history, a moment of irreversible dissolution for the old order, a wild warping of the social crust of the earth, as violent in its way as the war decade of the Forties but with its own war and its war against war. There are no smooth transitions in history, he thought, only the appearance of smoothness after the fact. There are no eras of peace, only breathing spells. All one could do was to delay the wars a little, for at a given signal such as the assassin's bullet hell would fling open its gates.

Tolstoy had said of history that nothing is the cause; scholars and historians supply the causes later. A gun is fired to start a foot race, all sports are war sports, and when the good psychologist William James said that athletics might be the moral equivalent for war he knew like Tolstoy that nothing is the cause. It would happen and nobody would ever know why, neither Socrates nor Marx nor the biologic historians who compared civilizations with the seasonal cycles of flora. And along with the fall of cities and cultures and forms would come a new kind of art which called itself anti-. Everything good would be anti- until this phase of the war was over, and he girded up his loins to try to deal with anti-poetry.

He had scented it in the air even before the time of the assassins. He had encouraged it, exploited it. That was why he claimed to understand the Sixties before anyone else. The existentialists and absurdists had propagandized for all the expressions of anti-culture, approved and even sanctified the other states of mind—the dream states, the mad states, the elevation of sensation to mysticism. Every mystical rite in the book was dusted off and trotted out for the young. He had read the Zen books before they were available in America and sent to Japan for the Blythe books on English poetry as Zen. He talked Zen to his students and even introduced astrology, being the first to ask his poetry students what signs they were born under, and his colleagues looked at him sideways and shrugged.

He first heard of marijuana from his daughter in junior high. It grew wild in Nebraska along the railroad tracks, and what had been a despised weed used only by hoboes and blacks in Harlem was about to become a sacred incense to the Sixties, one of the first of the Causes, one of the first instruments of the Revolution. The word revolution is dear to the American heart, and one way to sell a new product is to call it revolutionary. In a little while the term reached explosive revolutionary heights, with the sexual revolution, the consciousness revolution, the youth revolution, the food revolution with young people disdaining meats and munching alfalfa sprouts and tofu and nuts and grains, the organic food revolution which swept the land and helped the political revolution against pesticides and land development, the language revolution and the appearance and defense of obscenity, even pornography.

The poet was a part of this revolution, he would proudly claim, for he had written the essay about Henry Miller that helped get him sanctioned by the Massachusetts Supreme Court and make his works legal, and his essay would appear at the front of *The Tropic of Cancer* in every edition from now on. He had helped Ginsberg's *Howl* and the cause of the homosexuals and the street bards and was thanked for being on their side, the poet Snyder told him long after, until he began to see the revolution as a necessary evil at best and as self-aggrandizement at worst. He believed in the liberty of books simply, but was frequently horrified at the paths liberty could take, and as long as there was censorship he would defend the censored and make a case for them.

In his lectures and travels he would continue to speak for the revolutionists of the word of any stripe, offending the academicians who were having the same troubles with their students that he was having with his. He deplored the decline and fall of writing and speech at the same time that he praised the Burroughses and Ginsbergs. He assigned Camus's *The Rebel* as required reading in his poetry courses and even came to the last ditch, the defense of Sade. He had smuggled copies of *The Hundred and Twenty Days of Sodom* and copies of *Justine* and *Juliette*, and he expounded Sade as an early existentialist and a modern anti-novelist. He was not concerned about contradictions because he had no position, he said, only a sense of adventure and fair play. His defenses of the forbidden naturally led to accusations of mischief and frivolousness, but even this finger-pointing did not bother him. Mischief and frivolity were also part of human nature and art. He was an anarchist of sorts, and when the Phi Beta Kappa chapter at his university asked him to give a lecture he lectured on philosophical anarchism, citing Kropotkin and Tolstoy and Godwin and Gandhi. He wrote out of conviction and not to advance a position. He could no more stand still for a system than the plates of the earth could stay put without an earthquake. He was certainly not a pacifist, but he could understand pacifists and wrote a poem about a conscientious objector while he was in uniform which was so convincing that the *Conscientious Objector* magazine reprinted it and the editor asked him what prison he had been in.

Writing his conscientious objector poem explained his "politics" to himself, explained everything and explained nothing. It disturbed him sometimes that he could take a point of view opposite to his convictions. Other people were more consistent and worked from a base and could advance and retreat from a fixed point. But he had no fixed points, and at the same time didn't experience any vertigo or queasiness in his floating states of mind. If someone asked him if he believed in God, for instance, he might answer, I think so, not yes or no. He would question the question and begin to think about what I think so might mean—that is, he entertained all possibilities, not out of any sense of liberalism or logic but because he understood that people operated out of conviction and that most convictions were beyond examination. That's what conviction means, and there is nothing to be gained by trying to prove or disprove the existence of God. One did or did not believe it, or in his case thought either answer creditable and both equally valid.

A belief in God might be an expression of something else, the worship of a stick for instance, and it was really the instinct to worship that was the root of the question. Thus when he began to hear about young men he knew who had gone to prison for their belief in one of the gods, or for their belief in an abstraction like Peace, he would try to become such a person in his mind, would try to feel their feelings and act them out in the words of a poem. He felt to his surprise that he did this well, almost too well, as if he had no solid character of his own; and when he came back and looked at such a poem he would wonder how he had the imagination to write it and at the impulse behind it. It was, he decided, the act of a playwright. He, who could not write plays, would become the character he was writing about. The fact that Shakespeare had created Iago probably meant that there was an Iago in him as well as a Hamlet. There was a conscientious objector in the poet as well as a conscript, a draftee and by now a patriot.

The revolutions of the Sixties made a patriot of him. Those were the years when he sent for the silk American flag which to him was almost a mezuzah. He had a mezuzah on the door as a reminder to himself that he was a Jew and he had the rolled silk American flag in the closet to remind him that he was an American. Almost everyone he knew was a disgruntled American of some kind. Academics don't take easily to nationalism, and the more voluble were outspoken anti-Americans who grabbed at every liberal cause that came by on principle, like a reflex, no matter what it was so long as it irritated the government and produced a little friction.

In a department meeting he fought bitterly against the introduction of what was being called Black English. This is an English Department he said, and not a zoo. The liberals glared him down. Imagine a poet talking like that. We are committed to Affirmative Action, they said, it's the law now, and he answered, Affirmative Fascism. Luckily the black English program was shelved and he felt he might have won a point, but now his colleagues looked at him differently than they did when he was hired. A poet, they thought simplistically, was by definition a liberal or radical of some kind, certainly not a conservative or a bourgeois redneck. What had happened to him? they wondered. He was beginning to feel cut off from his fellow professors, especially the younger ones who were turning rabid in the wild climate of the Sixties, cut off from his students whom he could barely look at, barefooted girls and boys who would sometimes put their feet up on their desks for him to look at and he said nothing, did nothing and pretended that he didn't see them. He was turning into a stuffed shirt, he thought, and after a lecture to a large class a student came up to him and asked, Do you consider yourself a member of the Establishment? and he answered, Damn right, and knew he shouldn't have said that to a sophomore. He didn't even know what the buzzword meant, only that you weren't supposed to belong to it unless you were the enemy. He was turning into the enemy, all right. Somebody put an upside-down American flag sticker on his windshield and he stood in the parking lot for a half hour scraping it off with his pocket knife.

Half the cars had bumper stickers with slogans like Amerika— love it or leave it, using the German spelling which was supposed to signify that America was fascist. Some of the students were now wearing tattoos, whether real or decals was hard to tell but the emblems of savagery were showing. A doctor's wife up the street from him was raped in her house. There was a rush on locksmiths. Two young students who had just announced their engagement were found in a ditch with their throats cut. Rock music blared from every direction, even on campus. At every noon between classes there were meetings with sound trucks and banners and milling students. One of his poetry students was taken away with a violent breakdown—a Scientologist, he said—and was not seen again. Make love not war rang through the air, but the air was full of hate. The newspapers talked about letter bombs. He was nowhere and spent hours reading and watching the news, the actual killing in the war taking place in the living room, and except for his wife there was no one to talk to anymore. He wrote angry verses, "Sestina of the Militant Vocabulary," about the situation and sent them to *National Review* which turned them down, then to *Esquire* which printed them. One of the ringleader poets in San Francisco wrote to him: "I see you are writing for men's fashion magazines," a rather polite insult, considering the source.

He began to read histories of the Second World War, bought paperbacks and scoured the public library for old ones and the university library for official and scholarly works, becoming he thought an expert on Japanese foreign policy and the Battle of Midway. There was consolation in the replay of his War, the war which everyone was now beginning to say was the "good war" unlike the First World War which had no meaning to anybody, and most certainly not an evil adventure like Vietnam. But reading up on the Greater East Asia Co-prosperity Sphere, which was the name the Japanese imperialists gave their invasions, he had a different understanding of Vietnam. Japan had gone all the way to India, just scouting it but intended to return to pick this gigantic plum when it had the leisure, and he himself had been in Australia when the Japs were right on the doorstep and the Aussies and Yanks were digging in for the invasion. The map hadn't changed, only the names of the invaders. Now it was the Reds who already owned all of Asia but Japan and the Southeast, where the Americans had succeeded the French and British in trying to hold back the Communists.

The supply of WWII books was seemingly endless. New ones were being written every day, maybe it was just the battle nostalgia of his generation, maybe something deeper, as each generation loves its own war and tries to lessen the importance of all others. But he also was reading another favorite of so many Americans, the Civil War, or the War of Secession, as Whitman had called it. When Whitman had written about the ardent prayer of Europe, those were his words for the destruction of the United States. France, England, Germany, Spain all prayed the ardent prayer that the United

States might be split, crippled and dismembered by the War. Those were his words and every country in the world, said Whitman, shared in the death wish except one, Mexico of all countries, the only one, said Whitman, we had ever really done wrong. And now the death wish had come home, to the delight of the Communists who thought they saw a new dismemberment of the United States in the campus revolutions that were sweeping the land, and other lands as well.

BOOK III

Reports of My Death

11.

He had been uneasy about his own academic preferment from the start, unprepared to accept what he felt he had not earned, especially as they started him from the top and he would never know what the struggle up the ladder meant. He was catapulted into a tenured professorship after having dropped out as a sophomore, and there was more anguish than pleasure in it. It came home to him one day as he sat on an interview committee recruiting young candidates for the first step of the ladder, and one bright and eager young Ph.D. after another came and answered questions gently put. This was gentleman territory; manner was fifty percent of the battle. One young man with a very impressive dossier took his chair facing the half dozen committee people and he accepted some coffee in its Styrofoam cup, and as he took it in his hand his body shook like a convulsion and the coffee shot straight up the air in a column and came down in his lap. Someone brought a stack of paper napkins.

He saw the young man later hunched over coffee in a corridor of the lobby and wanted to go up to him and console him somehow, but there was no way to do that, his nervousness had ruined his chances maybe for good. The scene somehow made him feel guilty and resentful and definitely fraudulent. What right did he have interviewing doctors of philosophy in English studies or anybody else? But he had been hoisted to the top and was made to sit in the seat of judgment.

In fact, when he started as Professor he was only an experimental professor, an experiment. The awful phrase "creative writing" hadn't even been invented, and that was why when he asked the chairman what he was going to teach, the chairman replied, You don't have to teach at all if you don't want to. And characteristically he turned around and invented courses for himself and wrote pedantic lectures, though at the seminars or rather get-togethers of the writing students he felt more at home, measuring his tastes and abilities against theirs. What else can be done in these creative writing classes?

He would say that anybody can write a perfect sestina, and found himself saying it thirty years later, but to be able to write a sestina or any straitjacketed poem that would be read ten, fifty or a hundred years hence was a horse of a different color. What made that difference? Here all theory goes lame. There is no way either to explain or to create talent. You cannot create creativity. It is what most people call a gift, though others might call it a curse, and any good editor, even a good reader, can spot talent in a flash. It doesn't take genius to spot genius. People without it hunger for it and idolize it in someone else. The presence of beauty is always astonishing and unsettling, stopping the rational processes of the human mind and throwing it off the track, so that works of art are always ceremonious, processional, creating order out of no order. People who know how to do this are strange people and everyone is perfectly willing to confer names on them like magus or charmer or poet, if only to keep them at a safe distance. But at the same time one had to be suspicious of the ones who called themselves seers, voyants; they were people who took the name poet too literally, and nine times out of ten they were impostors. But of course there was always the tenth one.

This kind of talk never gets anywhere, and yet seems necessary, somehow, and what was one to do in these seminars but listen for the talented note, the authentic tone, the strange new turn, and nod approval? Or was it all a waste of everyone's time, a new form of self-indulgence very American? Only Americans could invent creative writing. It was part of the pragmatism of America to think that poetry could be produced like tomatoes. You could do anything with tomatoes. In California they even invented a square tomato to fit more economically into a box; round tomatoes waste too much space. Why not produce poetry and even poets? Soon the experimenters would begin to say that everyone is potentially a poet, even children and lunatics—especially children and lunatics—but even insurance salesmen and engineers, and it wasn't long before the government would begin to shower money on the experimenters, called innovators.

The word innovation is holy in America. Innovation means creative, good, and to oppose innovation is un-American, evil. Going to the moon is a drop in the bucket; we have to get the creative process in hand and put it to work. Though of course it wasn't put in such terms by the professors, who still used the vocabulary of the humanities and not psychology or sosh (sociology), or the professional literary scholars who held creative writing in contempt but appreciated its attraction to the administrators and the pursers of the institution. Monies were now available to bring poets to the public schools, to sell poetry as it were, and in order to have Poetry in the Schools one had to have real flesh and blood poets, and since there weren't enough of those on tap we had to turn out more from the universities and colleges, start more poetry magazines, first of all get an index of poets, a poets' phonebook listing every poet in the United States with his address and phone number. Letters are too slow for the now poets. Use the phone, reach out and touch a poet.

What the criteria for being listed in the directory were he wasn't sure. One had to publish something like some poems somewhere. Intention, however, carried a lot of weight. Reading circuits were set up for poets to travel from state to state. Poets were finally getting organized, and the President of the United States called for a national Poetry Day. After all, there is a national Mother's Day and a national Prune Day; why not set aside a day to honor our poets and even invite them to the White House for a party and let a few of them read to each other—not all five thousand of course, only the ones with a social conscience, perhaps.

Mr. Carter had to show his respect for the art. It was a democratic art, and all these minority poets milling around wouldn't hurt the President's image one bit. The President's wife would make a little speech of welcome, holding the hand of her scowling young daughter. He didn't want to go to the affair, but his wife did; she had never been to the White House. She even wanted to get in line and shake hands with the President. He did it to please her. He had never heard of half the poets there, and hadn't read many of them. He had given up their publications, partly paid for with public tax monies. The party lasted for hours, with wine and finger food and he couldn't get into any of the readings and wasn't asked to be one of the readers—not the right stuff for a national Poetry Day, though one of his books had been in the little library of every fighting ship during the War, he discovered thirty years later when the ships were being decommissioned one by one and the books sold.

The downhill speed of American poetry in the last decade has been breathtaking, he wrote, for those who watch the sport. Poetry plunged out of the classics, out of the modern masters, out of all standards, and plopped into the playpen. There we were entertained with the fecal-buccal carnival of the Naughties and the Uglies, who have their own magazines and publishing houses, and the lovelorn alienates, nihilists, disaffiliates who croon or "rock" their way into the legitimate publishing establishment. It was part of a talk he gave in San Francisco at the American Library Association convention. Newspaper reporters were present, reported what he had said on the wire services, and before he knew it he was being quoted all over the United States in newsprint.

In the beginning of his teaching life, poets were few and far between, and the ones who turned up in these primitive classes were really poets, really had the intention if not always the gift, and they had certain advantages. They knew there was no "future" in it as far as material recompense was concerned, and so were spared that kind of ambition. They knew that they would probably never have an audience for their work, more than a few hundred readers if that. They knew they would never have to worry about agents or contracts and would always consider the association of poetry and money morganatic, to say the least, knew that there would always be a gulf between them and the Serious World, and that even writers put them in a different category from themselves. Poets were not really writers, i.e., professionals; there was always something unprofessional about them, about poetry itself. So they were left alone, home free with their little company of fellow poets, who spoke a different language from every other language.

He remembered how after a book party for his second book—he was just weeks out of the Army—the publisher handed him a new contract for his next book, and to the astonishment of the publisher he didn't even read it, just signed it and handed it back with a smile. He remembered how when he was hired at Johns Hopkins, Associate Professor with Tenure he would always say as if the title was a visiting card, that he didn't even ask about salary, a measly four thousand a year. The Dean actually called him into his office and said that the salary was too low and they were adding another thousand, and he thanked the Dean and forgot about it.

Whether this was some kind of righteousness, or just plain stupidity, he never bothered to find out. It was not a stance of some kind. There was no principle behind it, only a personality, and his students were not after any dangling golden carrots, either. They only wanted to write their poems and have them commented on, favorably they hoped by a published poet, one who won acclaim and prizes. Prizes and acclaim were okay; that was the only kind of reward that mattered, and there was even something fishy about money attached to poetry. Money was for novelists and artists. A lot of artists would become millionaires. They were big business.

He thought of two great sad poets he had known at the Library of Congress. Both had won the Nobel Prize or would, both were exiles from their European countries and were being kept alive by the Library, their lives and works sheltered from their enemies at home. There was nobility about them, Jimenez and Leger, who called himself Perse and who wrote so deeply and lyrically about the princes of exile. Of course he was being unrealistic and ancien régime. The world had changed since he had discovered poetry back in the Twenties, the Thirties. The war had changed everything, even poetry and education. The G.I.'s were being rewarded for being G.I.'s. The colleges and universities were theirs. They were serious, more serious than students had ever been, and some of them wanted to be writers. Writing courses were invented for them. All of them had a lot to tell the world and they wanted to learn the know-how, the craft. It was still possible to teach the trappings and the suits of poetry, the forms. People still wrote the basic pentameter, the masters still used it, some of them, Frost and Auden and Cummings and Stevens. But the big break with the iambic "heave," as Pound called it, had come long ago and was still new, had come in the Tens and in the Twenties, and poetry would never be the same again. The barriers were down, the net was down, as in Frost's definition of free verse, with a snap.

But that was mostly surface, and he began to notice that a school for poetry had quickly turned into a school *of* poetry. Lines of force sprang into being, attitudes, dogmas, definitions, terms. They were to stay away from theory, but theory creeps in through the crevices of the poem and begins to exert its influence. There were big theories in the air, mostly wafted from overseas, from England, from Eliot and Pound specifically, big critical signs dropped on them like chunks of concrete—objective correlative, the dissociation of sensibility, the auditory imagination, the ideogram method. Students, even poets, can't resist these things; they have to talk about them. But such terminology is insidious and gets into the poems, as fog seeps through the window. There were prohibitions and inhibitions resulting; a poem is a turning away from emotion. Emotion must be depersonalized. Talk about the poet as a person is to commit the biographical fallacy. Poetry is intentionally ambiguous. Ambiguity can be stratified into types.

The new poetics were enough to prevent poetry altogether. Everyone became self-conscious about writing and even about reading, textures, structures. Ironies replaced the senses and feelings of the poem. Feeling could only be handled gingerly, objectively, without trust or directness. The one advantage of this kind of palaver was guild status, secrecy, for every trade must have its secret language and vocabulary, even shoemaking, but the amount of time and talent wasted on these talmudic exercises was costly and he grew restless and impatient with poems that reflected all this depersonalization.

Where was the voice, the cry, the hum, the music of the poem? It was psychology moving in on them; there was an establishment smell about it, even a theological odor of sanctity. Philosophy was putting its hand in. Eliot was a philosopher after all. Better the ravings of the romantic Shelley than this, but Shelley was already taboo, Whitman was taboo, even Shakespeare was being given a good shaking by the new theorists. The poet was all too innocent for this game and wanted out and began to plan his escape, even his escape from Tenure. Even at Iowa City, where Creative Writing had been incubated and the new poetics of structure-texture-irony was in full swing, he had hope for the program of salvaging poets, but the atmosphere got too thick, the bitterness and backbiting of the poets too shrill, the endless explications too microscopic. At one moment he thought he was back in the Middle Ages doing trivium-quadrivium lessons. At another he thought he was in a school for salesmen. The competition was acid, the conniving for scholarships and favors from the director disgusting, and he went to the director and said he must cancel his contract. It bothered him to see poets rushing at the sow—Iowa is pig-metaphor country—knocking each other over for the choice tit.

The Director was very upset at this kind of defection, but could do nothing about it, and immediately hired a poet who had won the Golden Albatross who was living in Rome. Anyone would have grabbed the job. For the established poets it was a preferment and gave prestige for the next round of applications and ladder climbing. It had already become fashionable to teach at the Iowa workshop in order to write an article blasting Iowa and the Middle West and American culture in general. Articles of this kind were a staple for magazines like the *New Yorker*, which regarded the Hudson River as the drop-off place of the flat world.

He taught It—Creative Writing—even in Chicago when he was the editor of *Poetry*, needing more pay which the famous but poor magazine couldn't supply—taught at Loyola University and had nuns in his class, excellent students, one of them talented, and regular students, two of them talented. It was more civilized than Iowa, stable with the kind of stability of an ocean liner or a cathedral.

When T. S. Eliot announced certain premises for his poetry, saying, "I am a royalist in politics, an Anglo-Catholic in religion, and a classicist in literature," he appeared to set a new standard for what a serious poet had to be made of—a program, a system, a metaphysics, an ideology, whatever. Ritual could stand in for God, and could cover both the religious and esthetic bases, as with Yeats. Myth could do the same for Pound, whose politics was also mythic, a combination of hero-autocrat worship and crackpot economic theory, and whose poetic was agglutinative, rococo shell-work, stuccoed all over not as Whitman had it with birds and rivers and occupations but with what Pound called ideas. This was his ideogram method, and only his staunchest defenders could put up with it. W. C. Williams's deity was place—his place—his poetics prose, his politics "un," to use Cummings's adjective, unpolitics in America, where the politician is held in utmost contempt. Wallace Stevens's politics were un, his god the imagination, his poetics priestcraftsmanship. These scaffoldings provided the critics with a basis for their estimations of the poetry. A poet who gave the critics no such ground to stand on was in trouble.

It was the age of criticism and there was no way to keep criticism out of the poetry workshop. Sometimes he would fly the banner of Shakespeare—you can prove or disprove anything by citing Shakespeare, one of the exceptions, Auden would say, that transcend all categories. Did Shakespeare believe in God? he would ask. What were Shakespeare's politics? What was his theory of poetry? and his answer was, Shakespeare saw the world as allegory, his poetics were that he sang English. But this was just marking time, giving the critics the slip, so that he could get back to the workshop, the workbench, the carpentry. Nobody could make a poet, you were one or you weren't, whether you got around to writing it or not, there were no mute inglorious Miltons in country churchyards or in Times Square, and the idea of a whole nation of poets is a good description of a funny-farm. Calling themselves poets was for some just a weird form of social protest in America.

Then why are we here? they would ask him. Was Creative Writing good for nothing, then? He would have to hedge. We are here to listen to each other's poems, we form an audience, a kind of guild. We are practicing a superior form of friendship. Sometimes there would come up a good line, several good lines, even a good passage, once in a blue moon a good poem, but they knew all that and were modest enough in their expectations of what they could achieve. One of the tests of a good poet, he would say, is editorial acumen, the ability to turn down your own work. It's the amateur who falls in love with his own written words and holds them sacrosanct. You would be amazed how many professors of literature hate literature, many of them failed writers. They can't wait for a contemporary poet to kick the bucket so they can feast on his remains, though most are faithful keepers of the text, enshriners of the artist and his work. All this circular talk served its purpose somehow, drew them closer together in a sense, gave them a purpose in congregating and exchanging their writings, a hope of minds reaching out to each other, minds touching, generating love out of solitude, perhaps. Poetry without love is a dry stick and will not put forth. We've had enough dry stick poetry, hollow and stuffed men, exhausted cisterns, etiolated cities and civilizations, Viconian Ferris wheels.

Now *The Waste Land*, which W. C. Williams said dropped like an atom bomb, had much to answer for. It made people see decline and fall everywhere, London Bridge was falling down. And when James Joyce said the Ferris wheel is falling down, down goes another civilization into chaos. Chaos is a time of extreme individualism and destruction like ours, according to this seer who got it from Vico. Man creates a theocracy first, which turns into an aristocracy, followed by democracy, which leads to chaos, us, death and ruin, every man armed to the teeth, every man his own Hitler. The arts go crazy, poetry is written execution-style, the Muse has murder in her heart, it all makes sense if you buy the premise. Here we are, headed for theocracy again, religious wars all over the place in the atheistic twentieth century, Israel and Iran, the State as deity, TV evangelism, the ultimate weapon for sale to savages.

They were all watching the revolution spread, the tide rising slowly and coming to their doorstep, wetting the campus grounds, turning everything to mud, leaking into the lobbies and vestibules of the administration buildings, into the classrooms, into Creative Writing—especially there, the distraught poets wild-eyed and hyper, the institutions in a state of panic. Chaos is come again, he thought, and he ran into the Chancellor of his new campus, who said that he didn't expect the university would stand; "they," meaning the rebels, would really shut it down. It wasn't a figure of speech, the Chancellor said. They were already making plans to put the university in mothballs. The poet didn't believe it but was worried about his classes. The poems had all turned obscene, graffiti, excrement and blood, imprecation and howling, love turned hate. He shuddered and wrote, I didn't go to the funeral of poetry, I stayed home and watched it on television.

He had had only three years at his Chicago professorship as the Sixties went into overdrive. A short reading tour to the West Coast ended Chicago and enrolled him as a permanent Californian. His common-law wife from Lincoln, Nebraska, was now free to marry again and they came to California man and wife. With his usual luck it happened quickly and without fuss; after a reading at Davis to an enthusiastic audience of students and faculty he was told that there was an opening for a professor and would he be interested. His chairman at the Circle Campus in Chicago tried to keep him with financial enticements but he was set on California, even though the fumes of revolution were beginning to seep like pollution up from the Bay Area to the Great Valley where the little "aggie" campus of Davis was situated.

The university in Davis, as in Chicago, tottered but didn't fall. Classes convened like a schizophrenic spiderweb. He had seen photographs of a schizo spiderweb; the scientists had given the spider LSD and the web that resulted had great gaps and lacunae, the manuscript was definitely defective. One suddenly could recall the exquisite perfection of the sane spiderweb. The students seemed disoriented. Everyone was badly shaken, and the poetry was bruised and angry and raw, and he didn't know how to handle it. He asked them about the "carpentry." The only thing they had to talk about was imagery, a bypass word that usually doesn't mean anything. No one even mentioned rhyme anymore; it was as obsolete as *thou*. They had given over rhyme to the rock lyricists. They could consider rhyme obscene, one of them said—it wasn't authentic, relevant, they said. Rhyme was for Madison Avenue advertisers and nightclubs, not for poets.

The rhythms, he said, what about them? A poem cannot exist outside of rhythms, even the so-called prose poem, which needs even fuller rhythm than metered verse, only the rhythms are larger, not looser, larger. But they didn't want to hear about rhythm. Rhythm was a control, and controls were off. After a while he gave up asking what the rationale was for ending a line where it did and getting no answer except that it felt right. It didn't feel right to him. They were flung back onto the content of the poem, what the poem was talking about. Singing was out of the question, wit was out of the question, even irony was obsolete, and the contents were a surprise. A surprising number of poems were about incest in the first person. He couldn't tell whether it was a device or a confession. He fumed against what was adulated as confessional poetry, called it a cop-out, and had the feeling that nothing he said would be accepted. He had lost his authority, and the best poems turned out to be lesbian love poems or gay love poems. He expatiated on the loss of the word *gay*, gone forever from the literary vocabulary like a bird shot down.

In a revolution, even a phony revolution, things go from bad to worse as a matter of course. The rug is pulled out from under the world of set values, fixed standards, and even without any kind of transvaluation there is chaos. Chaos is the first stage of the revolution; nobody knows who is doing what or why. It is the dismantling that occupies everyone. Physical destruction is very important, especially the destruction of symbolic property, banks, churches, official residences, monuments to the ancestral enemy. The smashing of icons of every description is necessary to block the bloodstream of tradition, and it is amazing how many structures, real and invisible, survive. The Kremlin stands, occupied by the latest set of tyrants, even the palaces stand. The new officials have to have status also, and after the slashing of paintings and the theft of plate they hang their own rags on the walls, usually red; red for danger. A society begins to reassert itself and rigidify, new uniforms are invented, very simple at first and gradually braided and bemedaled. A hierarchy of rewards is set up, titles are remade, heroes officialized, bayonets are replaced by discreet and ornamental firearms, but with live ammunition. Laws are laid down by fiat, rivals for the power are shot or disappear into prison or exile, and the revolution is over to await the next time.

That is the real revolution. The pseudo-revolution only mimics the bloodship, the mass meetings, the chaos. The pseudo-revolution knows that it is only playing at a power grab; it is a fun revolution. Make love not war is a fun slogan, almost an advertisement of adolescent longings. Even when real grievances are mounted, genuine wrongs angrily presented, there is no real hope of victory, because there is no simple aim, no party, no genius of leadership, no ringing manifesto, no plans for consolidation. Relentlessness is missing, madness is missing, do or die is missing, and it is hard to tell the roar of the pseudo-revolution from a football game or a rock festival, for in a sense the pseudo-revolution was only a rock festival after all.

Music was everywhere and integral to the swirling masses of young, drugs and flowers were intermixed. There are no drugs in a real revolution, or music either except in a particular song, one only, which is a battlecry, a "Marseillaise" or a "Star-Spangled Banner" or the "Internationale." You can tell if it's a real revolution if it leaves a song behind for posterity. But this pseudo-revolution had only Beatles songs or Pete Seeger, sad love songs mostly with electric guitars. This kind of revolution depends on electricity, even capitalist electricity. It depends on the internal combustion engine, that defeats it to begin with. It depends on the Means of Production and has no plans to capture the Means, no wherewithal. It is a rich revolution at bottom, well-shod and well-wheeled, even well-educated as such things go. But it is built only on negatives—a child banging its highchair, lots of negatives, hell no we won't go, even in child language, all monosyllables, serious enough for those who refused to go to the undefined war and get killed or gassed (and that was the core of a real revolution but it got nowhere except in the news).

The free speech movement down the road at Berkeley got nowhere except the freedom to yell *fuck* into a microphone. The clothes revolution got everywhere. Suddenly everyone started to wear blue denim work clothes. It was to become the international fashion overnight, a symbol of the pseudo-revolution, its color blue not red. Imagine a blue revolution! Blue is the love color, blue symbolizes peace, peace is no way to wage war. They needed a new color and got it—black, and all at once black became the color of the pseudo-revolution, though god knows the blacks needed a real revolution and they got that too, torching the urban landscape from sea to shining sea and throwing the big negative pseudo-revolutions into further confusion and factionalism.

Even the poetry turned black, leaning over backwards to integrate, as they called it in a kind of pig Latin. It must be violent, they said, incendiary, street level, a full expression of centuries-old hatreds and no holds barred. A black student burst into the poet's creative writing class and asked or rather demanded to read a poem. He stood in the middle of the room and read a long malediction against whitey and white education, picking on a kindergarten reader about Dick and Jane, two nice antiseptic middle-class children. Fuck you, Dick, fuck you, Jane, said the poem while the class stared at the unknown visitor, and he finished his poem and stalked out, mission accomplished. And that was only a sample. There were already cadres of blacks lying down in the middle of highways to stop traffic, shots were being fired in border neighborhoods, fires were beginning, like the Russian fires that had smoked

Napoleon out of Moscow, becoming an everyday event and on the campus the torching, as they called it, of ROTC buildings, the very symbol of the military. Chancellor's offices, administration building were occupied by singing shouting sloganizing students calling *shut it down.*

It would seem to be an ideal atmosphere for poets from one point of view, action and passion on the spot, but of course it had the opposite effect of ruining the poetry. No time for craftsmanship, poetry on the run, to hell with emotion recollected in tranquillity or in anguish, to hell with books, all books were irrelevant, the buzziest of the buzzwords irrelevant. By now there was full-blown chaos by the simple technique of stoppage and obstruction. Anybody could do it, from the elementary device of spray-painting a windshield or heaving a brick at it, to false alarm bomb scares, for at last the individual terror was born and everybody was a potential terrorist.

Years before this time of chaos, he had prided himself on the part he played in making black poetry known, when he had published Tolson in his magazine and written an introduction to one of Tolson's books, had visited him in the all-black town in Oklahoma. The poet was the only white person there and had come to meet the black poet and to lecture about him. He was put up at the president's house as an honor, the only solid middle-class stucco house in the tiny town. The poet Tolson was actually the mayor of the tiny black town, and two black girls, students, worked in the president's house and came up to him laughing and put their hands on his hair and exclaimed how soft it was and he didn't know how to respond. Fortunately the president happened to come in and gave him a slight scowl and the girls left. Tolson had been made poet laureate of the country of Liberia, the only free black country in all of Africa, not all that free what with the French and British trying to grab it and the American rubber plantations, but it recognized the

American black poet along with Duke Ellington as music laureate. This was long before Selma, Alabama, and the symbol of the bus.

Tolson's *Libretto*, his laureate poem, was a masterpiece, equivalent in power and beauty and significance to *The Waste Land*, but with no such press, no British establishment to put it on the map and keep it there, no scrolls of criticism to sanctify and keep it, on the contrary an almost dead silence. Who was going to honor a black poem about blackness, negritude? The poet had written about Tolson's *Libretto* that amazingly Tolson *wrote in Negro*, which puzzled and hurt some of the blacks. It was before black turned beautiful and the intellectual Negroes didn't know what the white poet meant, but he was right even if the terminology made the blacks twitch.

The Confederate poet Allen Tate had praised the poem to the skies. He was the American representative of T. S. Eliot himself, the apostle of the eliotic, and he had praised the black man's *Libretto* and acclaimed it as a first for an American Negro. Tolson, with piercing acumen and probably with tongue in cheek, had sent Tate his poem, a version of it, and received the reply, "I am not interested in the propaganda of Negro poets," and with advice. Tolson, instead of being offended, set about refashioning the poem, and it was this work that the Southern poet felt called upon to praise. William Carlos Williams also welcomed the poem, quoted a bit of it in *Paterson* and called Tolson by name. But mostly there was silence, the silence of the white critical eye that could not see black. And indeed the blacks themselves could not handle the poem, its languages and cultural references more numerous than those of *The Waste Land*. The blacks buried the poem as if it were not for them, the whites ignored it except for Tate and Shapiro, the British ignored it, even the French who generally know better, and in the black upheaval which quickly turned into black apartheid in America the blacks condemned the poets who had praised Tolson. Whites had no right to praise a black poet.

At one of those interracial symposiums in Berkeley the poet was on the stage with an Amerindian writer, an Hispanic poet, a Chinese poet, himself the Jew and a black poet, and when the white Jewish-American began to praise Tolson, the black poet leaped up and snatched the microphone out of his hand and denounced white interference with black writers. It was none of their mother-fucking business. The white Jewish-American snatched the microphone back and continued with his praise of Tolson, and a black woman in the audience jumped up and shouted at the white Jewish-American poet, and he finally gave up and sat down. Poor Tolson was dead. If only he were here he would put those black Nazis in their place, he thought, but there was no help for it now. He felt he had lost a friend in the melee. He was bitter about the arrogance of the black apartheids, the blacks had gone crazy. But a small voice inside him said, "and about time too." And the black poet said to him, that Tolson poem is bourgeois shit.

12.

In the handsome Guthrie Theatre in Minneapolis the poet had given a reading to a closely packed audience. A question period was to follow—he enjoyed parrying questions, hardly ever actually answering them. John Berryman, who was host that evening, rose from the back of the room and asked, "Do any of the books you've published embarrass you?" It was the kind of question that is carefully decided upon in advance, and that packs several varieties of wallops. Without pausing, the poet on the stage replied, "All of my books embarrass me," and there was a ripple of what is called nervous laughter.

The answer, of course, was untrue, a non-answer but one which served the purpose of disarming the question, turning the live charge into a blank. But he knew immediately that Berryman was making a public declaration of dissociation from him, and that saddened him. When he would tell the story later, it was always in the context of what he hoped was graceful surrender. He had outshone his contemporaries too long. Berryman was only a year his junior, and the older poet was being nudged to the side.

Sometimes he would receive letters from strangers, unknown poets, who would relay hearsay criticism of him by well-known poets. He had begun to notice that his name was no longer a sine qua non in the canon, and the newer anthologies were beginning to drop him from what had been a standard roster of poets of his age. He wondered how far the process would go, and maintained a kind of almost scientific impersonality about it. He was not going to let it eat him away. He hoarded his pride, the melancholy sweetness of adversity. He relished the idea of expecting the worst, almost encouraged it, leaving himself defenseless, aloof, arrogant in humility, too proud to stoop to self-justification. And yet the only criticism that ever hurt him was the criticism of other poets, especially those his own age. He had written great praise of Berryman's new work and would continue to do so, very impressed by the new idiom he was playing with like dynamite, and Berryman disdained to notice his commendations, which amounted to homage.

One morning when he had begun to feel the sense of banishment, expatriated from Parnassus, and was already contemplating his total withdrawal, the phone rang. He was still in bed with his wife. It was the poet Wilbur, calling from New York to tell the poet that he had just won the Bollingen Prize, the very prize that had caused the poet such anguish when it had first been bestowed on Ezra Pound. It was now the foremost poetry prize in the country, and now he had won it. But not alone; he was sharing it with Berryman, honor and money and all. But that made no difference to him and he clasped his wife and wept with relief at this redemption, as he thought of it. He was glad that it was not the kind of prize that the newspapers would recognize, and people would not even know how to pronounce it. It was a prize bestowed by pros and for pros, and he would always think of it as his best honor, one that ensured his poetic amour propre for keeps. They had not written him off after all.

He sent Berryman a joyous telegram but received no reply. Locked into alcoholism and megalomania, Berryman would in three years leap off the campus bridge in Minneapolis to his death on the frozen ground.

There was another story he told about himself, and once even used on the lecture platform, and that caused a roar of laughter. It was about a letter he had received. It was a time when teachers, for whatever reasons, encouraged or even directed students to write to authors and poets about what they called the artist's career. Even students in grade schools did this, and college students would frequently take to the telephone and call him to ask questions about certain poems of his which they were writing papers on. When this happened the poet was so astonished that he would try to answer them as best he could. The letters he almost never answered. Most of them were full of misspellings and bad constructions and showed plain ignorance of the poems. But this letter outdid them all.

Dear Dr. Shapiro—
I have been assigned to write a term paper about you and your career, where you were born and educated, what kind of degrees you have, your rise to publications, your wife and children, what prizes you have won, your definition of poetry, and your decline.

He thought, I would love to meet the teacher who directed that child. In a way the letter was a revelation to him. These people had a stock notion of decline, a kind of primitive biologic idea; but then so did more sophisticated people, the critics, the artists themselves. The idea of decline began to haunt him and tug at his mind. Maybe the Bollingen Prize was some kind of mark of punctuation, a period. Not a worrier, he found himself worrying about nameless things.

His new wife was going into depressions. It was her children, or rather their absence, she said. They had sent them back to Nebraska to live with their father because Chicago had been too dangerous for them, three girls at puberty, running around with the children of prostitutes and drug dealers off Clark Street where their public school was. They had failed to get them into private school; the waiting lists were years long. And the youngest child virtually alone, friendless in an apartment building where mostly newlyweds or old millionaires lived. So they were all sent back across the Missouri to become Nebraskans again, brought up by an authoritarian bully of a psychiatrist, the husband the poet's wife had fled from, who had kept her bathroom medicine cabinet stuffed with sleeping pills and other powerful drugs. She still had a big supply.

The two had landed in Davis, California, in the summer heat which was legendary to Californians and lived in a fairly cool old brick bungalow which they rented. Most of the time they were happy, and the professors and their wives who were staying behind for the summer or hadn't yet departed made them at home with endless favors and displays of hospitality. But sometimes the depression would fall upon her. She would chain-smoke and drink Scotch; they both did, but she would become morose and decide to take a walk alone. If it was nighttime he would be frightened, though he tried not to show it, but would now start to follow her in the car without her knowing it. She would walk to the edge of the little town and if she started down a highway he would follow slowly even with the car lights off, but if she struck across a field he would lose her and park the car and sit in the dark hoping she would find her way back. One night she told him on her return that a truck had stopped and the driver got out and asked if she was all right or needed a lift.

She had found a psychiatrist in the next town of Woodland and was now making regular visits, just as she had when he had met her and she was breaking up with her husband and drove regularly from Lincoln to the Omaha psychiatrist fifty miles away, top speed on the icy highway in the powerful Chrysler, surviving miraculously unscathed. The psychiatrist had a calming effect for a long time, and she and the poet talked psychiatry, though the poet felt conscience-stricken that he had failed her, or that love was no longer the protective force it had been. He knew that part of her was leaving him, and the dangerous night walks alarmed him. They had contracted for a new house. If only the house would be finished and they could move in and she could get her piano back. She missed it and needed it. It had been her triumph for a while and she had received a fellowship to study in Chicago when she was in high school, but her parents forbade her to go to the big city alone, and she remained a local concert pianist, giving recitals at benefits. But for now there was the psychiatrist and the visits to the new house, which rose rapidly and soon had walls and doors, and they spent time visiting drapers and carpenters, and read paint charts and looked through catalogues for light fixtures, and planned the Californian garden where almost anything would grow all year round. Probably because of his memory of Japan the poet persuaded her to have the house painted black outside, the only black house in town he said, and have bamboo planted all across the front, set in gray gravel, and this occupied them almost to the end of the summer and kept them going. But the night walks continued, along with the sleeping pills and the Scotch.

One morning he awoke to find his wife gone. He looked out onto the driveway. The car was gone. It was seven o'clock in the morning. In the bedroom there was no evidence of any kind of departure. Her coats were still hanging in the coat closet in the hall. He searched around for a note of some kind and was relieved to find none. He dressed automatically and was returning to the living room when he heard the front door open.

We must have had a lot to drink, she said. I decided to drive to Omaha. Home, the poet amended to himself. Omaha, almost two thousand miles away. His heart felt like a stone.

I was stopped on Donner Summit in the snow; I just had sandals on. The policeman was very nice, helpful. He didn't say anything about liquor. There wasn't any in the car. He asked me where I was going and I said Omaha. He took me into a cafe and bought me coffee. He told me to go back to Davis.

It was, he remembered afterwards, her last escape attempt, and the drive up and up to the top of the sawtooth mountains where so many travelers had died in the snow had frightened her. The higher she went the soberer she got. She could not have been driving well, for the police car had followed her, and when she had drunk as much coffee as she could she waited for dawn to return down the interstate and back into the valley.

He gave himself a new chore. He would now wait until she was sound asleep, and then get out of bed quietly and find her pocketbook and remove the keys. Then like a burglar he would place hers and his own bunch of keys under his side of the bed. If she reached down she would surely waken him. He practiced keeping the key rings silent by gripping them tightly and laying them on the carpeting without a sound. In the morning he would replace the keys. The sad operation became habitual.

The poet settled into his new job, which was not new to him, the same courses as in Chicago, modern poetry, creative writing. Part of his department even consisted of old friends from a dozen years before and his wife had found an old classmate of hers from the Omaha high school. All the transitions were easy, but the depression hung on and the strange night walks persisted, and one night he tried to dissuade her and even to restrain her, but she was stronger and taller than he and she struck him hard in the face and knocked him to the floor and left. His head had missed the edge of the raised brick fireplace by an inch. They never mentioned the incident and the poet wondered if she had been aware of hitting him and knocking him down. They had both been drinking through the afternoon.

A month later she took the pills. And now the psychiatrist ex-husband was tightening the noose, cutting down on the children's visiting rights, and even threatening not to let them come to California at all to visit their neurotic mother and the crazy poet she had married. The poet grew very heated and cursed her former husband, the psychiatrist, and they both got more and more angry, she said she was going to kill herself, went into the bathroom and locked the door, which she had never done before. He stood outside and listened and heard the medicine cabinet open and close several times and he called her. She refused to answer and he kept calling and started to knock and twist the knob. It was only a hollow-core door such as tract houses have, and he finally banged at it with his shoulder four or five times until the flimsy lock gave way and he saw her slumped on the floor breathing thickly. He saw at least four empty plastic pill bottles strewn around.

He dragged her to the bed, his arms under her arms, and dragged her up on the bed. He couldn't lift her. She weighed more than he did. In his moment of panic he remembered a remark Saul Bellow had made about her when they met, that he admired big handsome women. He managed to drag her up to the pillow, not sure that that was the right thing to do, for she was losing consciousness fast. He rushed across the street where a retired colonel lived, and rang and banged on the door until the colonel and his wife both came in their pajamas and he told them what had happened. They dressed swiftly, and soon the three of them lifted her into the car.

It was dawn when they emerged from the emergency room supporting her, now drowsily awake. Her stomach had been pumped, just in time. Her psychiatrist had been called and came at three o'clock in the morning. Of course the episode would be kept secret, he said, though nobody had made the suggestion. There is a shame to suicide or attempted suicide which touches everybody in the immediate vicinity of the act, and a pact of secrecy is formed in self-protection. But in the nature of things such secrets are never kept, they leak through the walls, even in the wee hours of the morning, and travel like ozone through the atmosphere to distant places. It would take a while but the secret would out, would take a strange twist of fact, as extreme events frequently do, and become a frightening and disgraceful distortion, one that would damage the poet worse than the actual truth.

He understood that the attempt ended a chapter of their life. This is where the walks had led, the striking out in the darkness across the tall fields, the agonizing wait for her return. He had what is called a lively imagination, and his mind in those days would alert him to every conceivable contingency while he sat waiting for the phone or the doorbell to ring. But she always returned and entered the front door, which he kept unlocked, and walked past him, pretending that nothing untoward had happened, and went to bed. He would wait until she was asleep before he followed her. Nothing was ever said about that night and the old pills all disappeared, only to be replaced by new ones which her psychiatrist ordered for her. She named one of them wolf pills because one night she woke and shook him and pointed to the foot of the bed. Do you see it? she asked. What? he answered. The white wolf, she said, and described it minutely. It was not threatening, just sitting there looking at her. She stopped taking the "wolf" pills and the animal stayed away.

They had reached a plateau now, and there was a kind of exhausted relief. As grass grows on a barren plain, and wild flowers find their way to the air, from seedlings dropped by fowl from the sky, they entered a land of peace and began the California moment which is without front or back, without clocks or calendars, without goals or ambition. They went about their business, real estate or teaching creative writing, but it was understood that nothing was serious and everything a pastime to provide table talk. It was why gardening was so important and the cultivation of roses more important than eating, why even sex was less important than athletics, why surfing was a form of social revolution.

The recovery, or what the poet thought of as a change of plan, seemed more than satisfactory. The night excursions ceased. They entertained and went to dinners and cocktail parties. She returned to school on campus to study Latin and the poet hoped she would become a graduate student in Latin, which was what he had wanted to be when he was a college student, hidden in the secrecies of a dead language which only a small brotherhood knew or cared about. She was a good student and made rapid progress until they came to the prosody. Was it the poetry or the prosody? He never knew which, but her interest flagged at this stage and eventually she dropped out.

Now and then she would ask about selling their house which they had built, and he was taken aback. The black exterior had taken on a kind of sinister aspect, instead of being smart and original, "Japanese" with its black bamboo, for even the bamboo was of the black variety, its twigs shading from pink to yellow to a kind of blue and finally a hard silky black. He would always respond with a surprised why about selling the house, and she would smile and shrug. But she had begun to study real estate now and was thinking of going to a real estate school to be able to pass the state examinations for agents of property. Unaware of such things, he did not know that there was a real estate boom all around and that people were buying and selling their houses for great profit. One day he asked her again why she wanted to move, or rather sell the house, and when she replied that they could make thirty thousand dollars profit, he said, surprised at his own voice, sell it.

It was as simple as that. She matriculated at the real estate school in Sacramento, did the work easily and passed the examinations, and even was hired by a large real estate agency. With the profit on their house she began to buy houses to rent, one at a time, carefully and with good advice from old hands. But she disliked the job at the big company in the quite big capital city; she disliked selling, as did the poet who had had a brush with it in the Depression when his father tried unsuccessfully to turn him into a salesman of office supplies. Before long she quit the real estate job and concentrated on her few houses.

She also tried to exercise her new skill in a very small real estate company in the little university town and sold one house, to a friend, but then let salesmanship drop for good. She was after all a desk person, like the poet, although he never knew what to do with a desk except to sign a paper or two on it when he had to write his name. He had never discovered the use of desks anywhere, whether in the Army or at home. He wrote sitting on chairs or on the ground or in bed, and he couldn't even type in the prescribed way but put the typewriter on a low stool and sat in a soft chair and pecked away with three or four fingers.

That he had been picked to be the company clerk years ago in the Army had astounded him, for there were plenty of real typists in the infinite pool of free talent. With his three-finger technique he could make the typewriter hum without trying, even though he had to eye the keyboard at every peck. It might have been his command of English which even the officer-doctors who were his superiors had admired, complimented him on, promoted him for. And his style. The dullest of communications he could give a twist to (out of boredom or actual creativity) that would make his memos call attention to themselves. He had been headquarters material, but he hadn't wanted to go where everybody, even in the jungle, was cleanly dressed and snapped to attention when top brass strolled in and out all day long. No desks for him.

His wife, on the other hand, was as much at home with desks as a cat with a velvet sofa. Her home office was beautifully organized, her accounts so exemplary that when they went to see their accountant on the annual tax roundup he was all smiles and wonder, and had little to do but chat to use up their accounted-for time like a psychiatrist.

It was tacitly understood that the poet would have no business duties. After all, he had been what the journalists called gainfully employed all his adult life and had never thought of money and accounts. His check came in and there was always enough and to spare. Besides, he had his royalties and lecture fees; he never thought of money. Sometimes he would study a dollar bill even with his magnifying glass, to fathom the secret of its power. In the first place, it was very ugly, covered with obsolete codes and execrable poetry—"This note is legal tender for all debts public and private," which was complete nonsense and an untruth, for even he knew that the dollar was worth not a hundred cents but only a fourth of that. He noted that it was even badly printed, the margins uneven, and the grandmotherly George Washington in his neckerchief—"her," William Carlos Williams said—looking sad and reprimanded. The poet's interest in finance stopped at his esthetic investigation, and his wife became the manager of all such things, to the satisfaction of both. She liked it, she enjoyed it; her knowledge became expert and *Wall Street Journals* and *Barron's* and *Money Market* magazines poured into the mailbox. He had few needs and had to be dragged into the store for a piece of clothing. Once when he had been on a clothing excursion with her to the only "good men's store" they had heard of in Sacramento and bought two suits and wore one to the campus, a colleague, an English professor to-the-shabby-born said to him, did your wife buy that suit? and he never wore it again, not to school.

The houses in the town were all more or less alike and the new ones were built by a man from the Ivy League Eastern schools who named all the streets after the best-known colleges. There were three or four plans he used, which had actually won an architecture prize in the new style of plywood on concrete slab with the pipes and plumbing all built in. The houses could be thrown up in a hurry and were all guaranteed to last the life of the mortgage, say twenty years, an excellent idea in a culture so fluid and at a time when such a thing as a family homestead was as obsolete as pithecanthropus. It didn't matter about the sameness of the houses in California, because in two years every house would be shrouded in cypress and eucalyptus and olive and orange and maytens and redwood and valley oak and god knows what greenery, with flowering ground cover or "Japanese" gravel or lawn or roses, some front yards with wagon-wheel motifs or driveways with little yachts or trailers and foreign cars and imported bicycles and mopeds. It was Hedonsville, U.S.A., and the inhabitants went half-naked all the time, on campus or off, except for the Easterners who took time to learn and the Europeans who never would succumb to the nude look.

This second house was in a cul-de-sac, and backed up onto a tomato plantation so unending that it ran straight to the next valley toward the Pacific. The poet had a steel cyclone fence erected through which he could see the little Vaca Mountains and watch the cultivation. He even had a gate put in facing the farm to be able to gather tomatoes during the harvest; a foreman told him that it was illegal but okay (like everything in California), but not to uproot any bushes. He could have all the tomatoes he wanted; they left tons on the ground, but the bushes should be unharmed until they were plucked by machine.

He enjoyed this house with its farm and mountain view and took a bedroom at the back for his study and helped transport a three-tier concrete fountain whose plash he could hear while he worked, the water sound soothing and musical, with the birds coming to drink at his fountain.

The "suicide" was never mentioned, as if it was something like a bad auto accident in which all the injured had recovered and would only shudder at the memory and not speak of it. But it was not forgotten. It would only return in a different form, masquerading as his own.

This was how they tried to reconstruct the event, so far-fetched and wildly improbable that they were never sure they had the right answer.

He opened his mail in his study one pretty afternoon—all the afternoons were pretty, with that Mediterranean sky and the little blue mountains across the tomato fields—and pulled a note from the envelope and a clipping from a magazine. The note said, You probably don't remember me, poet. We met at Jessamyn's. My husband and I had a hearty laugh at the report of your suicide. We know better.

It didn't register until some time after he read the article. The article was cut from the *Journal of the American Medical Association—JAMA* it called itself—and was about Sylvia Plath and all the American poets who had killed themselves. It began with a dramatic list, Hemingway of course, Hart Crane, Vachel Lindsay. John Gould Fletcher, John Berryman, Randall Jarrell, Karl Shapiro. It still didn't register.

Whenever something horrible happened, something out of normal perspective, something that would take years to assimilate or might never be assimilated at all, his mind shut off defensively, as it did during the all-night bombing in the Pacific. Everyone was splattered with everyone else's blood, yet he had gone on quietly opening cases of blood plasma and obeying orders about stretchers as if he were in a training class or a film. His mind shut down on this article now, and he laid it aside and opened other mail while the event took root in his thought. It was an hour before he picked up the article again.

His mind would do another operation simultaneously after a shock, a catastrophe, and would begin to sort out origins and purposes. Where did this thing start? What was it for? Who was to gain advantage? What sort of advantage? He was aware of this kind of thinking while he felt he wasn't participating in it at all; another defensive mechanism, a still different area of his mind said. He picked up the article and studied the name of the author and looked for some reference to her. To be established as a suicide in the journal of the powerful and feared American Medical Association was as good as a funeral, a statistic so absolute that even God couldn't strike it down.

When he discussed the article with his wife they both decided that it should be ignored. Nobody they knew, certainly not poets or English professors, would ever see the *Journal of the American Medical Association*. But the article had been written by a woman who was both an English professor and an M.D., obviously a person of peculiar and sweeping ambition. Did he know her? The woman who had sent the article was a doctor's wife, of course, and he thanked her wryly. And the woman who had written the article sent him an apology of sorts. "I hope you still have your old sense of humor," she said. "I made a slip." A poet at her university in the Midwest had seen her article, and had drawn her attention to the error.

So if the poet didn't know her, she knew him and had written his death warrant. The name now came back to him; she had been a graduate student at Nebraska when he was a professor of English there. She hadn't been a student of his but was writing her dissertation on John Donne. She wanted to be a writer, he recalled, and it was possible that he had read some of her work or even rejected it as editor.

It was the time of the Sylvia Plath bandwagon, when critics and even journalists and especially the new feminists were celebrating her suicide and her poetry as one and the same thing. American society was once again made the whipping boy of culture, and there was a great wailing and gnashing of teeth over this young woman with her history of suicide attempts, as if Society itself had grabbed her by the scruff of the neck and shoved her head in the oven. The article in *JAMA*, a name which the poet already relished, a kind of hydrophobic word, was this double-doctor's attempt to assert herself both as medical expert and literary expert. Of course, the contributor's note said, she was a professor of psychiatry, no less, at the Midwestern University Medical School, and literary suicide was right up her alley. He put the matter out of his mind, sat in his study and listened to his fountain making up tunes and watched the hummingbirds fluttering on the red hibiscus and watched the Rube Goldberg tomato-picking machines that had been contrapted at his campus and which were funnier than circus carts with tumbling clowns. They were big streetcarlike devices with running boards, on which stood shoulder to shoulder sorters of tomatoes, while the scoop at the front of the machine plucked up the bushes whole and dumped them into a net where the fruit tumbled down to the girls and boys, university students and Mexicans, who tossed the not-quites back into the fields for the gleaners or just for the rot. He read and wrote and listened to music, and was sad inside though it never showed. People always said how happy he was, and he laughed. That proved it.

His books now were redactions, recapitulations, rehashes, and he wanted to get done with it. As a writer one achieves a mountain status, or rather a Gutzon Borglum status, in which what you have done is not necessarily good but is ineradicable. Huge stone faces bigger than Sphinxes sitting in the middle of nowhere and depicting such visages as Theodore Roosevelt, or little faces, curios, but which have achieved not encyclopedia status, that's easy, or museum status, that's transitory, but *dictionary* status—that was the goal. In the dictionary you are inviolate, immortal, and there a name becomes a word. As a librarian he knew this.

He knew that his insurance was running out and this was his problem: not to regain it, "keep it up," but what to do in the void. It was what happened to skilled men who retire and who think of dying, what beautiful women think when they study their hands and eyes and hair and know that they have to create a new character to carry into the living room. And he asked himself why he had to do anything. What obligation did he have? In the mythic East a man of forty would say goodbye to all that and give away his substance and start up the hills to find a cave. He was in a cave. He liked the cave, the fountain, the hummingbirds, the tomato-picking contraptions, the razory glorious pampas thrashing around at the corner of the garden.

He didn't even think of sex. His wife was angry. She knew that the blood pressure pills he took were anti-sexual—she hadn't been married to a psychiatrist for nothing. His doctor was giving him female hormones; he thought he was even beginning to grow breasts. If he didn't speak to the doctor, then she would. He spoke to the doctor who gave him a different pill. Had the damage been done or was it just another vestibule of the void?

It was the second time a graduate student acted the bearer of bad tidings and brought him devastating news. The first time had been when he was editor of the literary journal at the University in Nebraska when an excellent little short story was "killed" by the Administration, and the graduate student, whose story it was, had received galley proofs with a red line struck through the long sheets. The story had mentioned in passing a conversation with the homosexuals in the English Department coffee room. Definitely unprintable to the minds of deans and such, the story was stricken from the proofs. The poet had known in a flash, as one knows certain things about the future almost by intuition, that the "kill" signaled his resignation from the magazine and even his eventual departure from the University. He would put up a daring fight, as his friends called it, would make his point about censorship and then lose the battle, himself as sacrifice. It was ever thus.

This was far worse and more than that. It was probably the worst thing that had ever happened to him in his life, and amounted to what medical journalists call life-threatening. His life was not only threatened, it was taken away from him. It conferred ghosthood on his years, and he was in a word *slain* and condemned to walk through his days under an ancient curse, as he thought of it, dramatizing his death sentence. For not only had the official journal of the American Medical Association written his obit but they had given his cause of death as suicide. He and his wife had long ago decided to forget the article in *JAMA* and never spoke of it to outsiders. The author of the article listing him as a suicide had apologized in a jocular vein and the issue was as good as buried. Or so he thought.

He was walking down the corridor of the Humanities building on his way home when the student stopped him and asked whether he had seen the article in the *Saturday Evening Post* that mentioned him. The poet answered with surprise that he didn't know that the magazine was still in existence. It had been his daddy's magazine, he said, ever since the poet was a child. It was the bible of the middle class, he went on, as *Time* was later to become; it encoded the value systems of H. L. Mencken's booboisie.

The graduate student interrupted, "There is an article about the death of Sylvia Plath by a psychiatrist. She lists seven famous American writers who committed suicide. You are one of them," he said and eyed the poet closely.

He could never remember whether there was any more talk with the student, but he knew he had heard the names of Hemingway and John Berryman. His mind had done its usual protective trick of slamming down the curtain. He did remember driving to the drugstore and buying two copies of the magazine, which looked exactly as it had when he was a child, except that it was smaller and didn't have a Norman Rockwell cover. He checked the table of contents and spotted "The Death of Sylvia Plath."

At home he felt a sudden wave of fear, as if a doctor had just condemned him to cancer. His wife read one copy and he the other. The first thing he did was to find the list of the proscribed. It was in an opening paragraph and read in a lip-smacking fashion, "To the death of Sylvia Plath must be added those of Ernest Hemingway, Hart Crane, Randall Jarrell, Karl Shapiro, William Inge and John Berryman." And then, being not only a psychiatrist but a professor of same at her Midwestern campus, she asked archly and the poet thought fatuously, "Does her suicide to any extent, illuminate theirs?" Illuminated suicide, the poet thought pointlessly when his wife asked if he knew her.

Know her? he answered. Yes and no. God help me, he thought, if they ever get me on a witness stand. Well, did you? she pursued, looking worried or impatient or both. He was already beginning to feel guilty. They would all make him feel guilty, as if he had done it. *JAMA* said he had done it. The *Saturday Evening Post* said he had done it. A professor of psychiatry had said he had done it. Who was he to contradict such authorities? And had he known the woman or not?

Whenever the poet felt he had answered a question directly he was uneasy, as if he had cheated on a test. He distrusted straight answers, which were not only boring but sophistical, he argued. The children had grown used to teasing him, even baiting him, about what they called his evasions, and would sometimes plant a question to see how he would reply and then look at each other and giggle with satisfaction, and he would feel offended and try not to show it. Their mother too had no sympathy for his style of dialectic and said so.

I remember, he answered, because I liked her name, a lovely name, a kind of Viking name, a skimming the waves kind of name, the name of a sailor's sweetheart. We had a song about it in school when I was little—But I didn't like *her*, he said.

His wife looked at him.

Nothing necessarily cause and effect, he said, but I'm sure she did come to me with her stories when I was editor in Nebraska, and I seem to remember that I gave her a poor opinion about them. She was a Ph.D. student but not mine. She wrote on John Donne. Did you know that John Donne once wrote a defense of suicide? (*Biathanatos* he said to himself).

All I know is that she got a Ph.D. in English and then went to med school and became, what is she? a professor of psychiatry, or an assistant professor. She'll go far.

It was all too insulting and contemptuous to let pass. The first time may have been a mistake; the re-publication was clearly not. The imputation of suicide would stick, any future readings of his poems would be tainted with it. Even though going to court meant a further debasement of himself and everything he felt he stood for, the slander could not be allowed to stand unchallenged. He would have to go to law, or to lawyers. The poet had no antipathy for lawyers, as he had for psychiatrists or rape-murderers, and he rather liked them and their eighteenth-century briefs, their cute hauteur and their grip on the almighty buck. And lawyers, those he had met, were soft on writers. They were writers themselves, and up and down the civilizations wrote the laws we live by. They even loved the swing and music of language and they practiced theory of behavior and action, such as what is *actionable*, and they were the keepers of the jurisprudence. The higher echelons dressed in black and in the older countries in perukes. There was a certain nobility about them, a bit tarnished perhaps, but still there was a residue of religion left in the crucifix of an old whore.

The poet wanted to approach one of the Clarence Darrows of the land who had at this time become public figures, celebrities always on television, who had books written about, not them, but just a particular case they had won. He knew he had the kind of case that would attract them—the AMA as adversary, a major university and a psychiatry professor as culprits, a national mass magazine with the sanctimoniousness of the Methodist Church. But his wife said no, they would use their local lawyer.

A huge dread, like a blanket of fog, hung in front of him. He was not sure why. His horror of publicity went back to the broadcast of the birth of his first child, when it came to him like a thunderclap that he never wanted notoriety, only recognition for his work, and then only by his peers and betters. He had grown up in a time when the only famous poets were dead poets and when literary notoriety of any kind was shameful and scandalous, infra dig, a time when real poetry was kept a secret from the masses, especially his middle-class masses. It was not for them. Now he himself was becoming a scandal, and he imagined that people in his little town were looking at him sideways and puzzling over his "suicide," for obviously such a juicy piece of gossip wasn't going to be ignored. Saddest of all, he now knew that no matter the outcome of the case, if there was to be a case, the accusation and the sentence would always remain. The cliche "Where there's smoke there's fire" kept running through his head, as it did everyone else's who troubled to think of the business. He began to be afraid of his fear, his sadness, and suddenly felt paralyzed in some part of his being. Part of him was stopped in its tracks, and he started to think of physical paralysis and what it must be like to have a limb disobey the natural command of the will—the cane, the wheelchair, the feeding by another's hand.

He remembered his associate editor at the Nebraska magazine who had to be helped up the steps by his wife every day, and with two canes, had to be lowered into his office chair, and he remembered too the associate's good humor, even his merriment at things, and the quiet peaceful mien of his wife, and the poet would watch them laboring toward their car afterward and he would watch them all the way as if he were helping too. Housebound, that was the word, for he was beginning to appreciate the sensation of being housebound. He discovered this one afternoon when he was about to go out front with his big garden shears to clip away some of the bamboo at his windows that was filtering out too much light. He had gone to the front door with the shears and suddenly stopped and came back into the house, and it was then he knew that *he didn't want to be seen.* By whom? There were only the neighbors across the street who had helped take his wife to the hospital the night of the—*suicide.* Was this a suicide house? Why had they decided to have the outside of the house painted black? Plant black bamboo?

Gradually his wish for absence or invisibility grew stronger and he began to dread going to school to teach. He had already begun to fear the jocular remark about Mark Twain which he had heard three times already, while part of his mind was drawing up a list of people who made the Mark Twain remark as people beyond his range of sensitivity, people trying to be nice and smooth things over but who dumped a whole box of salt into the wound. The report of my death is greatly exaggerated, the witty and bitter Samuel Clemens had said and got away with it. But even that was only a stupidly mistaken report of his death, not his suicide. To the poet, when the remark was made to him he considered it as confirmation of his own demise, an accepted fact or at least an acceptance of the accusation of what was already taken for granted, his "attempted suicide." The Mark Twain joke was supposed to comfort him by implying that his friends were glad he had failed in his attempt and were welcoming him back to the world. It was at this time that he began to refer to himself as posthumous, even taking a kind of vicious delight in saying it in letters when the occasion presented itself.

Their lawyer was a young, nice-looking, slightly porcine Californian, and a graduate from Cal. Cal is a magical term in California and is used only by graduates from the University in Berkeley; it is a password and a putdown, especially when used to a graduate from one of the eight other campuses. Even if the Cal alumnus got his degree from an inferior department at Cal the syllable was enough to give him or her status. He had been made a partner in a large family law firm in Sacramento, with quiet dignified offices on a tree-shaded side street. They handled all branches of the law but had never had a libel suit of such proportion, and the poet sensed that they were a little dazzled by it.

He was interviewed by several of the other lawyers in the firm, aware that they were sizing him up as a player in this law game. He was told right off that depositions would be taken by the other side, the enemy, and that they, his side, would instruct him about answering, which questions to avoid or parry, what kind of tone he should use, when to become indignant and even angry, but not too angry so as not to appear a "hostile witness." Hostility would cost him.

The poet sat through these sessions with his wife, growing more and more miserable at his "criminal" status—suicide is a felony in California—and he must strain his wits to the utmost to prove his innocence and assert Damage. Everything hinged on Damage, especially damage to his income, for in the long run, or even the short run, Law always comes down to money. If you can prove loss of income you have a case, and if you can't you might as well give it up. Psychological damage, yes, that was a factor of course, but he would have to prove that the accusation had damaged his psyche, or better still his health. Second to money damage, health damage was taken seriously in court. A kind of workman's compensation, the poet thought, because he had got his arm caught in a machine while he was on the job. Oh, and the lawyers explained, the other side will send you to a psychiatrist for a report. All the cogs of the machine would be set in motion, and he would be laid on the couch of guilt and inscribed with the name of his crime all over his body until he died. It was Kafka's *In the Penal Colony* nightmare and the poet was not prepared to go through this and was on the verge of quitting the case.

Psychiatrists stood at the bottom of his list of professionals, with their half-fraudulent science, their incredible money lust, their hatred of art. Of the theorists that he knew, the poet was most interested in Jung, as all the other academics were, because Jung had reinstated poetry and painting and the primitive and mythology and numerology and even astrology, a man with a world mind and not just a carrier of guilt. Jung had stolen the Freudian fire and carried it back to Olympus and the Academy loved him for it. Of course the poet would not be sent to a Jungian, nor were there any in the big California valley, but to one of the regulars who would write a report on the poet's state of mental health, or what they would conceive it to be according to their rules and definitions.

Had he had nervous breakdowns? Was he an alcoholic? Had he broken the law? Was he financially responsible? Did he have an acceptable sex life? Was he a productive citizen? Any psychiatrist could answer these questions any way he wanted or felt like, and it would go into the testimony. His side, on the other hand, could hire a friendly shrink to refute the enemy and then it would be up to the judge or jury to decide which shrink was more convincing. He understood that the use of psychiatrists was only another form of intimidation and harassment and that no lawyer took them seriously, but this thought drove him into a darker state of mind in which he felt that all his privacy was being torn to shreds, his poems being pawed by cheap detectives looking for hidden messages to a foreign power.

His lawyer and his wife were worried, knowing he would never withstand the onslaughts of the lawyers and the psychiatrists. Their concern made him even more anxious, and he said bitterly that maybe he should go to actors' school, and the lawyer answered that a lot of coaching was necessary in this kind of case, that there were a million tricks the other side could pull. They were driving back to Davis together and the poet wanted to jump out of the car, but just sat silently and chain-smoked.

Malice, said the poet's lawyer, as they entered his blue Mercedes, malice is all this case is about. You've got to prove malice, he said to the poet, looking at him in his mirror. The lawyer and the poet's wife began to make fun of his testimony at the deposition; after all, it was the poet who was on trial in front of the battery of *JAMA* lawyers in dark suits, flown out from Chicago to confront this suicide suspect. If he couldn't prove that the psychiatrist was malicious, then there was no case. They asked him why he didn't lie about his income which had diminished as the result of the libel, why he had been so gentlemanly, why he wasn't indignant. He would have to be coached, said his lawyer, the poet was ruining the case, and his wife agreed. He wanted to jump out of the Mercedes.

He thought of his sweet Uncle Jack who had jumped out of a moving car because he was being reprimanded, over-instructed, harassed. He didn't get hurt but fell down, got up and ran off through the park. Jack was his friend, the poet was probably his best friend. He was said to be retarded, the last of twelve children, *peculiar*, people called him, and went only to the fourth grade but held an important job in his brother's office all his life, still peculiar, they said. When he was a child the poet and Uncle Jack were inseparable, though Jack was five years his senior. When he was grown he would visit Jack in his one-room apartment, barely furnished because he had no use for what people call decorations and lived like a monk. Sometimes the poet and Jack would go to prostitutes together, for the uncle seemed to know where to find them and the poet didn't. The uncle pretended that the family was descended from aristocratic Spanish Jews and even studied Spanish at night school, after which he always threw his arms around the poet when he saw him and exclaimed *Mi sobrino!* and the poet would answer *Mi tio!* and they would go off into gales of laughter.

The lawyer's concern and impatience, his wife's concern and impatience made him feel surrounded, as if by caretakers, for in fact he felt peculiar, but he wasn't about to jump out of the car on the thundering freeway.

He lucked out with the psychiatrist, someone he knew, a New Yorker named Bluestone who had a rambling house with a brick wine cellar he had had built and was as proud of as if it were his masterpiece. The poet thought he could trust him, even though the Other Side had picked Bluestone. They talked for three hours, mostly about the poet's writing and teaching and only in passing about the woman who had slandered him in print. He had made a study of the mores of suicide, and to the poet's surprise said that there was no injunction against it in Judaism. It was such a friendly afternoon that he almost forgot why he had been sent there. A few days later he saw Bluestone emerge from a supermarket licking a tall double-dip ice cream cone and he felt assured that this shrink wasn't going to throw him to the wolves.

They had planned on going to Europe that summer, the poet and his wife, and were told by the lawyer that it would be months before the case got under way, there was so much preliminary work to be done, and that their absence wouldn't interfere with the proceedings. Besides, the lawyer was going to have to take depositions from the defendant back there in Middle America, and depositions from the editors at *JAMA* in Chicago, and the lawyer had never been to Chicago and was excited and happy for the opportunity. After all, it was a contingency case and expenditure was no big deal. Whether they raked in a million or just a few thousands it would be a good case, and they were bound to win unless the poet blew it by a lot of unfortunate answers. The mention of money in this connection made the poet feel queasy and again he wanted to quit, but knew he had to go through with it as a point of honor if nothing else.

He was one of those people who never get sick, never even get a cold, and except for the malaria in the tropics during the war—but that was a female anopheles bite, he would say—he had forgotten what illness was like. Was it true that he shoveled snow barefooted in Nebraska? People would ask him and he would nod, though he didn't make a fetish of his health. But now he began to have feelings of wilting. His muscles were weak, he was short of breath and at night he awoke soaking wet with perspiration. His wife wanted him to go to the doctor but he refused. He mentioned his sweats and the weakness to a friend who was an amateur diagnostician and she said those are the symptoms of tuberculosis, and he laughed.

He read the long Complaint for Damages, as it was named, in his copy of the long, thick legal document in which he was the complainer, thirty-two numbered lines to the page with a neat double rule on the left and a single rule on the right margin. Incontrovertibly legal-looking and sounding, drained of every milligram of human feeling, it was the perfect antithesis of a poem except for certain eighteenth-century flourishes of diction such as Wherefore, plaintiff prays: but followed by the hideous arithmetic of "1. For the sum of $1,000,000.00 general damages" followed by a series of other sums. The association of his name with the ideogram of a million dollars made him shudder, and he felt as if he had befouled himself. Naturally everybody within hearing distance would snicker that the poet was going to become a millionaire by virtue of the case, and to his suicide would be added the accusation of money-grubber, prostitute, god knows what. He had really fallen in the mire.

"Said publicity," the Complaint read, "exposed plaintiff to hatred, contempt, ridicule and obloquy, causing him to be shunned and avoided and proximately causing him to sustain a severe and continuing shock and strain, and to suffer great mental anguish, mortification, humiliation and shame; all to his damage in the sum of $1,000,000.00."

Was this gibberish? He couldn't decide. Was it just phraseology out of Blackstone, or some other ancient and honored tome that the law used as a smokescreen? He wasn't about to pursue the question. He knew that there he had lost the Case, that there wasn't any Case, and whether he got a million dollars or nothing was totally irrelevant. His execution was accomplished.

Another blow fell which to the poet was even worse than the libel suit: he was banished from his favorite anthology, *The Oxford Book of American Verse*. To him this had been his proudest prize, more than all the others put together, his stamp of approval and his passport to the Old World of literature. It was already twenty-five years old and had gone through fifteen editions, and the poet-librarian knew that it was in every library in Europe and was in a sense an official book, an Almanach de Gotha of American poets. He was handsomely represented, he thought, and fixed in a constellation that would never fade. After all, the editor was the famous Harvard professor Matthiessen whose encyclopedic works on American literature were universally honored and whose death was mourned by literature itself. For Matthiessen had leapt from a hotel window in Boston, despondent, the poet wrote in an elegy, over the Communist invasion of Czechoslovakia about which the professor had written a stirring book, a hopeful book which was thrown on the flames of the Russian invaders. And his lover had died, his hopes had died, and he leapt. Suicide again, and now his beautiful Oxford book had died and the poet along with it.

A Chicago professor with whom the poet had had furious battles over this same issue of Communism had been made the new editor of a new Oxford Book, and the Chicago professor, now an Oxford professor, had yanked him out of the canon completely, a total deletion. It was as if the proclamation of his own suicide was having a ripple effect, that people who knew poetry were conspiring to erase him from the map like Czechoslovakia. There were more signs as the libel spread. Another psychiatrist, one of those popularizers who batten on the misfortunes of the unhappy, published a book about mental depression in which he reprinted the suicide list, again including the poet's name—the kind of book that sells a million copies and is on everyone's lips for weeks or months or even years. The lawyer would happily bring suit against that psychiatrist and his publisher, and up the demand for money damages.

To cap it all he received a clipping in the mail, a cutting of the daily crossword puzzle in the *New York Times*, one of the few newspapers in America which are read not only in New York but all over the world. Someone had drawn an arrow to the seven-letter horizontal which was left blank by the sender. He looked at the legend for the seven-letter word and read "Late American poet." Death by crossword puzzle! crossed his mind but he had lost his sense of humor and only felt a chill. He filled in *Shapiro* and then completed all the verticals to prove the point. He tried to remember other poets with his name; one was the editor of the *New York Times Book Review* itself, but what would he have to do with crossword puzzles? He began to think of poets he had heard of who did crosswords, and immediately thought of Auden. He pictured Auden lying in bed with his martini at his side filling in the words of the day's puzzle and pausing at his name. He even thought of dropping Auden a postcard with a versified disclaimer, but decided to do nothing.

THE NEW YORK TIMES, SATURDAY, NOVEMBER 11, 1978

CROSSWORD PUZZLE

Edited by EUGENE T. MALESKA

ACROSS

1 Of a plant pore
7 Appropriate cry for G.B.S.
12 Late U.S. poet
13 Marries in haste
15 Naps
18 Corkers
19 Topgallants
20 Pro —
21 "— long way . . ."
22 Pier
23 — speak
24 This: Fr.
25 Kin in a G. & S. line
26 Prepare peas
27 Circular panel
29 Dressed — nines
30 London bus
33 Seed covering
34 Musical pieces
39 Money in Prague
40 Slow one
41 Church V.I.P.'s
43 Danube feeder
44 Commandment word
45 Venus de —
46 Writer Anaïs
47 Up
48 — energy
49 Naps
52 Go to bed
53 Wearer of a silver eagle
54 Campus brass
55 Accrued

DOWN

1 Tam-o'- —

2 Becomes habituated
3 Sills's milieu
4 Overlook
5 Sandy's sound
6 Became less severe
7 — fours (teacakes)
8 With craftiness
9 "— tricks?"
10 Bee: Prefix
11 Exited
12 Phlegmatic
14 Drawing
16 Diamondback

17 Turgenev novel
22 Self-defense system
23 In arrears
25 Sadat
26 Peculate
28 Pipe up
31 Fuse
32 Ply needles
33 "What Is This — Called Love?"
34 Not so arduous
35 Having a diagonal direction

37 Site of the Eisenhower Center
38 Spread out
40 Disgraces
42 City on the St. Lawrence
44 Avowed
45 Word with court or pool
47 Huge land mass
48 Pacific archipelago
50 Agnès or Jeanne
51 Sweetie

11/11/78

He went to the kitchen and made himself a martini and idiotically toasted Auden, his favorite poet in the language.

His wife noticed that he was losing weight and he noticed that his trousers were becoming looser. He ate and drank as usual, whenever and whatever he felt like, for he paid little attention to food and thought that gourmandizing was piggishness and a sign of stupidity. The loss of weight didn't particularly concern him, but he remembered his seldom-seen doctor asking at each checkup session every year or two whether he had had any "weight loss," as that could be a sign of cancer. Nevertheless he began to weigh himself and watched as he went down five, ten, fifteen pounds, then twenty, and he began to admire his looks in the mirror.

His own simple diagnosis was probably the right one: shock from the suicide accusation, night sweats as a preventive to nightmares, weakness as an expression of inner sadness, what the Victorians called a broken heart. He knew that something in him was broken, but he also knew that he wouldn't succumb to self-pity.

They landed at Heathrow in a blinding thunderstorm and went by taxi to the little flat they had rented and slept through the night, and the next day got up to see London. His wife, who had never been to Europe but from her reading was a London expert, insisting on taking the underground everywhere, though the poet, who was a taxi addict, said you can't see anything in a subway and what's the point of being in London if you can't see it? They shopped at a Safeway supermarket nearby.

The weaknesses had increased. He stayed in bed much of the day while his wife went on walking excursions in the city, photographing houses with a small camera. The London town houses intrigued her, coming from the American Midwest with its sprawling domiciles and lawns spread out all around like hoopskirts. The neat elegant facades of the London houses on good streets were her special province, though they visited the British Museum and the Tate and so on. At the British Museum she was hypnotized by Egyptian sarcophagi high up in the vastnesses of the collection, and couldn't be pulled away. Tired, he sat down and eventually told her he would meet her downstairs at the main entrance while she wandered from Pharaoh to Pharaoh.

Some days he felt strong enough to wander himself and walked, not sure where, until he sought a taxi to take him home. They had found a neighborhood doctor, the landlady's doctor, who came and examined him and gave him pills to cool him down, for he was running a slight fever. He went to the doctor's residence and was examined in what appeared to be the living room. The doctor suggested possible tuberculosis and took a patch test, but he was clearly puzzled. They were all puzzled, the poet included, and when he got back to California and had a whole week of tests for every known disease that matched his symptoms nobody could find anything, so that he came to the obvious conclusion that he had a psychosomatic something for which there was no cure except his own will.

His wife took a slightly different approach, knowing that he was sick and not sick, and treated his condition as a kind of malingering. He was spoiling their European trip, ruining it for her, and she was resentful. They went to the theater, once. They went up the river to Kew Gardens, and when he saw the immensity of the place they were to walk through he sank down on a bench and said he couldn't make it. She was silent, she even wept as they toiled slowly back to the train station, and they sat in the train all the way back without a word.

Even when they returned home and had reached San Francisco at the miserable ill-built airport, an evil construction designed to punish people who fly, and had to walk a semicircular mile with two heavy suitcases, she was angry, and when he sat down on a concrete barrier to catch his breath she said "Are you still doing your act?" He was crushed. That was the last straw. Did she really think he was faking night sweats, skinniness? for he was now skinny. She was tall and strong, very strong, and took great pride in her health and she carried the bags, for there were no porters anymore in liberated California, and he trailed behind her like a cur.

Back in Davis, the case went on, from bad to worse. The country lawyer was cut to ribbons by the sharpie lawyers from New York and Chicago. The poet was informed in no uncertain terms that the main thing now was to keep him out of court or he might even end up behind bars for perjury, so inept he was at dealing with reality, and they all caved in and agreed to "settle" out of court.

The money was enough to buy a couple of houses for investment, new small dwellings in Woodland,—a real town, a redneck town, not an ivory tower campus town,—dwellings in what approximated working-class neighborhoods. Young tattooed independent truck drivers parked their gleaming diesel "cabs" on the driveway and polished the gleaming chrome chimneys that rose up on the side of the cab, and the wives tended the exotic cacti gardens in front with a wagon wheel or two for ornament on the gravel "lawns," though some had real lawns which had to be nursed in the blaze of heat of the valley. And rose bushes, for roses loved the valley heat and bloomed nine months of the year. They were working people who used their hands on high tension wires and pylons, locksmiths, highway foremen for the vast California highway system that was the envy and the ridicule of the world. The poet liked these tenants and was astounded at his wife's business acumen. He was astounded too when a Mexican tenant had to be evicted on the complaints of his neighbors for wife-beating and destruction of the inside of the house, and the sheriff had to cruise up, a woman sheriff with thick pistols on both hips and spangled with chains and medals and walkie-talkie radio and wide-brimmed hat, to deliver the notice of eviction. There was more than one eviction, and books with names like *Landlording* began to appear in the house, along with books on Money Markets and finance. One of the tenants was a professional deadbeat, as he was called by all and sundry, an evangelist who used the phrase The Lord Jesus in every other sentence. He had a wife, a scared-looking, washed-out woman, and a scared-looking, washed-out child. The three moved from rented house to rented house after paying the initial deposits, and stayed without paying the rent until they were given notice to move. It was their way of life and the courts had no way to deal with him, a well-known local character who kept the sheriffs busy with summonses and deadlines for removing themselves to still another dwelling.

This way their life led into a calm and they even moved to the working-class farmer town, for the old rich owned the farms, which were some of the richest in the world and grew everything including rice which was exported to the Orient. Most of the old rich were White Protestant with white skins and blue eyes, and the wives all drove white Cadillacs and wore blue light wool dresses as a kind of uniform, the poet thought, to distinguish them as the Owners. There were also the postwar Japanese, who were getting just as rich but were less ostentatious about outward symbols. The friends of the poet and his wife were shocked that they were moving to Woodland —nobody moved to Woodland—and even their Woodland friends, doctors and lawyers, their own lawyer who had handled the suicide case, were shocked at the idea of leaving the university town of Davis for this backwater.

The new house was in an old almond orchard and hundreds of the trees were still bearing, although because of their great age about one or two would have to be cut down every year. The man next door, not really next door because the house was invisible behind the trees, a tall and bald psychiatrist, had an extra lot that belonged to him and owned about fifty of the beautiful trees. When the nuts started to fall he would have a professional shaker to shake the nuts down, have them dried on sheets in his driveway, shelled and bottled and put up for sale. His wife was a Quaker, the psychiatrist also, and the poet could see the connection between Quakerism and psychoanalysis, the inwardness and meditativeness of their practice. The poet had been taken aback by a remark she had made about his novel *Edsel* which she took out of the Woodland library. How could such a nice person write such a filthy book? He was immediately afraid of her; censors terrified him, and he could never feel at ease with her.

The house was large for two people, with four bedrooms and two living rooms and three baths. They had the entire establishment furnished with carpeting, expensive carpeting, especially in the main living room which held the grand piano, though it was silent now and had been for a long time except when the children came and dug out the music books and played in their amateur fashion and sang songs they had grown up with, and then the poet's wife would sit down and play seven or eight Schubert pieces expertly, and Rameau, and her favorite Chopin études.

She had learned to be an almost professional gardener in California and planted nearly thirty rose bushes, each with its own bubbler that worked on an automatic time clock, but she did the pruning and the systemic poisoning and fertilizing, always bare-armed and bare-handed though he begged her to wear gloves or gauntlets. But she always said she couldn't get into the bushes properly with gloves on, and her hands and arms were constantly scarred with crisscross scratches and new wounds and old, and when the doctor said that she had cancer he wondered if the constant assault on the roses and the revenge of the thorns and the poisons had something to do with it. Nobody would ever know. It was too much work harvesting the almonds and fighting off the bluejays and other birds that could break through the double shells and a certain amount of the take went to the rats, which fed on the nuts but were eradicated by their two Siamese cats, which in spite of their effete and helpless appearance were great hunters and eaters of rodents. When the poet and his wife wanted almonds they would buy them from the psychiatrist.

After a time they owned a half-dozen houses; the poet never knew precisely how many. The management was done smoothly and seemingly without much time-consuming work, and except for emergencies things ran themselves as long as there were overseers such as lawyers and accountants and his wife's knowledge of land-lording, so that she began to return to her first love, writing.

It was a different kind of writing she went back to—romance novels. She had attended writing conferences in the mountains and had run into commercial writers, people who made a living and a few a fortune from writing commercial best-sellers, formula books they called them, in which one wrote under an assumed name and sold the product outright, name included, to a big national publisher. The small paperback books were marketed in supermarkets like groceries, for in fact they were groceries to the millions of housewives who brought them home and devoured them. In her disciplined way she bought about a hundred of such books, read and analyzed them for plot, character and tone, and then wrote one and got an agent in New York and before long a publisher and contract. She loved the activity and the companionship with new romance-writing friends all up and down California, went to and participated in their conventions, sometimes with the poet along, who at one or two sessions read his poems when asked. She began to make good royalties and bought a word processor, the mysterious machine glowing green in her study when the processor was in operation. She went to the training class in Sacramento for instruction and felt very much at home with the processor.

The romances had specific settings. That was one of the rules, like travel books, and her first one took place in nearby Sacramento, the second in Carmel where they would go and spend a few days at a time to learn about this resort. She would do thorough research about the inns and the curious ordinances of the township that forbade sidewalks, for instance, where police were invisible and there was no jail because the town was too well watched and perhaps expensive for ordinary crime. A robber would be snatched immediately and whisked off to Monterey, a tough little city made famous by John Steinbeck.

The third novel was set in Sausalito and San Francisco across the beautiful bridge, but that one was never finished.

They were flying back to Davis from San Diego where they had spent a weekend visiting a retired couple who were thinking of moving there. San Diego, the poet thought, the lost city of dreams which his little friends back in Norfolk, Virginia, had never stopped praising and longing for, but then, they were Navy children used to living in exotic places. It was a short flight up the immense valley to Sacramento and he noticed something odd, or was he imagining it. The plane was almost full, and now and then one of the stewardesses would sit down on the arm of an aisle seat and whisper something in the passenger's ear. He watched this several times and was puzzled. Once a stewardess sat down in an empty seat next to a passenger and leaned head to head with him for several minutes and got up with a serious look before she rediscovered her professional smile. Is the plane in trouble? he asked himself. When they deplaned at Sacramento and boarded the little jitney to drive them to their parking lot, people were talking breathlessly. Marya asked, Is something wrong? A voice answered, The President has been shot. They don't know whether he'll live. When the poet looked at her she was in tears.

It was the week before Christmas and she went for her routine checkup at the clinic. It was about the tenth time they had x-rayed her for lower back pains. Gall bladder they said. Then operate, Marya said, and added to the surgeon, Do you think I'm a surgery freak? They laughed. She had had so many operations, major and minor, necessary or not, and did almost seem to welcome them. The poet had come to take it as routine.

It was after Christmas, after the operation. The surgeon had sat him in a small room and tried to explain. He heard only some of it after the dread word, the death sentence. He remembered the surgeon saying I don't think you've heard a word I said, and heard himself saying I'll tell her myself.

How long? said the oncologist, a sweet and saintly-looking man who had a bad stutter. Imagine having to deliver death sentences day after day. It could be six months, he said, or it could be twelve years. He explained all the organs involved, starting from the pancreas. The poet's hearing went on half-audio again.

Now there was the chemotherapy and the purchase of wigs, the stares into space, the unexpected visits from distant friends. The dosages increased. The last treatment was called platinum and she must stay overnight in the hospital to recover from that.

He and his younger stepdaughter stood at the foot of the bed while she lay there. After a while the stepdaughter had to leave. He stood and watched and thought she was too still. He watched her pajama lapel and could not see it moving. He went and looked

closely and thought she was not breathing. He raced to the nurses'
station and there was nobody there. He raced up the corridor until
he found someone in uniform and gesticulated wildly. There was
sudden activity and four people sped a gurney down the corridor.
By the time he got back to the room they were surrounding her,
one pounding on her chest, another hooking up a machine. You'd
better leave, one of them said.

It was, as the gentle oncologist had suggested, exactly six
months.

For many months he lived in a state of narcosis, continuing to
function outwardly, getting chores done, teaching, paying bills,
changing the oil, seeing friends at intervals. His life was over, he
was just going to wait it out as best he could. Then one Sunday
morning he was awakened at dawn, it seemed, by a phone call
from New York. The caller, former wife of his oldest friend now
dead, whom he had first met forty years ago when he had called
on the friend to say goodbye, in uniform, ready to be shipped out
to the Pacific, had overlooked the time differential and apologized
for waking him. She had read an old interview of his in a poetry
magazine and had written him a letter, then decided to check the
address with him. Dazed with sleep he said oh yes, he remembered
her, and gave her his current Davis address. It was the beginning
of a new phase of his life.

•   •   •

DEATH ONCE DEAD

I

The Ashes

Her ashes lie in a cardboard box
On a nearby table.
There used to be funerals and processions
And eventually a stone where dates were incised.

Now nobody knows what to do with the remains.
Her parents have never buried ashes.
I've never even buried a bird.

Should I look for an artist to make me an urn?
What would I do with an urn in a tract house,
House without niches for shrines?

Someone suggests, scatter the ashes over the High Sierras
Or over the nearby Pacific.
Someone says, there are companies that do that well.

I keep the carton with the remains of my wife
On a nearby table in my bedroom.
But I have fallen in love!
In the midst of all this I have fallen in love.

Each night I lift up the box and I cry.
Inside the box there are bones that are not ashes
And that rattle. There's an envelope taped on the lid
With the vital statistics,
And her wedding ring with the bones sits in the box.

I I

The Dinner Party

Home from the dinner party for the new poet
With the eye of a race horse, handsome and fine
As his poetry, proud
Strong and intelligent, which will go places,
The old poet closes his bedroom door
With bloodshot, tear-broken eyes
For the beloved who is no longer in his bed,
Though the new love has opened his life like a sky
From thousands of miles and forty years away.

III

Homework

Now that I am living in your house
My highest wish is something else,
That I will make you feel at home.

Domesticity, poets say,
Blights all passions but the dollar sign,
An adage not germane to this
Undomesticable group-of-two.

The sound of your typewriter
Is my kiss of welcome,
Your anger at phones a sensual trip.

You recover quickly from distractions
After a silence in your oasis,
Come back with your climactic eyes,
Heat-lightning flickering still.

Journeys below are difficult for us,
Makeup, dresses, menus,
Money something we pretend to manage.

Forget but don't forget that I am here
Without parole,
In love transcending hearth and home.

IV

Sea Dance

With a glance from your sky
With the susurra of your voice
You right me.
With the kiss of the tilt of your head
With the ecliptic of your mind
You right me.
My sailor, my astronomer,

Is this what Heraclitus meant
When our souls flow into one?
With the offshore fragrance of islands
Île sous le vent
Îlots de memoire
All our lost years come home like treasure
Fierce and acrid as copra.
With your lift to the sun
With your throat of drowning
You right me.
And steady with glistering ropes
I will pilot to haven your riches
And anchor you in my being.

13.

They were in Austria. He knelt at Auden's grave, not to pray
certainly, but to twist off a sprig of what he thought was rose-
mary. Do people plant herbs on graves? he wondered, and pocketed
the sprig before she noticed. She was Austrian-born herself and he
had come to Vienna with her to see the city she had grown up in and
to visit with Auden, as he would put it. The grave was crowded to
suffocation, the poet thought, with low plantings and small flowering creepers, a family plot on one side close, a family plot on the
other. Auden was at home now among the villagers he had chosen,
a Roman Catholic churchyard in Austria for the great poet, who
called himself a New Yorker, not an American. He knew he was
not an American: a Birmingham-Oxford Englishman who had lived
nearly all his life in exile. All poets live in exile, the kneeling visitor thought, and he and his wife strolled back across the road to the
little *Gasthaus* for a glass of beer under a chestnut tree.

He had known Auden well enough to call him by his beautiful
first name, he remembered that Auden had dropped his middle
name "Hugh" because of the anti-Semitic legend of Hugh of Lincoln, supposedly murdered by Jews for a blood ritual in the Dark
Ages; he would remain W. H., not Wystan Hugh. But the whole
name was on the gravestone reinstated in death in Kirchstetten just
at the Vienna woods, not far from the mountain retreat where Beethoven faced the horror of his deafness and wrote a will threatening
to kill himself, the Heiligenstadt Testament.

There was a wall between the grave and the *Gasthaus* and in front of the wall a statue in defeat. One almost never sees a war statue of defeat—except the great Vietnam memorial—and he remembered the Confederate statues all over the South, straight and defiant and each one facing North, no abject surrender here. But this Austrian fellow of World War I stood with bowed head and no helmet, his cartridge belt hung loose and empty, and on the base of the statue UNSEREN HELDEN for the fallen heroes who never came back, and the names of the killed were there. It was in its way a suitable reminder for Auden, whose early poetry spoke eloquently of that first of the World Wars, when the young American poet had discovered Auden during the Depression in a British leftish magazine. Now he heard Auden recite the failures of that war, he heard the bones of the German dead call Auden cousin, for the English and the Germans are at least cousins, the Saxon preceded the Norman in England, and the bones of the dead in the Auden poem said *Call us not tragic, Falseness made farcical our death, Nor brave, Ours was the will of the insane to suffer By which since we could not live we gladly died, And now we have gone forever to our foolish graves.*

Yes he had chosen the right place to make his last poems and to die and be buried among his German cousins. Though in Austria one is careful not to confuse Austrian with German; both parties are clear on the distinction. The poet's new wife had already translated half of *The Man Without Qualities*, by Robert Musil, Austria's answer to Thomas Mann, the epical novel of the last, almost surrealistic days of the Austro-Hungarian Empire, set at the moment before Austria lit the match that put the world to the torch. Auden and Spender and Isherwood were too young for the war, and grew up in its wake and tasted its bitterness in Germany where they all vacationed, and partook of the decadence and studied the despair and witnessed the birth of Hitlerism and its triumph. They issued warnings in their poems and stories. Too late; the dispersal of exiles all over the world had begun, Auden to exile himself to America with Isherwood and to cries of shame from British patriots.

They had encompassed it all, these writers, from Sarajevo to Yalta to Hiroshima, and were once more in the era of postwar, again *entre deux guerres*, though nobody could any longer comprehend the meaning of a war to come which was conducted in the language of the TV cartoon and the space movie. The very President of the United States had been elected to star in the space movie; it was his script and a redaction of T. S. Eliot's vatic poem which downgrades the apocalypse from a bang to a whimper. Auden disliked all that missile mythos and wrote a sneering poem about ejaculating penile dildoes to the moon, though he wrote a pretty one about battleships or flat-tops lying in the Bay of Naples perhaps; but then of course there were the sailors.

They went inside the inn and borrowed the key to the little village church, simple and unbaroque with very few pews. Auden had sung here when it was time for hymns, prayed here though Anglican. When he returned the key to the stout landlady she showed him a drawing of Auden above the corner table where he had sat, right opposite the corner where the local poet Josef Weinheber had his shrine, and Auden had written a touching and compromising poem to him. Auden had become one of the locals. He had found his home, his house, his cave-of-making as he called one of the rooms in a brilliant series of poems about the house, and they walked up the road to the house and were greeted by a smallish dog on a chain that barked and wagged its tail and a large black hen stalked around the corner and examined them. There was nobody home. The housekeeper was in the hospital. A long flight of wooden stairs led like a ladder up to Auden's attic study from the outside, a separate entrance as it were. He dissuaded his wife from climbing the stairs and they returned to the table outside the inn. A bee sipped at his beer and he evicted the bee and raised his glass to the statue, the wall, and the grave beyond.

Any elegy, no matter how inventive, is a formal construction, a ritual, and not his kind of poem, although he had written one in the Army that was widely reprinted over the years. But now he wanted to make an elegy for Auden and add his wreath to all those others. He felt he knew too much about Auden and too little. He was still too stimulated by his poetry, especially his late poems which were in many ways the best of all. He approached the job cautiously, thinking of openings as in a chess game, and he toyed with epigraphs, Auden quotes such as "reneighbored in the County of Consideration" the C's italicized. Auden was prone to personify physical areas. Geology had been his early love, his poetry is laden with geology. And another quote, one of Auden's penetrating shockers that he was so good at, "One should not stink of poetry." What a line from the century's greatest English poet. He knew what Auden meant: all that phony authenticity, the fallacy of authenticity you might say, poets who advertised the vocation like recruiting sergeants. Stink was the right word and Auden had a highly developed nose. In one of his *About the House* poems he dropped the casual line *Shakespeare probably stank, the Grand Monarque certainly did.* Maybe there was something homosexual about this olfactory obsession. Verlaine had played it up in his buggery poems that he wrote with Rimbaud, *a little cheese a little shit* went one of the tastier lines, but of course he didn't use either of these epigraphs. An elegy is epigraph enough. The poem started tentatively:

> I call you Wystan, as I did then
> In the days of the terrible Bollingen Prize
> In the days of the moral dilemma we never solved.
> When you visited us in Chicago, Wystan, I said
> But what do you want with a Woolworth's?
> To buy a collapsible cup to carry
> Aboard the train to sip my whiskey in
> Especially crossing Iowa, he said.

Auden had voted with Eliot and the rest of the poets in the room at the Library of Congress to give the first Bollingen Prize to Ezra Pound, the only dissenter being the only Jew naturally, and Auden had remarked, "Everyone is anti-Semitic sometimes," and let it go at that. He would know; his lover was Jewish and practiced infidelity all through their lifelong marriage.

The notes went on:

> Of the great princes of exile of our time
> You are the foremost even now as you lie
> In the churchyard near Audenstrasse,
> A shock to see your name changed to a street
> Or rather a painterly country lane
> With its inn where you sat and the valley views
> And the simple church with its fifty pews

and it was apparent that there was going to be some rhyme in this poem and a certain attention to iambic five. "There are the princes of exile," wrote the exiled French poet St. John Perse. It was his line in the beautiful prose poem *Exils* which Perse wrote while he was asylumed at the Library of Congress during the war—the princes of exile, those who do not forget the trust of their civilized knowledge in a dark age, and Auden was one of these princes.

> We went to Auden's village, his house, his church, his tavern
>   table in the inn, his grave
> He put Kirchstetten on the map among these charming farms
> The little road that turns towards his place
> Is Audenstrasse
> Who overdecorated your grave
> those Austrians
> The great poets spill over their banks

He had written with a red ballpoint pen in the margin of one scribbly draft "d. 29 Sept 73," and it was now eleven years that Auden had lain here. He should not have twisted off the sprig he had pocketed; Auden had already contributed to these roots. The dirt was wet and black, as if coagulated. Inevitably he thought of the bleeding trees in Dante.

One of his wife's Austrian translator friends had given him the

Kirchstetten edition of Auden, all the poems he wrote there, master-pieces among them, the English on the left and the German, very badly translated the friend insisted, on the right. He owned most of the editions of the poems but this was already his favorite. He couldn't read the German anyway, but knew how it would be all but impossible to bring over the nuances and endless modulations of the Auden voice, his own invented language, words that even schol-ars had to look up in the OED, turning nouns into verbs, elevating nursery words like *comfy*, balancing museum terms like *steatopy-gous* with bathroom language like *satisfactory dump*, recapitulating every form known to English prosody from the Anglo-Saxon to the New York newspaper, and coming to peace at the end with the Sap-phic stanza and the Horatian tone. Magpie they called him in the early days, but not for long. Like Horace he was a domestic poet:

> There's nobody home, the housekeepers are absent
> It's just as well, I don't want to enter your premises,
> Most undomestic of domestic poets
> But who epitomized the house
> Cellar to bedroom, attic to stool,
> Making an Austrian cottage everywhere

It was as if a child had asked for three wishes, a house, a church and a cenotaph, and got all three in the same place, though there were other wishes, a more faithful love for one, and the Nobel Prize for another. He had not moaned and cursed about not getting the prize like Robert Frost, but would say when the topic arose that he was on the Short List. He knew he wouldn't have the laurel of Sweden; you can't switch ideologies and impress the persnickety Swedes. You must embody a Tendency and live it through, Yeats midwifing Irish culture, Eliot as chief mourner of the Tradition, Bel-low as the American voice of the humanist Jew. In terms of sheer genius Auden could have won the prize several times over, but in literature it is not given for genius alone. It is probable that Auden didn't fret about the slight, although he always took care to garner the proper honors; with him it was as much a matter of manners as anything else.

Or was the Auden elegist making too much of the WWI statue? He hoped not, he was sure not. The fallen heroes of World War I had been his introduction to Auden back in the heart of the Depression, when only the writers and intellectuals were screaming against Hitler, Mussolini and Tojo, when the escaping Jews were already on the high seas and being denied admission to all the European countries and America as well. He had read Auden's words, *And when hatred promised a more immediate dividend, all of us hated,* the notes continued:

> Over the wall behind you, Auden
> An infantry statue mourns, head bowed
> Bareheaded for the heroes of World War One
> Who marched from this village and never returned
> While unbelievably apt and prompt
> A NATO fighter rips overhead and straight across your grave
> As if you were one of the fallen, a latter-day Rupert Brooke

During the Second World War Winston Churchill had flown over the Greek island of Skyros where Rupert Brooke was buried, the last sweet singer of the old imperialism. A wreath was dropped for the poet who wrote *If I should die think only this of me.* . . . His forever England still hung in the air, and Auden's plot in Austria was also a token of that forever England, just like the Protestant cemetery in Rome where other great English poets came to rest. The famous Keats epitaph: "Here lies one whose name was writ in water," could as well apply to Auden, a water-poet from beginning to end. Water gurgles under all his geology, dear water, clear water, he addresses his element; it is water that makes man's wonders happen, that and fire, but Auden is not a fire poet. In the days when Auden was suffering the disappointments of the fallen idols of revolution, in the

year that Freud died and Yeats died and the new world war had
begun, Auden wrote in his elegy for Yeats one of his astonishing
dicta—Poetry makes nothing happen

>In your tribute to Yeats in your rather baroque poetic
>You astonished us once, as you always astonished
>By writing that poetry makes nothing happen
>You made a generation of makers happen
>You changed the tune of poetry for our time
>You left the examples
>Volunteer exile, man without a country.
>Dialectician of our age.
>You never ran from, you always ran to
>Like Alice your friend and when you got there
>You had to confront your mountainous Gertrude,
>   Dame Kind
>Who bellowed at you, Wystan, there's no there there.
>There's never a There there, Auden,
>Except in your Austrian graveyard,
>Except at your slab in Westminster Abbey
>Rubbing shoulders with T. S. Eliot,
>Watched over by Chaucer,
>Slyboots Wystan, you outfoxed us all,
>You turned the screw of modern poetry,
>You changed the tune of English,
>Left us the models

Auden had felt more at home in the twentieth century than any other
poet, in Iceland, Italy, China, Manhattan, though always with an
Edwardian nostalgia for the steam engine and the hydraulic pump.
He cursed the diesel engine and mourned in horror the decay and
violence of cities, robbed and assaulted even at Oxford where he
was the honored guest. It would be different in Austria; safety was
the order of the day. Tourists back from Vienna said you can eat

off the sidewalk and stroll the streets at midnight, and who would assault Auden on the road named Audenstrasse:

> Sandwiched between two families, in a cozy Austrian
>   churchyard,
> Safe in his compromise country,
> No more the potential of Manhattan muggers or Oxford
>   punks,
> His ideologies weathered, his reputation ripened,
> Even his epitaphs penned and readied

Was the elegist making too much of the Nazi connection, that Josef Weinheber who had apparently killed himself in 1945 in fear of the Nazis he had espoused a while? Auden had written a longish poem to Weinheber. They might have been friends; and after all, hadn't the Austrian poet turned down Goebbels' invitation to Nazi culture with the rude *in Ruhe lassen!* leave me in peace. Buzz off!

But there it was, the ambiguity again, the Auden double play, for in apologizing for Weinheber wasn't Auden apologizing for himself?

> Quaint village which not long ago
> Rang loud with the Nazi salute,
> Here lies a world poet who lighted
> From nowhere to sleep in your lanes,
> The gesture of civilized man
> Who loved and co-opted the hatred

The handwritten notes had gone on too long and were beginning to move in circles, repeating the same lines again and again, and he knew the poem was beginning to crystallize out. The runniness was beginning to jell into something, at which point he took to the typewriter and began to *stanza* (to use a late-Auden device of verbing the noun). He began in his usual once-upon-a-time manner of inviting the reader on the train with him en route from Vienna to Kirchstetten, looking out the window at the scenery

From Vienna it's picture-postcard all the way.
Jesus, was ever such a land at ease!

Wondering if *Jesus* would have to go, too coarse in this *Grüss Gott*
landscape, and he would perhaps soften *Jesus* to *Tell me* and he
typed out the opening stanza in penultimate form

> From Vienna it's picture-postcard all the way.
>   Jesus, was ever such a land at ease!
> The fat farms glistening, the polished pigs,
>   Each carven windowbox gushing with red
> Geraniums, pencil pines and chestnut trees,
>   The gaily-painted tractor rigs,
> Steeples with onion domes that seem to say
>   *Grüss Gott,* come lie here in our flowerbed.

then typed all the rest of the poem, about nine stanzas, salvaging
the lines and sections he wanted to keep, after which he would begin to edit and revise line by line again. But something intervened
as he began to type. He scrawled a tercet to use in italics as the
heading of the poem. It read, after the title At Auden's Grave:

> Poetry is homosexual, every mother knows,
> A high security risk, all fathers suppose.
> Ambiguous Auden ran the gamut of all those.

He knew that this three-liner had no place in his poem and was
not even sure it would stand on its own three feet someplace else.
It had sneaked in the back door and sat up front. He stared at it
until he recognized that it was a kind of valediction, the end of
a lifelong interior debate about art and homosexuality, about the
double nature of the poem, about Auden himself. But the closet
door had long since been taken away—unscrew the locks from the
doors, Whitman had yawped, Unscrew the doors themselves from
the jambs; and so it had happened, after a hundred years, though

even in Auden's youth he had had to hide the facts and fox the pronouns.

Emily Dickinson had had to fox the pronouns, changing the he's to she's and back again. Whitman had had to, but not very successfully; the Secretary of the Interior of the United States where Whitman was working was prowling through Whitman's desk and found the blue edition of *Leaves of Grass* Whitman was working on. Secretary of the Interior Harlan promptly fired Walt Whitman from his job. That was all ancient history, at least till the middle of the twentieth century, when the closet doors came tumbling down, but the bio-esthetic-moral problem remained, even though at long last, as the tercet seemed to say, there was no problem after all, simply an equation, a fact of life; there was Auden to prove it in word and deed. He crossed out the three-line poem, slightly proud that he had escaped the vulgarization of a discussion of the poet's sexual nature. Instead, in the next to last stanza, where he made a kind of summary list of Auden-faults, he called him only misogynist and wasn't even sure of that. Homosexuals don't hate women, quite the contrary. But he had overheard a remark once by a friend of the poet's, Wystan says that after five o'clock he can't stand the sight of a woman.

No, the faults of Auden the poem enumerated were more various and more or less serious. That life was not his bag, most poets live lives of noisy desperation. That he was old hat, Edwardian, longing for the days when locomotives ran on hissing steam, the last days of Empire in fact. Greenwich Villager was not much of a charge, a kind of obsolete expression like bohemian, and of course his apartment was legendary for filth, always the unwashed dishes stacked and the roaches. New York is the cockroach capital of the world. And the mice, Auden had his pet mouse, somebody said, that would eat from his plate. The elegist had only recently walked by the building on St. Marks Place in the Village where the Auden-Kallman apartment was. Now there was a plaque on the wall for

Auden, high enough up to escape the vandalism. It was dusk and the sidewalks were already busy with knots of drug pushers and dealers. He had never been to Auden's apartment himself, Wystan and Chester were strict about visitors. Tennessee Williams had come to the door and had been turned away. Not Our Sort, said Auden; NOS in the private language of snobs. Who crossed his threshold had to pass muster.

Drifter, the finger-pointing went on, yes typically for the artist in the modern world, as the sad expression goes. Auden had drifted everywhere, never really settling until he reached his Austrian hamlet and his house and grave. But intellectual drifter too; magpie, the early critics called him. And coward; this was the most unkindest cut of all. He should have stayed in England like Eliot and helped put the fires out, so said many in those days. And traitorous clerk, this was Auden's own expression. Make intercession for all traitorous clerks, he wrote in a poem, clerk being priest of sorts in the old diction. Auden always felt the intellectual guilts of the age and acted them through. All of his ideologies were founded on guilt, the guilt of Marx, the guilt of Freud, the Christian guilt, the Fall. The Treason of the Intellectuals was a slightly French, slightly fascist idea, and Auden felt the pressure of the guilt to the end, starting as a revolutionary and ending in prayer.

Lastly, his own self-accusation of genteel anti-Semite in an early anguished love letter to Chester, a kind of prose-poem found in Chester's papers, the Oxonian young genius head over heels in love with the Brooklyn Jewboy, the love of his life. Auden even pretended that Chester had a poetic gift—greater love hath no man— and lured him to write, to keep him perhaps.

The heuristic line that the elegist prized most was one which he thought the best tribute to Auden ever made, and he wanted it engraved in marble and bronze *aere perennius* to read

> I come to bless this plot where you are lain,
> Poet who made poetry whole again.

For Auden had ended the era of fragmentation. No more heaps of broken images, no more hoards of destruction, no more slogans saying that the fragment is king. He had miraculously healed the poem and given it back to the world. The final poem would read:

AT AUDEN'S GRAVE

From Vienna it's picture-postcard all the way,
Jesus, was ever such a land at ease!
The fat farms glistening, the polished pigs,
Each carven windowbox disgorging red
Geraniums, pencil pines and chestnut trees,
The gaily painted tractor rigs,
Steeples with onion domes that seem to say
Grüss Gott, come lie here in our flowerbed.

How many times did Auden take this train
Till that bright autumn day when he was borne
Back in a baggage car after his last
Recital, back to his Horatian house,
His cave of making, now the mask outworn,
The geographical visage consummated,
Back to the village, home to the country man
Without a country, home to the urban bard
Without a city he could call his own.

But suddenly a startling word
Leaps from the signpost of the country lane,
It's AUDENSTRASSE—
The poet becomes a street, the street a poet,
English with German music mated.

Here will arrive no pilgrim mob
As in Westminster Abbey, where his name
Is chiseled next to Eliot's. The sole cab

Has never heard of Auden, has to ask
Gasthaus directions, but we find him there
Ten yards away and settled with his slab,
The bracketed dates, the modest designation,
His plot planted to suffocation
In the country style of *horror vacui*.

Close by, a granite soldier stands
Bareheaded, bowed, without a gun,
Wearing his empty cartridge belt,
A blunt reminder of the First World War,
Signed *Unseren Helden* for those villagers
Who never returned and lay somewhere in France
Entre deux guerres before the next
World War should be begun
By the ultimate twentieth century hun.

Far from his foggy isle
The poet rests in self-exile.
Earth of the great composers of the wordless art
Enshrouds this master of the English tune
Not many miles from where Beethoven scrawled his will
When he could no longer hear the trill
Of the little yellow-hammer, nor the titanic storm.
In such a place Dame Kind
Released the intellectual minstrel's form.

Across the *Audenstrasse* from the grave
A bee drops from the chestnut, sips my beer,
brings back his image to me, on a day
I bought him a tin collapsible cup to sip
His whiskey from on some Iowa train,
Knowing his dread of that vertiginous plain.
Now all is comfy in his delectable cave
I scatter the bee and greet him with my lip.

Whatever commentators come to say—
That life was not your bag—Edwardian—
Misogynist—Greenwich Villager—
Drifter—coward—traitorous clerk—or you,
In your own language, genteel anti-Jew—
I come to bless this plot where you are lain,
Poet who made poetry whole again.

Sandwiched between two families Auden lies,
At last one of the locals, over his grave
A cross, a battle monument, and a name
History will polish to a shrine.
Down in the valley hums the Autobahn,
Up here the poet lies sleeping in a vale
That has no exits. All the same,
Right on target and just in time
A NATO fighter rips open the skies
Straight over Auden's domus and is gone.